Eco-Justice—The Unfinished Journey

Eco-Justice—The Unfinished Journey

EDITED BY

William E. Gibson

STATE UNIVERSITY OF NEW YORK PRESS

Published by
State University of New York Press, Albany

Printed in the United States of America

♻ This book has been printed on recycled paper.

For information, address State University of New York Press,
90 State Street, Suite 700, Albany, NY 12207

Production by Diane Ganeles
Marketing by Anne M. Valentine

Library of Congress Cataloging-in-Publication Data

Eco-justice—the unfinished journey / edited by William E. Gibson
    p. cm.
   Includes bibliographical references and index.
   ISBN 0-7914-5991-8 (alk. paper).
    1. Environmental justice. 2. Environmental education. I. Gibson,
William E.

GE220.E26 2004
363.7—dc21   2003045656

10 9 8 7 6 5 4 3 2 1

This book is dedicated
to two friends:

Senja Radcliffe,
who typed the manuscript
and had served the Eco-Justice Project for many years
with exceptional loyalty and skill
when her speed and accuracy were indispensable, and

Dieter T. Hessel,
who in his denominational and ecumenical roles
gave early and critical support to the Eco-Justice Project
and the dissemination of its message
and is now a foremost leader in the continuing journey.

Contents

Foreword

Dieter T. Hessel

The essays collected in this book chronicle the development of a movement linking ecology and justice, which was cultivated for more than two decades through a campus ministry program in upstate New York headquartered at Cornell University. That influential endeavor was initiated, with others, by William E. Gibson, coordinator of the Eco-Justice Project and Network, and editor of a modest quarterly journal named *The Egg*, in which most of the following articles appeared. Being a coparticipant in the movement as well as Bill's friend has been, and continues to be, a great personal pleasure. On behalf of the other contributors, let me express our gratitude for his gracious, tireless efforts during the last third of the twentieth century to advance the eco-justice paradigm for a world in peril.

Numerous faculty, students, and leaders of religious and environmental organizations, with whom Gibson interacted and from whom he often learned, were mentored by him. He not only wrote persuasively and encouraged others to reflect in depth on this subject; Bill practiced what he preached, inspiring many to follow up in daily life and chosen work. He motivated a network of individuals and institutions to counteract earth-destroying habits by caring for ecological integrity together with socioeconomic justice, for the good of all.

The essays selected for publication here explore the vision, values, and virtues that comprise eco-justice ethics. No doubt, much more praxis—in other words, ethically focused thinking and doing—of this kind is needed in twenty-first century education, religion, business, media, and politics for there to be a constructive response to the reality of a hotter, stormier, less biodiverse, more crowded, unequal, and violent Earth. As the crisis of Earth community deepens, mature eco-justice ethics become even more relevant.

It is encouraging to note that an approach initiated by a few ecumenical Christians after the first Earth Day, to bridge conflicts between environmentalists and social justice advocates, has evolved into a general ethic for earth community with interreligious[1] and crosscultural salience. Today, across social sectors and in diverse countries, there is growing appreciation for and "construction of what is often called an 'eco-justice' ethic . . . that holds together concerns for the natural world and for human life, that recognizes that devastation of the environment and economic injustice go hand in hand, and that affirms that environmental and human rights are indivisible."[2] The eco-justice movement now has global reach, as evidenced by the ethical principles enunciated in the Earth Charter.[3]

To read this book is to step into a moving system of thought and action that flows toward healthy earth community. In the following points, let me briefly specify what a mature eco-justice ethic contributes to shaping just and sustainable community in a socially conflicted and ecologically stressed world.

First, an eco-justice ethic views *interhuman justice as part of environmental wholeness*, because environmental health is inseparable from human well-being. This insight challenges the popular assumption that environmental issues involve caring for an external natural world apart from humans. The problem is that nature's health will never get the priority attention it deserves if nature is viewed as external to human society, or we to it.

Environmentally destructive policies and practices break down or decrease wild and managed ecosystems. At the same time, environmentally destructive activities intensify socially unjust scarcity and maldistribution of natural resources, threatening basic livelihoods. Polluting production and overconsumption are interconnected with impoverishment, abuse of human rights, armed violence, and hazards to the health of everykind.[4] Therefore, all who care about protecting ecosystems, preserving biodiversity, or reducing threats to public health must at the same time act for socioeconomic justice. As emphasized in the next point, the reverse is also true.

Second, an eco-justice ethic fosters *ecological sustainability as part of, and simultaneous with, social and economic justice*. It turns out that the ethical imperatives of economic just and ecological protection are not sequential, contrary to prevailing development theory. Affluent people on every continent still wrongly believe that economic development eventually leads to environment protection—in that order. But not in today's crowded and technologically toxic world, facing severe biophysical limits and increasing socioeconomic inequity. Economic developers and social activists, take note: healthy society depends upon ecological security. Justice and sustainability increase together or not at all. If either is treated as merely instrumental to the other, neither justice nor sustainability will be achieved.

Bill Gibson wrote two decades ago, "Eco-justice is the well-being of all humankind on a thriving earth. It is acceptance of the truth that only on a thriving earth is human well-being possible—an earth productive of sufficient food, with water fit for all to drink, air fit to breathe, forests kept replenished, renewable resources continuously renewed, nonrenewable resources used as sparingly as possible so that they will be available for their most important uses as long as possible or until a renewable alternative can be utilized. On a thriving earth, human well-being is nurtured not only by the provision of these material necessities but also by a way of living with the natural world that is *fitting*: respectful of the integrity of natural systems and of the worth of nonhuman creatures, appreciative of the beauty and the mystery of the world of nature. . . . A thriving earth is not conquered but cared for."[5]

Third, an eco-justice ethic *applies comprehensively* in a world where ominous environmental threats intersect major social problems and affect every sector of society. The concerns or issues to pursue, therefore, range far beyond what is conventionally thought to be "environmental." The eco-justice topics introduced in this volume include: toxic pollution and environmental justice, technology and energy, refocusing religious thought and ethical education, integral development versus mindless growth, duties to animals and ecosystems, hunger and agriculture, population policy and gender perspectives, good work, green economics, corporate accountability, appropriate lifestyles, and ways to build sustainable community.

In each area of concern the point is to do an eco-social analysis that explores the links between ecology and justice, and then to implement the basic eco-justice norms: solidarity, sustainability, sufficiency, and participation. These ethical norms are both ends-oriented and means-clarifying: they illumine our goals (where we should go) and ways to reach them (how to get there). As this book's title indicates, eco-justice is both a destination and the path of a continuing journey.

Fourth, an eco-justice ethic is *relational and contextual.* Contemporary cosmology and green sciences teach us that everything is internally related. The universe that flared forth more than ten billion years ago eventually produced galaxies and stars and, about four billion years ago, brought forth life on planet Earth, evolving into the richly diverse, infinitely interesting forms we know—from beetles to behemoths, mushrooms to mice, wheat to giant cedars, fish and birds, fungi and frogs to chimpanzees and whales and human beings. We all come from the same beginning and share common elements. Otherkind are kin to us; we are all related in an earth community alive with interdependent diversity. This profound cosmological, ecological insight decenters and resituates the sovereign human self that has dominated modern philosophy and science since Francis Bacon. The subjecthood of all created beings underscores an urgent need for earth-enhancing human behavior. It challenges our foolish domination and manipulation of the "external world" for convenience and profit, and it calls us to right (i.e., wise and just) relationships.

A relational ethic of eco-justice is contextual, not absolutist. Eco-justice norms inform immediate choices at any given time and place, but do not tell us exactly what to do. In light of social experience, religious/philosophical tradition, and critical reason (including scientific knowledge), our ethical task is to discern among available options the path of right relations, or the good to be achieved, through policies and practices that respect both biotic and cultural diversity.

Solidarity with earth and people, ecological sustainability, basic sufficiency, and fair participation all matter as mutually reinforcing and correcting norms that inform and qualify each other. Full-orbed efforts to achieve just and sustainable community, therefore, encompass these deep, practical values as essential, interactive components of a healthy future—that is, what earth community requires, and thrives on.

Fifth, this ethic projects *a hopeful vision of an alternative future* for global society, to be embodied in ecologically and socially appropriate public policies, technologies, and institutional and individual lifestyles, as well as meaningful democratic processes. An ethic of eco-justice nurtures just and sustainable ways of working, living, and reshaping community that respect and care for diverse beings while showing responsibility toward other humans and future generations. This is in sharp contrast to the socially cruel and ecologically destructive policies of economic globalization (including transgenic biomanipulation) that business and political elites around the world are busy fostering. The following essays on eco-justice journeying indicate what it will take to move toward the healthy, alternative paradigm of mutually enhancing human-earth relations. These essays also exemplify ways to embody the paradigm by living, working, educating, and advocating for a better future.

Sixth, by continuing the eco-justice journey, articulators and exemplars of this ethic are contributing to *an ecological reformation*. An eco-justice ethic, deeply rooted in nature and religion, enlivens the practice of ministry and theological-ethical reflection, as Bill Gibson himself exemplifies so well. Through frequent writing and speaking when he was coordinator of the Eco-Justice Project at Cornell University, Bill challenged the religious community in general and ecumenical churches in particular to join the journey. In the late 1980s, he became the prime drafter of the first major denominational report on this subject.[6] And he was quite active in ecumenical gatherings on eco-justice concerns. Meanwhile, a growing number of other writers also helped to refocus theology and ethics in ways that encompass ecology and justice.[7]

An ecological reformation poses an alternative to the insidiously dominant culture of hyperproduction and overconsumption, and shifts the axis of theology, ethics, and liturgy so as to focus on the real biophysical limits of threatened Earth and to highlight the human vocation of seeking human rights together with otherkind's well-being. To move in this direction involves abandoning old theological bad habits of separating history and humanity from nature, and separating human salvation from the redemption of creation. Another reforming step is to reread sacred texts with the view from outdoors, while continuing to read those same texts in light of the view from abroad and below (perspectives of the disregarded and powerless). With such fresh insight, it becomes natural to represent theology in terms that are both ecologically and socially alert, with the salutary effect of recycling traditional affirmations about God, Spirit, world, church, soul/body, sin and evil, community, redemption, and new earth.[8]

Seventh, an ethic of eco-justice challenges *interpreters of sustainable practices to encompass social justice*. This impels leaders and members of educational, business, and religious organizations to model a wider sense of sustainability in earth-honoring or "green" practices.[9] It recognizes that transformation is needed in our production, consumption, and investment patterns, what and how we learn, work and play, and the action networks we join, to show respect for nature's diversity, to respond to the world's abject poor, and to build sustainable community.

Are we here for creation's sake, or does Earth exist mostly for us humans? What is our responsibility to future generations, and to everykind now alive? As the following essays show, the eco-*in*justice crisis demands a coherent, spirited ethical response that attends to ecological integrity and social equity together—the well-being of humankind with otherkind in one Earth community over time.

Notes

1. For example, there is strong emphasis on eco-justice in Hebrew covenant law and Confucian humanism. Similar themes of just and sustainable community are emerging steadily in other religions. For perspectives on religion and ecology, see *Daedalus* 130 (4) (Fall 2001), and the ten-volume series on World Religions and Ecology published by the Harvard University Center for the Study of World Religions, Cambridge, Massachusetts.

2. Kusumita P. Pedersen, "Environmentalism in Interreligious Perspective," in *Explorations in Global Ethics,* Sumner B. Twiss and Bruce Grelle, eds. (Boulder, Colo.: Westview Press, 1998), 254.

3. The text of the Earth Charter, released in March 2000 by the Earth Council in Costa Rica, is available on the internet at <u>www.earthcharter.org</u>. The sixteen principles in this inclusive statement of global ethics are presented in four parts concerning (1) respect and care for the community of life, (2) ecological integrity, (3) social and economic justice, and (4) democracy, nonviolence, and peace. [The Earth Charter is Selection 24 in this volume.]

4. Aaron Sachs, *Eco-Justice: Linking Human Rights and the Environment,* Worldwatch Paper 127 (Washington, D.C.: Worldwatch Institute, 1998).

5. William E. Gibson, "Eco-Justice: New Perspective for a Time of Turning," in *For Creation's Sake: Preaching, Ecology and Justice,* Dieter T. Hessel, ed. (Louisville, Ky: Geneva Press, 1985), 25.

6. As then Director of Social Witness Policy for the Presbyterian Church (U.S.A.), I formed an Eco-Justice Task Force with Bill Gibson as member. For and with the task force, he drafted a study book, *Keeping and Healing the Creation* (Louisville, Ky.: Presbyterian Committee on Social Witness Policy, 1989), and then a report, *Restoring Creation for Ecology and Justice,* which was debated and adopted by the 202d General Assembly of the Presbyterian Church (U.S.A.) (Louisville, Ky.: Office of the General Assembly, 1990).

7. See the definitive bibliography in Peter W. Bakken, Joan Gibb Engel, and J. Ronald Engel, *Ecology, Justice, and Christian Faith: A Critical Guide to the Literature* (Westport, Conn.: Greenwood Press, 1995).

8. For a fuller discussion, see my concluding chapter, "The Church Ecologically Reformed," in *Earth Habitat: Eco-Injustice and the Church's Response,* Dieter T. Hessel and Larry Rasmussen, eds. (Minneapolis, Minn.: Fortress Press, 2001).

9. Higher education is the matrix for energetic eco-justice-oriented curriculum initiatives and leadership to institutionalize sustainable practices. For more information contact Campus Ecology (www.campus@nwf.org) and University Leaders for a Sustainable Future (www.ulsf.org).

Acknowledgments

I acknowledge with much gratitude the following:

The authors of the articles included in this book; the team, including especially Ingrid Olsen-Tjensvold, who conceived *The Egg / Eco-Justice Quarterly* and got it "hatched"; Sharon Lloyd O'Conner and Dieter T. Hessel, each of whom served as editor for a time; and *all* the contributors who made this journal truly one of its kind, including the many authors whose contributions I intended to use here but had to cut for lack of space.

My colleagues and companions in the founding and journeying of the Eco-Justice Project and Network—students, faculty members, church folks, EJ staff, coordinating committee members and chairs, subscribers, program participants—with special mention only of these very few: my colleague the late Frank Snow of the Genesee Area Campus Ministries, long-time Associate Coordinator Earl Arnold, and Willem Bodisco Massink, who chaired the coordinating committee for many years.

The various church agencies, small foundations, and many individuals whose financial support and encouragement kept the project and the journal precariously but vigorously alive, with particular thanks to our two most generous grantors, the Presbyterian Hunger Program and the United Methodist Board of Discipleship.

And family members whose always-willing help with the mysteries of the computer was indispensable: my daughter and son-in-law Debbie and Ron Jaworski, and my two grandsons Dan Jaworski and Carl Gibson.

Grateful acknowledgment is made for permission to reprint the following: Charles A. S. Hall's article, "Sanctioning Resource Depletion," which appeared first in *The Ecologist* 20 (3) May/June 1990; Holmes Rolston III's article, "Duties to Animals, Plants, Species and Ecosystems: Challenges to Christians," which appeared first as "Environmental Ethics: Some Challenges for Christians," in *The Annual: Society of Christian Ethics* (Washington, D.C.: Georgetown University Press, 1993), 37–50; and the quoted material in Larry

Introduction to the Journey

This book recounts a journey. It took place over the last several decades of the twentieth century. It continues into the twenty-first century, with new impetus, louder wake-up calls, and evidence still accumulating that a good future depends upon staying the course. **Eco-justice** is the journey itself as well as the outcome toward which it aims. The course is rocky, with enormous obstacles. They include not only the shortsighted self-interest of the powerful but also the deep, pervasive assumptions of our culture about progress and growth, the good life, and the relationship of humankind with nature.

The essays in this book exemplify a fresh grappling with the idea and the issues of eco-justice over a period of two decades. They provide a significant historical account of the eco-justice journey, largely from the standpoint of the formation, program, and publications of the Eco-Justice Project and Network, which was based at Cornell University in Ithaca, New York. The authors demonstrate a decidedly new awareness of reality and a distinctively contemporary perspective on nature and history. In my introductory Editor's Notes, looking back from the turn into the twenty-first century, I seek to maintain the theme of a journey against obstacles, reflecting a momentous time and imparting lessons for ongoing response and struggle.

I speak of the journey as one deeply engaged in it. I believe that my personal awakening and involvement were to a large extent representative of the Eco-Justice Network. Of course we—colleagues and companions—had considerable diversity among us, particularly in regard to the deepest roots of our embrace of the eco-justice values. But my participation enabled me to develop a reasonably comprehensive and coherent framework of thought for describing and interpreting the movement in which we were engaged.

The Times and the Movements

I had served as a minister in higher education for some twenty years before turning on to eco-justice. In all that time I believed firmly that justice in the social order was inescapably imperative for Christian faithfulness and responsible human action, but I did not yet understand justice in its ecological connections and dimensions. A major early step in my awakening came with the first Earth Day, in April 1970—not just the day itself but the entire academic year leading to it. Until that year I had no idea of the extent of the poisonous pollution from industrial production. Some years before, however, I had been roused to concern about population growth, by the message that natural and social systems could not indefinitely withstand the "explosion" of human numbers.

In 1970 I began to ask questions about the American economy. Through phenomenal growth in the post-World War II years it had extended a comfortable standard of living, for the first time, to a majority of the population, though still leaving a large minority behind. Could any eventual inclusion of these nonparticipants and the impoverished majorities in Third World countries continue to hinge upon ever greater economic growth in a world with more and more people? With questions like this I began my own journey toward eco-justice.

In 1970 and 1971 I was finally completing my doctoral program at Union Theological Seminary in New York, with a thesis on "Contextualism in Contemporary American Protestant Ethics." I examined several types of ethics, each of which put ethical decision into a context of something happening. Contextual ethics, I wrote, emphasizes the importance of the context in shaping the content of decisions about the right or the good or the fitting thing to do.

I did not examine a specifically ecological context of decision, as I surely would have if my project had been undertaken a few years later. Nevertheless, the emphasis on what was happening— on contemporary conditions and events—prepared me for an analysis of the "eco-justice crisis." I subjected the conditions and events of our time to the basic, abiding biblical, Christian norm of love inclusive of justice. I combined this abiding norm with the biblical, Christian understanding of God as involved in this world's affairs, the contemporary no less than the ancient. The context subjected to the norm and understood as important to God was the tumultuous time of the early 1970s. Several dynamic movements for justice for oppressed people were proceeding and converging. And now came a renewed and passionate mobilization in behalf of nature.

As the 1970s began, the civil rights movement, following the marches, riots, and gains of the 1960s, had turned its attention to persistent poverty and the subtle (or not so subtle) exclusions of

African Americans from full participation in the economy of abundance. The women's movement, protesting male domination and asserting equality and partnership with men, was gathering momentum. A little later came an increased national awareness of the magnitude (and obscenity) of hunger around the world, and new efforts by the churches to address or alleviate this global problem. But the most dramatic and strident mobilization in the new decade opposed the unjust war in Vietnam. This movement peaked with the "incursion" into Cambodia, the fatal shots at Kent State, and the mounting toll of death and destruction suffered by the Vietnamese people, the U.S. soldiers, and the Vietnamese landscape.

These drives and mobilizations sought justice. In one way or another they protested the afflictions of the vulnerable, the marginalized, and the weak at the hand of established power. As student protests against the war intensified, with nonviolent and sometimes violent resistance, the nation and the churches became severely divided. When some legal defense funds of the United Presbyterian Church were allocated to Angela Davis, a storm of protest arose within the denomination. She was black, female, antiwar, and anticapitalism.

In the midst of the complexities and turmoil of these justice movements came the resurgent environmentalism. Many Americans, wearied by the controversies and the abrasiveness of black and antiwar activism, welcomed the environmental movement as a blessed relief from the justice struggles. Surely everyone wanted clean air and water. On the other hand, many civil rights and antiwar activists rejected environmentalism as a craven cop-out from the struggles for justice to people.

The Eco-Justice Project and Network was founded on the conviction that both of these ways of viewing and shaping environmentalism had to be emphatically rejected. Concern for the earth and its myriad creatures and systems should not, must not, be a turning away from the cause of oppressed and suffering people. The concept of justice must be expanded to embrace all creation, human and nonhuman. Earth and people would thrive together or not at all. And the road to eco-justice would be no relief from controversy and opposition.

Launching the Project

In 1972 I was transferred by United Ministries in Higher Education (UMHE) in New York from my position with the Board for

Campus Ministry of the Rochester Area to the staff of the Southern Tier Area Council of UMHE, with a base at Cornell University in Ithaca. In the summer of that year as I prepared to move, I read *The Limits to Growth* by Donella and Dennis Meadows and their colleagues at Massachusetts Institute of Technology. The authors, a team of systems analysts, reported their computer-based projections of five interacting global trends—population growth, the application of capital to industrial production (economic growth), food production, environmental pollution, and resource depletion. Their projections indicated that the world was heading for "overshoot and collapse" sometime in the twenty-first century if these trends continued. Human numbers and industrial output would grow beyond the capacity of planetary systems to sustain them, and then would decline or collapse more or less precipitously. Obviously that would entail massive suffering, premature deaths, and social as well as environmental breakdowns and upheavals.[1]

This book galvanized and focused the concern I had begun to feel, that human beings were carelessly and cruelly abusing nature and doing so in ways that would redound harshly and perhaps fatally upon themselves. In those days, UMHE in New York was seeking ideas for area-based ministries that would be responsive to the times and capable of drawing together the resources of church and university in a common concern for the larger society. I worked with Frank Snow, who had succeeded me in the Rochester area, and others to develop a project that would combine the concerns of ecology and justice. It was indeed a response to the times: the radically new awareness of the limits imposed by nature upon human behavior and demands together with continuing struggle against old injustices in their distinctively contemporary forms.

Throughout 1973 we had monthly meetings in Seneca Falls, halfway between Rochester and Ithaca, of a small study group composed mainly of campus ministers and faculty people. We examined this new consciousness of ecological limits and its implications for justice, survival, and the values by which people live. Only half facetiously, we sometimes dubbed ourselves the "Club of Seneca Falls," a takeoff on the Club of Rome, the international group of scholars and industrialists to which *The Limits to Growth* had been a report.

From the study group came the convening of a regional consultation of church and university people from three of the areas—Southern Tier, Genesee (Rochester), and Central New York—into which UMHE had divided its work. We asked participants to consider themselves the Eco-Justice Task Force,[2] with intention to stay involved. The theme of the consultation was "Coming to Terms with the Limits to Growth: Fact, Value and Practice." The keynote speaker was Norman Faramelli of the Boston Industrial Mission, one of those who had already given currency to the term eco-justice.[3]

Because there was no way for a task force on eco-justice to complete its "task," our task force evolved into the Eco-Justice Project and Network (EJPN). The project was sponsored by the Center for Religion, Ethics and Social Policy (CRESP) at Cornell University and by UMHE in New York. Upon the dissolution after a few years of the latter organization, Genesee Area Campus Ministries became cosponsor with CRESP, while the project maintained its headquarters in Anabel Taylor Hall, the religious affairs building on the Cornell campus.

Addressing the Issues

EJPN put on a remarkable series of local/regional/national conferences, colloquia, and forums from 1974 to 1992. These presented the big picture of the global eco-justice crisis: the environmental degradation and ecological constraints and limits, on the one hand, and, on the other hand, the massive deprivation, hunger, suffering, and inequality among people, most of which were unnecessary and therefore unjust. We defined a number of major issues of the day as eco-justice issues, so-called because they could not be addressed responsibly without the eco-justice perspective: hunger, energy, lifestyle, economics, good work, and peacemaking, as well as specific environmental problems. We dealt with practical matters of solid waste, the particular concerns of women in the eco-justice crisis, and the emergence of "eco-communities." Speakers and panelists included Kenneth Boulding, Roger Shinn, Hazel Henderson, John B. Cobb, Jr., E. F. Schumacher, Amory Lovins, Barry Commoner, Hans Bethe, Kenneth Cauthen, Paul Sweezy, Murray Bookchin, Robert Lekachman, Jeremy Rifkin, Herman Daly, Elizabeth Dodson Gray, Donella and Dennis Meadows, Gar Alperovitz, Larry Rasmussen, Gerald Barney, Maurice Hinchey, Lois Gibbs, John Haught, William Clark, William K. Tabb, Heidi Hadsell, and James A. Nash.

EJPN carried on extensive education and outreach addressed to churches, campuses, and communities. Programs included a minicourse taken to church and other groups on "Eco-Justice: Crisis and Response"; a Fact-Value-Policy Colloquium on energy issues and another on steady-state economics; a long-running Cornell faculty study group on The Global 2000 Report to the President; collaboration with Rochester Area Colleges on Peace Education and Global Studies; a continuing education course for clergy and lay leaders; and a "Beyond the Year 2000" academic course at Cornell. We prepared several slide presentations, notably one shown many times on "Untangling the Waste Knot," developed by Will Burbank, my successor as EJPN Coordinator. Mary Jeanette Ebenhack, Burbank's successor, put together a year-long forum series in connection with the EcoVillage development in Ithaca.

EJPN staff contributed to national denominational and ecumenical responses to the eco-justice crisis, including the launching of the Eco-Justice Working Group of the National Council of Churches in 1984, and the policy statement of the Presbyterian Church (U.S.A.) entitled *Restoring Creation for Ecology and Justice*, adopted in 1990. A study and program group of EJPN produced a curriculum manual, *A Covenant Group for Lifestyle Assessment*, which was published (1978 and 1981) by the United Presbyterian Program Agency and used extensively by four denominations. The United Methodist Board of Discipleship made it the basis for a year-long series of lifestyle conferences around the country, led by a Roman Catholic sister. I took advantage of fairly frequent opportunities to contribute to journals or books, as did EJPN's Associate Coordinator, Earl Arnold.[4]

The Journal of Eco-Justice

EJPN initiated its own publication in January 1981 under the leadership of Associate Coordinator Ingrid Olsen-Tjensvold. This was an outgrowth of our mimeographed newsletter, *Eco-Justice Themes*, which had begun in 1974. We called the new journal *The Egg*, a name inspired by a poem of Nikos Kazantzakos. The poem speaks of the present and the coming moments as "horrifying." "But the moment further on . . . will be utterly brilliant . . . [for the] belly of the earth is still full of eggs."[5]

There was always a bit of friendly contention about the name. We became careful to add *A Journal of Eco-Justice*. Some of our folks tired of needing to recover and explain the name's origin. In 1993 it was changed to *Eco-Justice Quarterly*.

The first editors were Ingrid Olsen-Tjensvold and her successor as Associate Coordinator, Sharon Lynn Lloyd (now Sharon Lloyd-O'Conner). When a staff reduction became necessary in late 1983, the editorship fell to me. I continued until 1991, when Dieter T. Hessel took over for a two-year period as editor with me as senior editor. In national Presbyterian staff roles, Hessel had given institutional and theological leadership to denominational and ecumenical incorporation of eco-justice into church program and mission. During the final two years of the journal there were guest editors under the oversight of Dana Horrell, who was EJPN Director from 1992 to 1995.

In 1985 the Eco-Justice Working Group of the National Council of Churches became a cosponsor of the journal. Denominational members of the Working Group ordered copies in bulk and distributed them to their own constituencies. Subscribers, EJPN members, exchanges, copies for conferences, and persons and offices we kept in touch with but never charged added up to only a few thousand but were spread throughout the country and reached a few overseas destinations as well. We believe *The Egg/Eco-Justice Quarterly* had influence and impact greater than the small circulation would suggest, and greater than might have been expected from the limited resources of budget and part-time staff that kept it going.

No other journal has been as intentional and consistent in maintaining an explicit emphasis on eco-justice—ecological wholeness and social and economic justice in their essential connection.

Meaning, Values, and Vision

The ecology-justice connection belongs to the meaning of the term as we insisted on defining it. Eco-justice does not mean merely another aspect of justice, so that now we have to speak of social justice *and* eco-justice. The term eco-justice retains the ancient claim upon human moral agents to build and nurture responsible, equitable, compassionate relationships among humans in the social order. And it incorporates the realization that has come like a revelation to our own time, that human societies cannot flourish unless natural systems flourish too. It affirms, moreover, that the nonhuman realm is not merely instrumental to human well-being but intrinsically value-laden in its own right.

Explaining eco-justice, I have sometimes said that the "eco" is for ecology and the "justice" is for Jeremiah—reflecting my indebtedness to the prophetic strand central to the biblical story as well as to the ongoing prophetic tradition in Judaism and Christianity. As for the intrinsic value not only of human but of nonhuman being, this is rooted, I find, in the biblical, Christian understanding of God as Creator, the source, lover, ruler, sustainer, and ultimate redeemer of all creatures, all that is. The Creator's creation encompasses the long evolutionary process and the cycles, systems, interdependencies, balances, and beauty that make life possible and good.

The EJPN originated out of Christian campus ministry, and the greater part of its financial support over the years came from church bodies. Certainly not all EJPN members, however, nor all the readers of the journal, acknowledged a biblical or Christian rooting. We sought a membership and a readership inclusive of any who actually or potentially felt the power of the claim to care about both earth and people. For Christians speaking to Christians, it was appropriate to appeal to the biblical, Christian story and to make a contextual, contemporary analysis of that story's valuation of justice, creation, and community. At the same time, however, we found throughout EJPN a shared commitment to certain eco-justice values, and we generally could agree as to which contemporary issues most urgently needed to be subjected to those values.

It was actually a bit tricky to make the journal speak to people of faith and show how their faith made those values integral to faithfulness, and at the same time to keep with us those persons genuinely committed to eco-justice but resistant to any implication that their commitment needed to depend upon religious belief and affiliation, Christian or otherwise. Perhaps there were some who thought the journal was too Christian and others who thought it not Christian enough. On the whole, I think we succeeded in speaking with integrity to inform and challenge Christians, without losing the EJPN companions with a different grounding.

We in the Eco-Justice Project participated in the development of an eco-justice ethic, which has become characteristic of denominational and ecumenical thinking, reporting, and writing on ecology and justice. This is evident in the policy statements and study materials coming from the churches belonging to the National and World Councils of Churches and from those Councils themselves.

Four eco-justice norms or values (normative values) emerged as particularly relevant to this time in history, the time of the eco-justice crisis, a momentous time of turning from one historical era to the next. Although the number of values on the list (we started with three) sometimes got larger, I felt that the additions were actually encompassed by the four. It seemed useful to keep the number short.

Selection 2 elaborates the four norms of participation, sufficiency, sustainability, and solidarity. The first two—participation and sufficiency—convey the distinctive contemporary meaning of justice. Because of their necessary connection with sustainability and solidarity, justice has to be understood as eco-justice.

These normative values provide the basis for envisioning an eco-just future. Eco-justice means a world with various forms and levels of community in which all members participate in obtaining and enjoying sufficient sustenance from nature. It means a world in which the arrangements for drawing sustenance are shaped, not only by human need and want, but also by appreciation of the natural world and respect for the rightful place of nonhuman creatures, the integrity of natural systems, and the claim for a viable habitat that all the future generations of creatures, human and nonhuman, make upon the present. Eco-justice means the well-being of all humankind on a thriving earth. It means a sustainable sufficiency for all.

The Rocky Road Ahead

We do not imagine that the journey to eco-justice leads to a utopian future. Neither eco-justice nor the kingdom of God will come to more than partial realization in the historical drama. But we are called to participate in the drama, the continuing story, and to respond to our best discernment of God's project in our time. The stark realities of our time—and, to the eyes of faith, God's judging, liberating presence in them—make the journey necessary. These realities contradict the modern view of the world and demand a new perspective that acknowledges the interdependencies necessary for life and rejects the anthropocentric assumption that human beings have the right and the wit to conquer nature.

The sustainability factor shows that we humans cannot long continue to dominate nature as in the modern era we have tried to do. Nor can we satisfy the needs of the human family unless we in the developed world reduce our material wants and build communities and economies of cooperation, sharing, and equitable distribution. In solidarity, we have to see how sustainability and sufficiency depend upon each other. We have to both "till and keep the garden"—to draw earth's bounty carefully and share it equitably. To come to these realizations and act upon them is to journey toward eco-justice.

The articles that follow elaborate upon the values and the vision of eco-justice and their implications for policy and practice. In the commentary that accompanies them and in my concluding chapter, it is important to keep in view the rough and rocky character of the road upon which we travel.

The obstacles to eco-justice are powerful, formidable, deeply rooted and entrenched. This has become increasingly apparent over the years of the Eco-Justice Project and the publication of the journal. To note the original publication dates of the articles will help to show that only as we sought to move toward eco-justice could we come to grasp the monumental difficulty of effecting the societal changes in thinking, valuing, policy making and daily living that eco-justice requires. We travel on a rocky road toward a sustainable sufficiency for all, and we have a long, hard way to go.

Notes

1. Donella H. Meadows, Dennis L. Meadows, Jørge Randers, and William W. Behrens III, *The Limits to Growth* (New York: Universe Books, 1972).

2. We took the word "eco-justice" with the meaning given to it, a few years earlier, as an outcome of a notable effort at the national level of the American Baptist Churches to relate the evangelical Christian faith to the contemporary situation. Owen D. Owens gave an account of the origin of the word in a 1999 paper entitled "Choose Life." Jitsuo Morikawa, who in 1956 became secretary for evangelism in the American Baptist Home Mission Societies, started a program to train Christian lay people to be agents of the transformation of the major institutions that shape society, for the sake of justice and liberation. In the 1960s Morikawa headed up a sweeping reorganization of the Home Mission Societies (a name changed later to National Ministries). He directed an intensive study to collect data on the major institutions and to identify the leading social trends, and thus to determine the contemporary context of the church's mission. Heading the list of trends were several having to do either with ecology or with justice. Owen Owens, a staff associate in the reorganization process, argued that there could be no choice between ecology and justice, or between nature and history. Another staff person, Richard Jones, coined the word *eco-justice* to mean both ecological wholeness and social justice. Out of the reorganization, the American Baptist Board of National Ministries in 1972 adopted the goal of "structural change of institutions toward ecological wholeness and social justice at their points of intersection."

3. Norman J. Faramelli's article, "Ecological Responsibility and Economic Justice" in the *Andover Newton Quarterly* 11 (November 1970), contributed to my new awareness of the need to connect ecology and economics.

4. William E. Gibson and Earl B. Arnold contributed to *A Covenant Group for Lifestyle Assessment* and to *Shalom Connections in Personal and Congregational Life*, edited by Dieter T. Hessel (Ellenwood, Ga.: Alternatives, 1981). Gibson's published articles include: "Eco-Justice: New Perspective for a Time of Turning," Dieter T. Hessel, ed., *For Creation's Sake:*

Preaching, Ecology and Justice (Philadelphia: Geneva Press, 1985); "An Order in Crisis and the Declaration of New Things," Robert L. Stivers, ed., *Reformed Faith and Economics* (Lanham, Md.: University Press of America, 1989); "Global Warming as a Theological-Ethical Concern," Dieter T. Hessel, ed., *After Nature's Revolt: Eco-Justice and Theology* (Minneapolis, Minn.: Fortress Press, 1992); "Eco-Justice and the Reality of God," *Church and Society*, July/August 1996; "The Obstacles to Changing Course," *Church and Society*, January/February 1997; and "The Sustainability Factor and the Work of God in Our Time," *Earth Letter*, November 1998. Arnold's include: "Changing Our Lifestyles, Changing Our World," Nadine Hundertmark, ed., *Pro-Earth* (New York: Friendship Press, 1985); and "The Solid Waste Crisis," *Church and Society*, March/April 1990.

5. I do not know which member of the team that worked on launching the journal came up with Kazantzakos's poem, or whether what we had was the entire poem or part of a longer one. I have tried unsuccessfully to locate the poem.

Part I

The Eco-Justice Perspective:
Crisis, Meaning, and Motivation

In many articles in *The Egg: A Journal of Eco-Justice*, which became the *Eco-Justice Quarterly*, the editors and authors aimed to change radically the way people looked at the world. We did not want only to extend spirituality to their relationship with nature, or to rouse them to action on specific cases of pollution, or to encourage lifestyles less oriented to consumption. We sought to portray the big picture within which those things make sense. The big picture is the rationale for the journey to eco-justice.

The journey entails new ways of seeing, thinking, valuing, worshipping, working, and playing and engenders new habits for day-to-day living and new foci for acting politically. But the various kinds of new doing and not doing to which people may be drawn need to be motivated by a sense of meaning and direction, a sense of appropriateness to the salient realities of the times together with a vision, however limited, of the better times worth seeking. Without motivation stemming from clarity about the eco-justice crisis and the adventurous worthwhileness of responding to it, travelers find it all too tempting to turn aside from the journey.

1

Not Just Ecology, Not Just Economics—ECO-JUSTICE

Chris Cowap

Editor's Notes

In early 1984 representatives of Canadian and U.S. churches convened in Toronto for an international consultation on acid rain. The prime initiator of the event, David Hallman of the United Church of Canada, had invited Chris Cowap of the National Council of the Churches of Christ in the United States of America to recruit an appropriate U.S. delegation. Among those who went was a core group of national denominational staff persons whose portfolios did or might include concern for the environment. The Toronto event gave impetus to a feeling that it would be useful to have a new vehicle whereby those persons, plus regional and local thinkers and activists, might collaborate ecumenically on the issues of ecology and justice. For several years the Responsible Lifestyle Task Force of an ecumenical agency, the Joint Strategy and Action Committee (JSAC), had been exploring the issues and visiting local sites of concern and activity. With collaboration by JSAC (which was in the final years of its own life), the Eco-Justice Working Group of the National Council of Churches (NCC) was established in late 1984 and early 1985.

Chris Cowap was the Director of Economic and Social Justice in the NCC's Division of Church and Society. Until her untimely

*death in 1988, she gave invaluable leadership to the formation
and the identity of the Working Group. The initial projects and
programs of the Group culminated in a December 1–3, 1986 national ecumenical consultation, "For the Love of Earth and People:
The Eco-Justice Agenda." Indeed it proved to be a major consultation, with consequences, and I shall make further references to it
in my notes. In the article that follows, Chris Cowap announces
the consultation and expresses her hopes for the relationships and
mechanisms that it may generate.*

*This article is a good introduction to the eco-justice perspec-
tive. In brief compass, Cowap's grounding for the consultation includes the following key elements of the way today's world is viewed
and understood from the perspective of eco-justice:*

> 1. *Rejection of the anthropocentric valuation of the nonhu-
> man strictly in terms of what is good for humans.*
>
> 2. *Recognition that the anthropocentric way of valuing and
> devaluing nature is deeply imbedded in Western techno-
> cratic civilization.*
>
> 3. *Acknowledgment of Christian implication in the misuse of
> the verses in Genesis 1 telling humans to "subdue" the
> earth and exercise "dominion."*
>
> 4. *Acceptance of scientific findings that the harsh treatment
> of nature by humans has become destructive to themselves.*
>
> 5. *Insistence on the inseparability of ecology and economics
> and the folly of treating them as competing concerns.*
>
> 6. *Recognition of the herculean difficulties of changing an-
> thropocentric assumptions and making economics ecologi-
> cally responsible.*
>
> 7. *Affirmation of ecology/justice as a religious concern pos-
> ing major new challenges to the churches.*

*The concern of the churches for economic justice, to which
Cowap refers, had begun to wane somewhat even as she wrote. Her
reference reflects the prophetic voice for justice of mainstream
Christianity, which had been raised with some vigor in the 1960s
and continued into the 1970s. I think, however, that the slowness
of the churches to accept eco-justice as a religious concern was not
because they saw environmentalism as competitive with economic
justice. It was related more to a turning inward and a general
weakening of their prophetic role in society, which became apparent in the 1980s and continued through the 1990s.*

Not Just Ecology, Not Just Economics— ECO-JUSTICE

(The Egg 6 [3], Fall 1986)

Once upon a time the sanctity of creation was integral to Judeo-Christian faith. Gradually that respect for the intrinsic worth of all God has created and will create degenerated into human arrogance, as Western civilization implemented the Genesis mandate to "fill the earth and subdue it; and have dominion over . . . every living thing." Though biblical scholars now interpret dominion as caretaking, in practice Genesis was and is translated into "conquer the earth and dominate everything in it, because no thing has value except as it is useful to us human beings."

Finding a New Way of Looking

Only in the last couple of decades has the realization that such heedless destruction cannot continue begun to spread from ecologists to ordinary residents of technocratic society. Now many of the people are way ahead of their "leaders" in understanding that today's toxic dump is tomorrow's poisoned water and malformed babies. More than 80 percent of U.S. residents now profess themselves willing to pay higher taxes for a cleaner environment. Many of them proclaim ecological health to be the top priority that must take precedence over all other issues: "If we're all poisoned, it does not matter who has or doesn't have a job."

Meanwhile, the churches have continued to show lively concern for economic justice issues. Intensive campaigns for full employment or better income maintenance and just treatment of the poor mark progressive Christianity's last few decades. Our prayers that justice may roll like mighty waters have usually meant *economic* justice. Many local church and community leaders insist that the immediate needs of persons for jobs and economic security must take precedence over all other issues: "It won't matter if the water is sparkling clean if people's families are hungry and homeless."

To pose these two issues—ecological wholeness and economic justice—against each other is to invite a debilitating struggle which nobody can win, with energies turned against each other instead of against the common enemies of both causes. We need to shake our kaleidoscopes and find a different, creative pattern, a new way of looking at the world.

Erroneous Beliefs and the Difficulty of Change

All industrialized societies of whatever political hue have built themselves on two erroneous beliefs: that the natural resources necessary for material well-being are essentially infinite and available to be harnessed technologically for the common good, and that the biosphere (air, land, and water) is capable of endlessly absorbing poisonous wastes without itself being poisoned and poisoning creatures or things that depend on it. Simply to recognize the wrongheadedness of these two assumptions and to adapt our actions to ecological reality will be a herculean task involving revolutionary changes in industrial methods, cessation of some kinds of production, and a lifestyle of curtailed consumption for some that is potentially richer in quality for everyone. The *Global 2000 Report* to President Carter attempted to make this point, but most people were paralyzed at the prospect and still refuse to face ecological reality, vainly hoping that it will go away.

Undergirding our present mindset are the familiar sins of pride and idolatry. We have imagined creation to be a hierarchical pyramid with ourselves at the top, and used or accepted the use of Scripture to justify this arrogance, or remained silent when political theorists asserted the sanctity of human freedom to exploit resources. We have relied on our own wits to solve the problems arising from acting on such a misconception of reality, counting on the next "techno-fix" to rescue us from our own folly. And we have put our trust in an ever-growing supply of material resources to avoid the hard, self-sacrificial, sharing actions that the contemporary situation requires of us.

The struggle to reach a new acceptance of our own fallibility and the interconnectedness of all of creation is daunting. But it is almost dwarfed by the dilemmas that necessarily accompany significant implementation of a sounder vision: how to achieve a reversal of careless planet rape or poisoning while ensuring just distribution of the costs and benefits of doing so. This translates most obviously into questions of employment, investment of capital, and "cost" redefined to include what have been brushed aside as "externalities" (loss of jobs, community disruption, effects of pollution on people and eco-systems, and everything else not directly affecting the producer), as well as the urgent need to develop methods of citizen participation that allow those who will be affected by such actions to be involved efficiently and effectively in policy decision-making.

To give one concrete example: numerous versions of legislation designed to prevent further ecological damage caused by acid rain were stalled in Congress because they failed to address adequately two problems of economic justice: how to reduce sulfur dioxide emissions in ways that would preserve the threatened jobs of soft coal miners, and how to pay for cleanup in ways that would shield low-income people from utility rate increases. Politically vehement forces, abetted by utility companies already troubled with overcapacity to generate electricity, had each other at a standstill. It has taken some very intricate bargaining to craft legislation that can become politically viable by meeting demands to: clean up emissions, protect jobs, distribute costs fairly, and shelter the poor. The prospects for equitable acid rain legislation improved as parties to the conflict came to realize that seemingly competitive issues were inextricably linked. Political pragmatism, if nothing else, had insisted on a new bifocal response.

Call to Consultation

"For the Love of Earth and People: The Eco-Justice Agenda," a national ecumenical consultation to be held December 1–3, 1986 at Stony Point Center, Stony Point, New York, brings people together around the new bifocal vision. Called by the Eco-Justice Working Group of the National Council of Churches of Christ and of the Joint Strategy and Action Committee, this event challenges each of us to comprehend the context in which all current and emerging justice issues, whether understood as "economic" or "ecological," must be judged. Our objective is to look at economic issues through the lens of environmental sustainability, and to look at environmental issues through the lens of economic justice. Enabling people to use these "bifocals" is critical to the effective solution of both kinds of issues.

Even the contemporary language necessary to define the problem beclouds it, since the point is that there are *not* two separate categories of issues (economic and ecological) but rather two facets of the same concern for earth and all creatures. The New Testament understanding of *oikonomia* of the *oikos*—stewardship of the whole inhabited earth—expresses the unity of justice to creation.

The churches acting ecumenically and coalitionally may be the most capable of healing the often bitter distrust and disdain felt by activists who have been working for either economic justice or environmental renewal. By bringing together a mix of religious and secular environmental leaders, community economic justice organizers and clean air/water/earth activists, we hope to weave connections that will bind together heretofore divided and separate elements of the caring community. We also plan to launch more effective ecumenical mechanisms for educating the public and acting for ecology/justice. May those few days in December come to be seen as an important step toward overcoming the wariness and obsolete thinking that hamper us, and the beginning of a mutual embrace that strengthens us all for effective action around our common concern for the "well-being of all humankind on a thriving earth."

2

Eco-Justice: What Is It?

William E. Gibson

Editor's Notes

The term "eco-justice" is not a household word. The Eco-Justice Project and Network (EJPN) and the EJ Working Group of the National Council of Churches intentionally put meaning into it and made consistent efforts both to explain it and to guard against the misunderstanding or watering down of its meaning.

Sometimes people think the "eco" means "economic," and we have to say, no, it means "ecology." But because "justice" refers prominently to economic justice, we must add quickly that economic justice is very much a part of eco-justice.

Sometimes the term has been used to mean only ecological justice, that is, fair and caring treatment of natural systems and nonhuman creatures. We must say, no, it means ecological wholeness and economic and social justice. I have always insisted on the hyphen in eco-justice; it makes the and more apparent, the two sides of one concern.

In the early days of The Egg *we devoted an issue to "Eco-Justice: Probing the Meaning." It was not just about defining the term. Various members of EJPN illustrated the meaning by telling what their involvement had meant to them. Their testimonies showed that EJPN was not just a think tank: it was a community.*

Wayne Heym, a former Cornell graduate student who had become a computer programmer, wrote: "A Covenant Group for

21

Lifestyle Assessment [the name of EJPN's curriculum and of the group it called for], in which I participated, really helped me not only to learn, in my head, the connections between my lifestyle, the choices I make, and destitute poverty and ecological problems in the world. It helped me to put [these connections] more into myself as a whole—into my being and make them important to me."

Diane Knispel (now Diane Gibbons), at the time a theology student in Rochester, said: "I was having a very difficult time when I was in college—taking courses in environmental education and religion. And while I felt personally interested in both, I couldn't see how I could combine them into a career. So it was really exciting and transforming when I discovered Eco-Justice. . . . People at Eco-Justice had integrated both concerns. They were coming from a spiritual perspective and engaging in issues of justice and ecology."

Anita Jaehn, who was coordinating Monroe Community College's program on Women in Technologies, had this to say: "Eco-Justice has been part of my life for a long time, and I cannot separate it from my religion. It is really my conscience, as I am always asking myself, 'Is this something I really need to buy or is it something that I want?' I am also constantly asking myself questions in terms of my work . . . questions such as, 'Am I encouraging women to train for work that is not eco-just?'"

Marian Shearer, a U.C.C. clergywoman who served on the Eco-Justice Coordinating Committee for many years, wrote: "Even at the point when I was most involved and would say, 'Oh do I need one more meeting!' I still would not have given up the link to people all over the state who were struggling just as hard as I was with how do we address world hunger, how do we address our threatened ecology, how do we address the problems of the world in war and peace issues. I'm glad to be in touch with people who know more than I know about economics, nuclear physics and all the rest of it, and who respect what I know about lifestyle and theology."

I have said, in more recent times, that the church should be a community of support for adventurous faithfulness in response to God in the eco-justice crisis. It wasn't exactly church, but the EJPN was that kind of community.

The following article offers a fuller explanation of eco-justice than was possible in the Introduction. It shows more explicitly how the eco-justice norms or values are necessary contemporary expressions of the abiding biblical themes of justice, stewardship, and community.

Here I used the word "trusteeship" for stewardship—avoiding a word church people tend to use too glibly, as they overstress the managerial role of humans in relating to nature. Too much of the management has been egregious, and what now is most needed is for humans to draw back and let nature heal itself. Still, in great humility, we cannot shed our responsibility for what we do or do not do, for the healing of creation.

The article has been slightly revised since first published, to make explicit the value or norm of participation (together with sufficiency) as the distinctive contemporary meaning of justice.

Eco-Justice: What Is It?

(*The Egg* 2 [4], December 1982)

I. Ecological Awareness and the Common Good

The idea of eco-justice draws together the essential considerations for understanding and influencing the great transition. I mean the historic movement from one age to another that someday will be written up as the story of our time. Perhaps I tend toward grandiosity in talking about eco-justice—or formulating goals for funding proposals. Only half facetiously have I remarked that the Eco-Justice Project aims to save the world before it is too late. I am in fact dead serious in believing it is precisely that goal to which we who participate in Eco-Justice, the network and the project, seek to make a modest contribution.

Of course our accomplishments are modest, but they tie in with the efforts of thousands and thousands of persons and networks, organizations, and movements all over the world. I think they tie in with the momentum of history, the wave of the future, the purpose of God. But there I go getting grandiose again.

Let me try to put it soberly. We live in a time of more-than-ordinary change; and the efforts of human beings to shape the future are more-than-usually significant. If we understand what is happening, we see where to exert our influence. If we realize what is at stake, we have an inescapable responsibility to do all we can to shape a world society that will be fulfilling and fair to all its human members and at the same time sound and sustainable with respect to the whole ecology of life on this planet.

I have often said that eco-justice means ecology and justice. More accurately, it means justice in the context of a new ecological awareness. This new awareness is so momentous that it requires a far-reaching extension of our old ideas of justice.

Those ideas have to do with fairness and the common good—with the claim that all persons make claims to be respected and valued and included in the arrangements that a society makes for meeting the various needs of its members. Justice in society means a set of arrangements or institutions that foster the good of all. They make it possible for everyone to have a proportionate, appropriate share of the ingredients of a fulfilling existence.

Those who seek a just society must take account of the forces opposing such arrangements. Even the best society remains a compromise between justice ideally conceived and the hard realities of human self-centeredness. A rough justice in the real world prevails when moral values and norms and institutionalized restraints adequately limit the power and wealth of those who would otherwise promote their own advantage at the expense of others.

The new idea of eco-justice holds on to the old ideas of human justice, with their idealism and their realism, and extends them to the realm of the nonhuman.

Without letting go of the claim as made by persons, eco-justice recognizes in other creatures and natural systems the claim to be respected and valued and taken into account in societal arrangements. It is not enough for human values, practices, and institutions to foster the good of all the people; they must become eco-just by seeking human good in harmony with nature.

Eco-justice is more than a prudential reminder to people that they had better protect the environment in order to protect themselves. It sees humans as bound up with, and integral to, that larger living fabric of all that is, which some call simply nature and some call God's good creation. Eco-justice finds value in the health and integrity of the whole natural order. The concern for ecological soundness and sustainability includes but transcends the concern of human beings for themselves.

II. A Response to What is Happening

You have to have a keen sense of what is happening in the world in order to appreciate what eco-justice is all about. You have to feel like a participant in history as a story unfolding now, a pivotal chapter in the process, the journey, the struggle that engages us humans who, remembering the past and envisioning the future, strive to live fittingly in the present. The idea of eco-justice capsulizes what has to have priority if a viable future is to emerge from the agonies and dangers of our present circumstances.

Although I did not hear the term till later, the idea of eco-justice was taking shape for me in 1970, a dozen years ago. The protests against the Vietnam War reached their peak that year. And the first Earth Day drove home to my consciousness the enormity of environmental degradation. The war brought a deeper dimension to my analysis of the ancient struggle for social justice. And the Earth Day observance provided a new context so full of implications for dealing with the justice question that it could never be ignored again.

The protracted disaster in Vietnam sharpened my existential realization of the power and the intransigence, the cruelty, and the hypocrisy of the forces, individual and collective, that put narrow and self-serving interests before the common good. I cannot give the details now. Suffice it to say that I came to a keener realization of the existence and operation of those forces in my own country—not that they were here and therefore not elsewhere, but that they were here as well as elsewhere. It became clear that the struggle for justice must entail a fundamental critique of the expansionist drive of the U.S. economy and the role of the United States in the world. That critique would surely lead, if we cared about justice, to the acceptance of fundamental changes in our system, our institutions, our operative values with respect to the control of the resources of the earth and the distribution of the benefits derived therefrom.

At the same time, from Earth Day I began to see what the ruthlessness and violence of the expansionist capitalist economy was doing to the landscape and to the life-supporting capability of the air, the water, and the soil. I began to see that the treatment of nature in modern industrial society posed a threat to human and planetary survival. Two years later this new ecological awareness was further intensified by my reading *The Limits to Growth*. The problems created by industry could not be solved simply by imposing pollution controls (important as those were). The indiscriminate growth of resource-intensive industry, like the soaring of the population, was inherently unsustainable and suicidal on this finite planet.

If economic growth could not be sustained, this would enormously compound the problem of distributive justice. It was bad enough to have the world hunger crisis of 1973–75 dramatize in excruciating detail the agony of malnutrition and starvation and the widening chasm between the poor majority and the affluent minority of the planet's people. (The shame of the rich-poor gap was that it did not need to be. The fruitfulness of the earth and the available techniques for production and distribution could have been employed to provide the basic necessities of life to all.) But if the industrial economies could not grow on much longer and if the Western model of development could not be the key to overcoming Third World poverty, those already impoverished and oppressed by the global economic order would be driven down still deeper into the mire of wretchedness and dependency. When I viewed the struggle for justice in the context of ecological limits, it became painfully apparent, not only that modern technology and industry had failed to prevent massive poverty, but that they would surely continue to fail if their success depended upon the ever more intensive exploitation of finite resources. Those resources were being degraded and devoured.

Eco-justice means a whole new way of looking at the world. It has become the indispensable perspective for criticizing *economics*: determining *good work*; making the *lifestyle* of persons and institutions responsible; overcoming *hunger*; addressing the *energy* crisis; and *making peace*. Those tasks or issues, plus that of protecting the *environment* itself, have been identified as eco-justice issues. All interconnected, they represent the particular concerns of Eco-Justice as a network of caring people. In Eco-Justice as a project we have studied and analyzed them all—in EJ gatherings, EJ publications, and EJ outreach—and worked on the matter of next steps that we and others can take to address them through personal practice and public policy advocacy.

III. Values For an Eco-Just Future

From first to last the participation of persons in our network has been motivated, informed, and sustained by a set of values and underlying beliefs. Since we are a pluralistic network, we do not express in just one way the foundation of eco-justice values. For me these values are not new; they represent the translation of old and enduring values into radically new relevance to conditions and events in the present time. I draw these values from the biblical story and from a Christian conception of life's meaning.

In the biblical story the word for justice is the word for righteousness and is always the expression of God's steadfast, compassionate love. Over and over again we find this love directed particularly to the poor and the oppressed—"the widow, the fatherless, and the sojourner," the victims of greed, cruelty, and carelessness and those who are peculiarly vulnerable to being victimized. God regards the hunger and suffering of the victims as the intolerable consequence of oppression, stemming from hardness of heart and faithlessness. Clearly God wills sufficiency through sharing. The Apostle Paul, therefore, appeals to the Christians in Corinth: give as generously as you are able to the offering for the poor in Jerusalem, "that as a matter of equality your abundance at the present time [may] supply their want . . ."; for "God is able to provide you with every blessing in abundance, so that you may always have *enough.* . . ." (II Cor. 8:14 and 9:8)

Applied to the "eco-justice crisis"—compounded of distributive injustice and ecological limits—these verses provide the clue to the norms of justice for our time: participation and sufficiency. Justice entails *participation* in the important decisions that affect one's life. There are to be no marginalized, disregarded people. This norm means the right and the opportunity to participate in the life of one's community, including the life of its economy. Participation requires democratic institutions. And it means that each person takes part as able and gifted in "good work," the work needing to be done, and thereby in the enjoyment of "good things," the sustenance made available. It means participation in sufficiency.

Sufficiency means enough. It does not mean bare necessities only, but enough for basic securities and a fulfilling life, as qualified by universal participation and nature's limits. Because sufficiency is a norm for everyone—toward which some move "up" and others "down"—it points in the direction of equality. It requires a movement away from the two extremes of misery and luxury. In the United States this would represent a radical value shift. The American people have been conditioned to aspire to more and more, never to take satisfaction in enough. In an expanding economy sharing seems unimportant, sacrifice unnecessary, justice cheap. The comfortable and the wealthy rise to higher levels of material plenty and excess, but the poor may at least find minimum wage, or even "livable wage," employment. [The paradox or scandal of the 1990s is that the "booming" economy and low unemployment failed at reducing poverty, even for many hard-working people.] With slow growth or no growth, however, it can no longer be pretended that a tolerable economic minimum can be achieved without a greater measure of equality. In the face of persistent poverty and inexorable ecological limits, the world no longer can afford the wasteful lifestyle of the affluent. We have to face hard questions about the control and organization of resources, employment, productive capacity, compensation, and mechanisms for redistribution. But it is at bottom a question of value, of justice as sufficiency.

In the biblical story the God of justice, engaged in the work of deliverance and liberation from bondage and oppression, is also the God of creation, who cares for all the creatures and engages in the work of protecting and restoring the earth as well as the poor. This God entrusts the human creature with the privilege and the responsibility of participating in the care of creation, beginning with the respectful use of creation for his or her sufficient sustenance. The role of man and woman is that of trustee for the Creator, the owner, who, far from handing it over to humans for heedless exploitation, still reminds them, " . . . the world and all that is in it is mine." (Psalm 50:12)

Applied to the eco-justice crisis, the biblical theme of human trusteeship translates into the norm of *sustainability*. Far beyond any previous period in history, the present situation confronts humankind with the earth as co-victim with the poor. Trusteeship has been bungled and betrayed; modern civilization has entailed a violent profligacy in the squandering of nature's riches. Sustainability becomes the norm requiring our diligent protection and restoration of the natural order, that it may be in good and fit condition for all God's creatures throughout the generations still to come.

A fourth eco-justice normative value emerges from the biblical theme of loving community under God, the key ingredient in human happiness and fulfillment. Applied to the eco-justice crisis, this translates into a powerful assertion of *solidarity*: the oneness of the whole human family in a world of unprecedented interdependence; the identification of caring people with oppressed people in their suffering and their struggle; acceptance of the costs as well as the joys of neighbor love and the struggle for justice and the common good; the priority of mutually supportive and enriching relationships over the accumulation of possessions; and the harmonious, integral relationship of humankind with the rest of nature.

I have made a personal statement about eco-justice as an idea, a perspective, a way of looking at this present perilous time and envisioning a more humane and viable future. The idea is rooted in the salient facts about the present momentous turning point in history. Intrinsic to the idea, however, is an evaluative judgment about those facts, a judgment that the reality to which they point has to be turned around. Eco-justice is the hoped-for, intended reality of a global society that more nearly embodies enduring values that always give definition, I believe, to human existence. But those values now become norms formulated to give impetus and guidance to the transformation of present reality. Living by the norms for our time, we shall seek a *sustainable sufficiency for all*. And that is eco-justice.

Involvement in eco-justice for me has meant good work, more rewarding personally and more important, I think, to others than anything else I have done. I have a community of colleagues and the support of fantastic folks in the Eco-Justice Network. My salary is substantially lower than it was before my old job was dissolved; but my wife is employed too, and we have enough. Our lifestyles have changed in lots of modest ways. Responding to the energy crunch and the high price of oil, we decided to heat with wood, since we live in a neighborhood where housing is not too dense to make this acceptable, and in a county where forests provide a sustainable yield of firewood. We are growing more of our food, doing that organically, participating in a co-op, lending equipment more freely to friends who need it, writing more letters to public officials . . . endeavoring to take the steps we can see to take. I am not an expert on saving the world before it is too late, but I believe and trust that small steps do anticipate the eco-just future and hasten its emergence. On the journey, communicating the message, straining to do that better and to move on faster, my life is very full.

3

Growth as Metaphor, Growth as Politics

Richard Grossman

Editor's Notes

Richard Grossman wrote this article for his own publication, which he had recently initiated and titled The Wrenching Debate Gazette. *It appeared there as a double issue, Nos. 2 and 3, in July 1985. I was grateful to be included on his mailing list. A veritable manifesto, this essay struck me as both eloquent and taxing in its style, trenchant in its analysis, and right on target in aiming to generate the wrenching debate so urgently needed and so slow in coming. I requested and received permission to carry it in* The Egg, *and he trusted me to shorten it a little and do a bit of editing.*

As I related in the Introduction, the challenge to growth, with its announcement of limits, had triggered the discussions that led to the formation of the Eco-Justice Project and Network. At this point in the narrative of the rocky journey toward eco-justice, it is fitting to examine in some depth the phenomenon and mythology of growth as it pertains to justice and ecology. Remembering that Grossman wrote this essay in 1985, the reader may ask himself or herself how differently the matter might be stated if such a piece were written today. The reader should ponder whether and how the essential debate can still take place. Can it go on at a level deep enough and persuasive enough to change the assumptions, perceptions, and commitments of the U.S. people and their leaders, so that they may surmount the obstacles to eco-justice?

31

Introducing the article in The Egg, *I encouraged readers to respond, suggesting that a bit of the debate might take place in the pages of the journal. It did not happen. Even environmentalists and justice advocates are ill-equipped to escape from the frame of reference within which discourse, private and public, generally proceeds in the modern world. It is hard to erase the usually unquestioned assumption that continuous "progress" through economic growth is possible, necessary, and good. It is hard to expunge the predilection toward growth as such and seriously discuss what is desired* from *growth, or what the economy is really* for, *and to begin to conceive an economy of sufficiency for all, made possible by the reduction of nonessential production.*

With growth exposed as a "dead" but still taken-for-granted metaphor for a good political economy, Grossman exposes and attacks various further assumptions (or sub-assumptions) that follow from the entrenched yet obsolete growth assumption:

- *that we can have justice via abundance, and thus that justice can be cheap;*

- *that the impersonal victimization of unfortunate people, or the destructive treatment of other species and natural systems, can be an acceptable, somehow necessary "episode" in material "progress";*

- *that the ills, inequities, wastes, and destructions in industrial society are merely side effects of growth that can be fixed and left behind (no, says Grossman, they* are *growth); and*

- *that growth—rather than popular educating, organizing, and pressuring—should get credit for the social improvements and the reductions in poverty that did occur in the 1960s and 1970s.*

Environmental organizations themselves, with few exceptions, have succumbed to the metaphor of growth and the politics of growth—largely concentrating their operations in Washington, seeking the best possible compromises and reforms without basically challenging the growth system and capitalism itself. But Grossman points to the ever-smaller circles of decisionmaking, the ever-greater concentrations of power and control. If these circles of power have been coerced into making or allowing some concessions or reforms, they are constantly bent on "strengthening their control over the processes of growth to take it all back, and more."

Nevertheless, Grossman expresses hope for a revitalization of democracy, economic as well as political. It would happen in conjunction with the debate that may finally show that the alternative to more *need not be simply* less, *that there are choices to make life* better. *Such choices—and the renewed and intensified organizing and pressuring that they would entail—would challenge and change the crucial matter of* control.

Growth as Metaphor, Growth as Politics

(*The Egg* 5 [4], December 1985)

Discussions of the nation's future typically focus on the promises and strategies of M-O-R-E. Producing more. Selling more. Buying more. Having more.

The purveyors of M-O-R-E want us to infer that human wants and needs are self-evidently fulfilled by these promises and strategies. Growth has brought us our fantastic wealth. It will do the same again and again for us, and for anyone. It will eradicate undesirable isms, free the oppressed, restore the environment. It will stimulate the arts, save our cities, decrease human reproduction, save our farms.

My purpose is not to rail against growth, not to offer an alternative to growth, not to suggest growth reform. Rather, I urge the complete expunging of the language of growth and the system of growth from the hearts and minds of those seeking democracy, fairer sharing of the world's wealth, and the integration of ecological principles into our lives and works.

Quick and Dead

Quantity has not been Earthlings' only preoccupation. People have been concerned with quality and equity. They have sought to institutionalize fairly the ways by which societies handle production and distribution.

But today, quantity and the language of quantity predominate. The imagery of quantity has driven out other models from our brains and guts. The power of metaphor, backed by economic and political power, is not to be sneezed at. Whereas, according to philologist Willard Espey, similes are mostly decorative, metaphors are tools to convey the "otherwise inexpressible." Espey reminds us of two kinds of metaphors—"the quick and the dead." The dead are those become so common and accepted that we no longer think about their original, literal meanings. We are not inclined to examine what biases they conceal, what values they imply. "Sifting the evidence" is one example. "Short shrift" is another.

Donald McCloskey noted in *The Rhetoric of Economics*: "A good metaphor depends on the ability of its audience to suppress incredulities . . . to suppress imagination. . . . An unexamined metaphor is a substitute for thinking." Growth as used by the purveyors is just such a good metaphor. It has become so dead as to be worshipped safely—often elaborately—by people with vastly different needs.

Even when growth is our goal, it turns out also to be our idealized means. It is O.K. not to have as much growth as promised as long as we are in the state of having growth. If what we are having is defined, measured and accepted as growth, we need not worry about people's lack of involvement in resource and labor decisions, about not having what we need, or about destruction caused by the arrangements for growth. For to extend democracy, to get what we need, and to clean up any messes, all we have to do is redouble our efforts to get growth.

Pigs Is Pigs

The defining and accepting of growth as means and end enable the salespeople of growth perpetually to sell and resell us pigs in pokes. Isn't it amazing how many times we have actually bought back our own resources and tools and sold our labor for a song and volunteered for cleanup without forcing the purveyors to specify what we were getting, without forcing them to make good on deliveries, to take back bad deliveries? And salespeople today are still at it. "Post-war growth in California," writes James Fallows in the March 1985 *Atlantic*, "did more for the people of Appalachia and the midwest than had any targeted assistance program."

Particularly fascinating to me is that just as growth itself is both end and means, the basic means of growth turns out also to be an end . . . to be aspired to, to have praises heaped upon, to be glorified. I refer to the free market. This is yet another good dead metaphor to which all kinds of qualities are attributed. Caught in its grip, people, social relations, communities, and the Earth itself are invisible and irrelevant, if not actually in the way.

Growth, as metaphor and as politics, rationalizes that harm to individuals or communities or to the Earth pales in comparison with having growth and free markets. Just having growth and free markets absolves the purveyors of any responsibilities. The role of growth and free markets is to help controllers of quantity to suppress incredulous tendencies afoot in the land. Quantity is so easy to measure, given our elaborate counting machines. But quality has no measure in the language of growth, and inequality has no column. Therefore, as long as quantity is linked with success, with justice, with peace, and as long as the purveyors of quantity control and evaluate the investments, it is difficult for the extant incredulous to point out what is not being counted, i.e., what is not professionally seen or linguistically recorded.

What growth as metaphor and as politics conceals most are the social relations, the investments, technologies, and production processes which the controllers of growth utilize to maintain their control and cause harm. As Frances Moore Lappe and Joseph Collins note in *World Hunger: Ten Myths* (1979), referring to agricultural business growth: "We must come to understand that a strategy emphasizing increased production while ignoring who is in control of that production is not a neutral strategy. It does not 'buy time'— that is, feed people while the more difficult social questions of control can be addressed. No. Such a strategy is taking us backward, itself creating even greater impoverishment and hunger." Growth becomes a "smoke screen for usurpation of . . . resources by a few for a few."

Adjectival Growth

With few exceptions, reformers in the left-liberal-progressive folds are no less locked into growth. They argue with the purveyors and salespeople of growth in the language of growth, trying to mobilize masses behind adjustments to growth, the fixing up of growth.

The outpouring of books in the last few years by people concerned with community and equity and justice (by Bluestone/Harrison/Faux/Alperovitz/Shearer/Carnoy/Bowles/Gordon/Weisskopf/Kuttner/Etcetera) are predominantly in the language of growth. There is little break from the politics of growth. We do not find last chapters which build upon the data and analysis so painstakingly produced to announce: and now, a whole new context, a new language, some live metaphors, wherein people and resources are not, in the words of Polanyi, "utilitarian atoms."

Few advocates of equity and justice acknowledge that the political and social relationships comprising the great growth dynamic *are what have created* the very inequities and destruction they are seeking to change. And so, for the most part, economic debate has been limited to putting cosmetics on a dead metaphor, like lipstick on a corpse: balanced growth/solid growth/natural growth/long-term growth/sustainable growth/equitable growth/overall growth/deliberate growth/restored growth/robust growth/limited growth/export-led growth/productivity-led growth/qualitative growth.

Expunge, Expunge

We have taken this metaphor growth to our hearts. When it comes to political discourse, we speak and think predominantly in the language of quantity, that is, the language of sameness and more. In groping to answer Friedman and Gilder and Reagan and the neo-oldies, in struggling for ideas and strategies and cross-issue connections, we never seem to get out of the growth lanes. What we need now is to expunge growth—the metaphor, the language, the politics—from our brains. We need to expunge it in ways which expose the hands behind growth, which enable people to see and feel the strength in their own hands. Then could we talk clearly and directly about what we want and need, about food and trees and schools, heat and transportation, money and homes and the land . . . in the language not of the dead but of the quick.

In "Standing by Words" (1979), (in *Poetry and Politics*, 1985), Wendell Berry encourages me to believe that I am not indulging in semantic quibble. Berry writes: "When language is detached from its origins in communal experience, it becomes 'arbitrary and impersonal.' If one wishes to promote the life of language, one must promote the life of community." As Fallows shows in his *Atlantic* article, entitled "America's Changing Economic Landscape," immersion in dead metaphors leads to extolling of destruction. For example: "An increasingly productive economy should be recognized as necessitating simultaneous painful growth and shrinkage, disinvestment and reinvestment. . . . Capitalism is one of the world's most disruptive forces . . . [with] constant churning of people from place to place . . . wrenching episodes in American life . . . social and economic fluidity created by industries on the rise. . . ."

The salespeople of the purveyors of growth appreciate that Fallows is not talking about people and community, that the pain he describes is "growth and shrinkage," not men, women, and children in despair over destruction of life. To them, the wrenched *are* "episodes," not human beings. The language he uses and the actions he endorses are those which enable "industries and governments, while *talking* of the 'betterment of the human condition,' [to] *act* to enrich and empower themselves," as Berry says. A smoke screen is at work. Fallows does not reflect for us what it means, for example, that those who are enriched and empowered by the "constant churning"—namely the merchants and the bankers—happen not to be the ones who have to hit the road for their or our own good. And he certainly is not thinking about the wrenching of the air, water, land, and neighborhoods.

Growth as Strategy

E. F. Schumacher, urging us to use our ingenuity with regard to our productive capacity, challenged the principal proposition of the metaphor of growth. Do you remember the opening lines of *Small Is Beautiful* (1973)? "One of the most fateful errors of our age is the belief that the 'problem of production' has been solved." What happened in post-World War II Europe and America to inspire Schumacher to such heretical dissent?

Alan Wolfe, in *America's Impasse: The Rise and Fall of the Politics of Growth* (1981), brilliantly describes the mass mobilizations which occurred around M-O-R-E. He details how growth became the dominant political strategy for so many, the dominant metaphor for the collective dream, the dominant tongue, the dominant measure, the master camouflager.

Wolfe suggests that what did not happen after World War II was the threshing out in community and national debate and experiment the difficult, explosive issues which lingered from the 1930s:

- Should the economic system be based on the market or the state?

- To what degree should public policies be addressed to the needs of a particular class (i.e., growth purveyors, workers, the poor, etc.)?

- Should government be coordinated and national, or local and decentralized?

Instead, many different voices and political power bases gathered around growth and the language of growth to "pursue economic expansion at home through growth and overseas through empire."

Justice via Abundance

Growth politics became the means for maximizing control over labor, resources and community by a few in the name of M-O-R-E for many. Growth politics became the way to launder people and resources into utilitarian atoms. Growth politics became the "safe" way to prevent large numbers of people from deciding where their money went, and to avoid the blame for disempowering people and communities. No one actually had to go on record against integration, employment, worker rights, and environmental protection. Under the growth metaphor it was hard to finger who should take the rap for rotten schools, inhuman health care, inefficient and destructive transportation and energy systems, destructive farming and financing, industries which made products people did not need in ways which created mayhem in workplaces and beyond, and unchanging inequalities. Since the purveyors of growth could safely be *for everything*, they were able to get away with being *responsible for nothing* in particular.

Equity and justice would be related directly to production. To quantity. The more America produced, and the more America helped the world to produce, sell and buy, the faster people across the world would be freed from drudgery and oppression. Shooting for justice via abundance, the nation could embrace righteousness without accountability. Goals became synonymous with means—never mind that the means were facilitating greater and greater concentrations of wealth and power, which in turn were blocking extensions of democracy and the ability of people to protect themselves.

But why worry? The post-World War II growth coalition was accompanied by fantastic leaps in industrial production. In the decade which was the apotheosis of growth—the 1960s—GNP just about doubled. In Wolfe's words, Kennedy unleashed "the twin forces of increasing [economic] concentration and greater public spending [which] were laying the ground work for further consolidation of the growth coalition." And yes, the number of people living in poverty began to decline. And unemployment went down. Civil rights laws were passed, nutrition and education and housing benefits were extended to more and more people. Even GNP's in developing countries were on the rise. To the growth coalition and to most of the nation, all this was the self-evident result of the arrangements and the processes of growth.

And people asked: If so much had been achieved, why not more? Besides, the ticket window to American politics would come crashing down upon the knuckles of any who asked: What's really growing? Growth for whom? At what cost? Decided by whom? What are the engines of growth doing to our neighborhoods and communities, to our ecosystems and habitats? To our fellow earthlings overseas? To our technological imaginations? To ask these questions was to attack those leaders who, for the promises of growth, had chosen to serve as police officers for the purveyors and pledged never to think such thoughts.

Left Out

Despite some efforts by some people, there has not been a locus among liberal-left-progressives where these questions have been raised. Most importantly, what they have failed to address is that the perpetuation of skewered divisions of wealth, persistent un- and underemployment, the wasting of huge sums of money, the destruction of public health and the environment, the setting up of barriers to hinder people from changing the status quo, the playing off of people against each other, *are* growth.

In other words, far from being side effects or impacts, today's inequities and ecological messes are the societal arrangements for control and quantity. The difficulties people experience gaining access to decision making and protecting themselves are deliberate, because the purpose of growth politics is control, and the purpose of finances and technologies which serve growth politics is M-O-R-E. The purveyors get their control by destroying people's ability to decide where the money goes; they get their M-O-R-E by destroying the earth. And they masquerade their purposes and their mayhem within the metaphors of growth.

And mayhem there began to be galore. As Schumacher, Bookchin, Carson, Henderson, Commoner, and others had been pointing out, the great leap in production which began with World War II had introduced huge amounts of new substances into the world. These were unpredictable, cumulative, and, as was becoming increasingly apparent, lethal. These substances, along with massive construction and destruction planned by the arbiters of growth, were heavily subsidized by taxpayers and supported by our elected representatives. As E.F. Schumacher wrote in *Small Is Beautiful*: "Both in quantity and quality of man's industrial processes [there was] an entirely new situation—a situation resulting not from our failures but from what we thought were our greatest successes."

Looking Backward

Today, it is vital to look again at cause and effect. The extensions of democracy in so many arenas—civil rights, housing, employment; the increased access to education, to food, to social services; the reduction of poverty; the public health and environmental improvements—all of which occurred from 1960 to 1980—came from the organizing which swept society beginning with the stirrings of the modern civil rights movement in the late 1950s. It was not "growth" which brought nutrition to the malnourished, but political organizing. It was not "growth" which ended segregation, but planning, marching, demonstrating, politicking, dying, the scaring of legislators, editors and civic leaders into action. It was not "growth" which brought millions out of poverty, but intentional shifts of investments by industry and government coerced by people who had educated themselves and mobilized themselves. It was not "growth" which raised consciousness about health and environment, but educating and organizing. On issue after issue, people forced themselves into closed circles of decision making with specific demands and backed by organized public pressure.

For awhile, people were successful at changing values, changing criteria, changing investments. But their reforms did not go to the heart of the growth process. And as victories were being chalked up, the purveyors of growth were methodically building credit for whatever progress was occurring into the language and process of growth. At the same time, they were shrinking the circles of decision making, strengthening their control over the processes of growth to take it all back, and more.

The Fly

There was a problem during those years for the purveyors: environmentalists. These folks burst as if from the blue. They had been influenced some by the cultural and political upheavals of the day, but essentially the environmentalists strode alone—without genuine roots in other movements and disciplines. As the Conservation Foundation's Grant Thompson recently wrote, environmentalists were motivated by "widespread dissatisfaction with the costs that careless technology was imposing on the common good." (*Environment,* May 1985). Basically, they brought new information, the beginnings of new language, energy and creativity, and they hollered:

there are too many side effects, too many people, we've got to start looking at the whole Earth.

Environmentalism was asking the nation to scrutinize particular technologies and development projects such as the supersonic transport, nuclear power and weapons, the Alaska Pipeline, dams, highways, chemicals, etc. Environmentalism was asking that purveyors consider specifics and quality, and be accountable. Of course, the purveyors rushed with their subscribers and enforcers to make environmentalists into one more special interest group. And that is how environmentalism, now institutionalizing, began to be perceived by the constituencies of growth, by the media, by politicians, and by the left.

But this is not how environmentalists wanted to see themselves. Imagine their surprise and heartburn when they found they were being confronted not only by the purveyors of growth but also by righteous constituencies of consumers, wage earners, and the discriminated against. Imagine the confusion of antipollutionists, people who believed they were alerting the world to real danger, when the growth coalition branded them antiprogress, antigrowth, antiworker, antitechnology, and Luddites to boot. Even though polls showed deep and consistent support for the environment by Americans from all walks of life, environmentalists (as one union bumper sticker said) were P-O-L-L-U-T-I-N-G T-H-E E-C-O-N-O-M-Y.

No Help

People coming to the political arena motivated by health and environmental issues in the early 1970s thus found themselves put on the defensive by fellow victims of the growth system who had embraced the promises and strategies of growth. As the movement institutionalized, following labor and civil rights models, it sought the credibility and respectability which came from being permitted past the growth ticket window. Environmental organizations were settling for curbs, for pollution control, for amelioration of side effects, for laws which were licenses to pollute, with government bureaucracies to define and enforce those laws. Rather than harm the source of all success—economic growth—the environmentalists sought to encourage corporate and government investment in sustainable growth.

Gradually, the locus of environmentalism began to shift from cities and towns around the country to Washington, D.C. The taming of environmentalists, and the guiding of environmentalism into the growth framework, was assured. Today most environmental group officials believe that effectiveness requires focusing attention on specific acts of polluters, not on the investments and empire of polluters/employers. They are careful not to draw attention to the institutional arrangements which (predictably) lead to destructive and inequitable societal decisions. "Pragmatic" Senators and Congress people achieve "the best they can," and help make environmental lobbyists pragmatic as well.

Though some environmentalists resisted, the temptation to cut deals behind closed class doors, to slice off pieces of the ecology, rather than fight out underlying questions of control, has proved as great for environmentalists as similar temptations have been to labor and civil rights leaders. This means that inherent in the framing of just about every "environmental" issue have been built-in contradictions between quantity and quality . . . between control and democracy . . . between jobs and the environment. It means that each struggle fomented by the environmental movement has highlighted these contradictions and run into the brick wall of growth.

Trends, Trends, Trends

The Club of Rome's 198 page volume, *The Limits to Growth,* set out to ask: "How much growth will the physical system [the Earth] support?" On one level, the *Limits* message was simple enough: trends in industrialization, population, malnutrition, depletion of nonrenewable resources, and deteriorating environments indicated that without major changes the industrialized world was headed for serious trouble. And *Limits* dared to suggest that the answer to the world's needs was not simply M-O-R-E. But given that the book defined growth problems only as destructive side effects; given the absence of channels for debating what to do with our productive capacity; given the absence of discussion on extending democratic processes to investment and work realms, *Limits* could offer only one alternative to save the planet: L-E-S-S.

But L-E-S-S was not likely to be popular among people putting up with inequities only because they harbored hope for M-O-R-E.

The Debate That Wasn't

Even though the debate following publication of *The Limits to Growth* lacked a persistently radical ecological analysis, it was long and passionate. And because we have had that debate on growth versus no growth, many people today believe we have had Wolfe's debate on production and control. The purveyors of growth, who knew better, understood that before the whole pollution and inequity mess blew up in their faces, they needed to step up their economic and political controls over money, resources, technology, workers, and consumers—their control over basic governance. And they saw that to the extent to which they could get the press and politicians, and even environmentalists and workers, to see "growth versus no growth" everywhere, the purveyors would hold the advantage. For in a contextless contest far from specifics, accountability and live metaphor—that is, in a debate between M-O-R-E and L-E-S-S—it is easy to isolate the advocates of L-E-S-S by manipulating the victims of M-O-R-E: labor, minorities, farmers, military industry workers, etc.—all those with hopes linked to growth.

Limits, and the debate it stimulated and the memories it leaves, did their share to scare off many within the left and labor and other constituencies who might have been open to helping integrate ecological values into broader equity agendas beyond growth politics. Struggles were not planned and conducted in ways which helped educate environmentally interested people about the threads which wound through so many political issues, which linked the so-called "single issues." Paths were not opened to the heart of the growth system. The hands of the growth purveyors were not revealed. In the late 1970s, for example, when antinuclear, safe energy, and prosolar movements were at their peak, many institutional advocates—myself included—tried to keep our critique and recommendations in the safe context of M-O-R-E. We said the nation could grow with solar and conservation investments. In addition, many solar advocates scurried to distance themselves from people seeking dismantling of the petroleum and nuclear industries despite understanding the need to force the shift of hundreds of billions of dollars out of these industries' pockets. Political strategies focused on reassuring the growth coalition that no one was really after their control and profits. Let the purveyors bring us solar energy and provide all the appropriate technologies, and even many environmentalists will be happy.

We Know Better

We know better. There have been many efforts over recent year to expose muddying language and systems, to break through the antidemocratic and anti-environmental grip of growth politics. Little in this article is new. But we need to keep raising these points again and again . . . especially today when M-O-R-E is not only beautiful but sanctified as well.

The time has come for the liberal/progressive/left to see ecological factors as production and democracy issues, not as social causes. And it is time for environmentalists to consider that creating democracy, here and abroad, can help undo the arrangements and end the practices which cause ecological destruction.

Precedents exist. There *are* people come to the political arena because of environmental destruction and human suffering, along with people energized because of inequity and human suffering, who understand that social justice and ecological sanity require democracy. They see the need to talk about what we make and how, about money and decision making, about work and resources, about vegetables and trains, electricity and heat, day care and schools, poisons and health, income and jobs, neighborhoods, farms, recycling, conservation, and direct democracy.

Grassroots Greens are talking and assembling here and in other countries. They are trying to penetrate production and work issues, to find energizing and innovative organizing strategies. The Greens's New England Committee of Correspondence, for example, is talking about "a decentralized world of self-governing but cooperatively interrelated communities and regions in which *both* political and economic democracy are joined, in which *both* social and ecological responsibility are practiced."

Deep Ecologists are trying to redefine human relationships with all living creatures and with the earth. They are creating new language characterized by accountability and quality, and groping for cosmologies rooted in appreciation of and defense of the natural world . . . with an eye on the political process.

So

So let us talk specifics. What do we want? What are our principles? Do we seek justice and democracy within an ecological world view? Do we wish to create fewer needs, to satisfy them "with smaller expenditures of materials, energy, and work, and imposing the least possible burden on the environment?" (Gorz) Do we value strong communities and the rights of individuals? Do we want to close equity gaps here and abroad?

Are we really talking about significant shifts in individual and societal values which result in Americans' taking smaller and smaller shares of the world's resources? Could we simultaneously bring about equitable financial and trading relationships with less powerful countries, and broaden democratic participation in resource, labor, and production decisions across the globe? How are we going to tackle global corporations and giant militarized governments, create alternative institutions and decision-making processes, generate less toxic material, refurbish people and the Earth on the grand scale required?

What do *you* talk about when you talk about growth? Tell us. Lay out precisely what you mean. Think what the effects will be on your favorite principles/constituencies/organizations/leaders if you and they walk away from the growth ticket window.

Let's open it up—beyond just radical ecologists and progressive economists. Let's see if we can cross issue lines and constituency lines long enough simultaneously to pursue equity agendas in ways which also promote ecological sanity. Let's see if people can hear us talking, not L-E-S-S, but different and better.

And whenever we sense incipient movement around growth in the larynxes of politicians, constituency leaders, editors, economists, and pundits of every variety, let us immediately issue a challenge: be specific. Where are the people, the air, the land, the water, the concern for species and future generations, for equity and quality, in your words? What is it you want to take from people, to take from the Earth? What will you put back? To whom do you think you are accountable?

People from different realms and perspectives need to move into the political arena. Together we can expose the phony assumptions, bury the dead metaphors, create new and energizing language and plans based on our principles, our wants and needs. Jeremy Rifkin, in *Entropy* (1980), for example, suggested we substitute "borrow" for "growth." Think about that for a minute: What would this little word change do to the way people view the planet, time, and people's lives on Earth?

Why would anyone allow the purveyors of endless M-O-R-E to keep filling our heads with the dead and delusional? Surely, people can seize control over their tongues and their minds. Surely, people can lead the nation through vital debates so long overdue—on production and democracy, commerce and democracy, equity and democracy, law and democracy, ecology and democracy, "democracy" and democracy.

We can talk in the language of free human beings, using real words and live metaphors.

And we can take action to govern ourselves.

4

Come Inside the Circle of Creation

Elizabeth Dodson Gray

Editor's Notes

In the article that follows, Elizabeth Dodson Gray, as an environmental, feminist theologian and ethicist, contributes her own distinctive, concise portrayal of what I have been calling the rocky road to eco-justice, together with her understanding of the ethic necessary to overcome the obstacles in the way. She targets a view of nature and the world that sees a hierarchy of being and value. This view, she says, has come down to the present time through the Judeo-Christian tradition and from incorporation into Western industrial, technological civilization.

Like Richard Grossman in the previous article, Dodson Gray calls for a radically changed view of the kind of life and the kind of economy that in the end make sense. "Do we really comprehend," she asks, "the full absurdity of a wealthy corporation on a dying planet?" She calls for an ethic of "attunement," of a keen sensitivity to the whole life system in its manifold diversity. Technology should be monitored to trace its impact, actual and potential, on the whole life system into the long-term future. Yes. And what of the power realities that stand in the way?

Elizabeth Dodson Gray spoke at the Eco-Justice Conference on "EcoCommunities." Her conference presentation was a strong and stimulating development of the ideas in the following article. This article condenses a paper presented at the "Theory Meets

47

Practice" International Symposium on Environmental Ethics in Atlanta, Georgia, April 5–7, 1992.

Come Inside the Circle of Creation

(*The Egg: Eco-Justice Quarterly* 12 [3], Summer 1992)

Our world view is basic to our morality. Our old world view, rooted in our Judeo-Christian tradition and recapitulated in the evolutionary pyramid, was one of a cosmic ranking-of-diversity hierarchy. The ethic born from this world view was one of atomized self-interest and the anthropocentric illusion of modern science and technology—that we could function "as we pleased" on the planet because we were "above" in dominion or "superior" as a species.

I argued in my book *Green Paradise Lost* that our view of our place in creation came to us as part of our Judeo-Christian tradition. Our whole Western civilization with its science and industrial system is built upon this cultural foundation and is still shaped by it. That creation theology from the Bible translates into a set of relationships we hold in our heads and which we have been deeply socialized into. I've found it useful to diagram those relationships as in the diagram below:

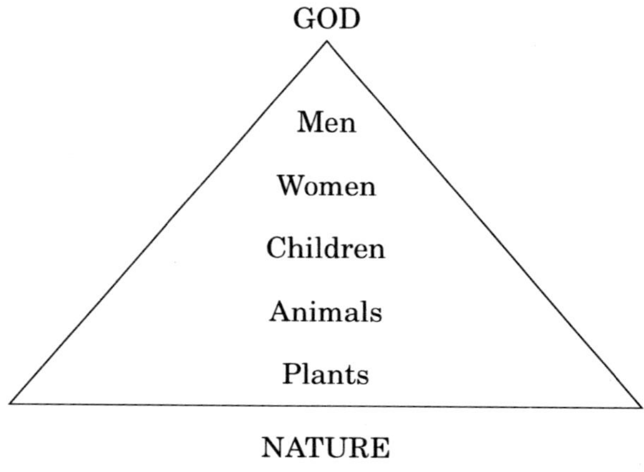

Figure 4.1

We have confused our human uniqueness with superiority—even though any biologist will tell us that *each* species is one-of-a-kind, unique. We never asked ourselves if we, as a species, had the best eyes, or ears, or sense of smell, or fleetness of foot—because the answer would be "no." We never asked ourselves if what humans do is as remarkable as the photosynthesis that plants do. Instead, we convinced ourselves that "big brains" are the mark of a superior species. But recent research has revealed that cetaceans (whales, dolphins, porpoises) have an equally large and convoluted brain cortex. By the sonar of echo-location, they can detect sickness, health, happiness, sadness, and sexual arousal in fellow cetaceans. If we could echo-locate, we would be certain we were the superior species!

A new world view has been ushered in by the sciences of ecology and sub-atomic physics. It is the systemic world view—that everything in our living earth system affects everything else. Humans are *within* the biospheral cycles of that interconnected system. The only way of life appropriate to such a systemic world view is an all-win ethic with its practical path of "attunement."

An Ethic of "Attunement"

Attunement. Let it be written on our hearts. It means that we are to open ourselves, we are to listen and look, we are to pay attention.

Why? Because we are *within* life, not above it, and we see life incompletely and often dimly, and we cannot afford *not* to attune ourselves. Not paying attention to our life-supporting systems in the earth's biosphere will no longer work for us.

Is it *possible* to attune ourselves to trees and rivers? After all, they don't talk. Christopher Stone, writing in *Should Trees Have Standing*, said ". . . natural objects *can* communicate their wants (needs) to us, and in ways that are not terribly ambiguous. I am sure I can judge with more certainty and meaningfulness whether and when my lawn wants (needs) water, than the Attorney General can judge whether and when the United States wants (needs) to take an appeal from an adverse judgment by a lower court. . . . For similar reasons, the guardian-attorney for a smog-endangered stand of pines could venture with more confidence that his client wants the smog stopped, than the directors of a corporation can assert that 'the corporation' wants dividends declared."

What Stone is proposing for "natural objects" is similar to what parents do when they "attune" themselves to the nonverbal body language of infants. Body language speaks volumes in parenting, in sexuality, in friendship. The earth also has nonverbal body language. When the air smells bad, when the trees on the crests of hills and mountains die, when the waters are fouled to the eye and nose, it does not take a genius to know that we are doing something wrong—and to *stop* doing it.

"What we most need," says the poet Thich Nhat Hanh, "is to hear within ourselves the sounds of the earth crying." Can we hear the plant in the tropical rain forest, the plant which may have the cure for cancer or for AIDS? Can we hear that plant calling out just before the bulldozers reach it? The extinction of species is as silent as the holocaust furnaces were for individuals. The world did not hear a cry then. Can we listen now? Can we hear and attune ourselves at all?

How—in practical terms—do we do this attuning? Well, the overall task is largely to redesign our technologies, indeed our whole industrial system, so that it "fits within" rather than blasts gaping holes in the biological fabric that is life.

Hand-in-Glove Technology

The ecologist Dr. Bettie Willard has said of our technology that it must be like a hand in a glove. It must be designed and used with such sensitivity and attunement that it fits *within* the biospheral systems just as a hand fits into a glove and does not destroy that glove.

Be clear that the ethic of attunement is *not antitechnology*. It is not Luddite. We need technology to help us with this redesigning of our industrial system. But it must be *technology used with sensitivity*, technology that is carefully and consistently *monitored* to track its impacts upon air and water and natural systems and habitats. What is needed is technology *motivated* not only by profit but by a profound appreciation of our true place *within* the living earth system, and *marked by a commitment* to stop using harmful techniques.

So how do we do that? Willard suggests what she calls *ecological reconnaissance*. By this she means our sending out ecologically trained advance patrols to scout out what is ahead of us. Otherwise, we will continue to face dumb choices—between, say, a massive dam project and the tiny endangered snail darter species; or between a logging industry which is client to the Forest Service and the last remaining habitat of an endangered owl species. Those are the alternatives we have created for ourselves when by inadvertence, and by a lack of ecological attunement at the start, we created a faulty original design.

Beyond Self-Interest to All-Win

Every decision we make, to be a good decision, must be good for the whole system. If a decision is good for the corporation but not for its environment, then it is a bad decision and we will come to regret it. If a decision is good for humans but not for trees or tundra or permafrost or Biscayne Bay, it is a bad decision.

If a decision is good for men, and not for women, then it is a bad decision and we will also live to regret it. The truth is we cannot affirm life unless we affirm women, because women are the life-bearers of the human species. This is why the so-called pro-life movement is not really pro-life—because it is not pro-women.

But also, if a decision is good for adults, and not children— good for whites and not people of color, good for rich and not for poor, good for the First World and not the Third World, good for humans and not good for plants, animals, the ozone layer and air and water, good for the present but not the future—it is a BAD decision and we will come to regret it.

The alternative whole system ethic can say, as does Native American spirituality, "With all beings and all things we shall be as relatives." It is foolishness to say, "Your end of the life-boat is sinking." Do we really comprehend the full absurdity of a wealthy corporation on a dying planet? I once saw a sign in a vegetarian restaurant that read, "Only when the last tree is cut down, when the last river is poisoned, and the last fish is caught, will we realize we can't eat money."

The ethic of attunement *within* an interconnected system calls us to learn to get comfortable with diversity, to praise and celebrate it—to honor the diversity that holds all life in place. Diversity is life-affirming, so to affirm diversity, human and nonhuman, is to affirm life. Within an interconnected system everything, and everyone, wins—or nothing wins. The huge elephant in the forest—we, the human species—can only act out that all-win ethic with an exquisite dance of attunement, trying hard to pay attention to what is, so that we may walk lightly upon the earth.

5

Creation and Liberation as a Continuing Story

William E. Gibson

Editor's Notes

I have already referred (see Editor's Notes, Selection 1) to the December 1986 national ecumenical consultation, "For the Love of Earth and People: the Eco-Justice Agenda." This event gave a large boost to denominational incorporation of this agenda into program and structure.

For example, the Presbyterians caucused at the consultation and decided to press their national governing body, the General Assembly, to undertake a major study of existing and still-needed church policy pertaining to eco-justice, as the basis for new mission initiatives. Several individuals in the caucus went back to their presbyteries and got them to submit overtures to the General Assembly calling upon it to take action that was essentially in line with what the caucus had proposed. The Assembly responded positively, and the Presbyterian Eco-Justice Task Force was formed by the Committee on Social Witness Policy (CSWP). Dieter Hessel was director of CSWP, and I served the Task Force as consultant and writer.

The work of the Task Force came to fruition when the 1990 General Assembly adopted the policy report entitled Restoring Creation for Ecology and Justice. *The Assembly thus declared: it*

53

"recognizes and accepts restoring creation [human and nonhuman] as a central concern of the church to be incorporated into its life and mission at every level." Implementation of this declaration was to be twofold: new mission initiatives for ecology and justice, and the infusion of the eco-justice perspective and concern into existing church agencies and programs. This is not the place to assess the quality and extent of the implementation (see Selection 26), but certainly the Restoring Creation *report has made a difference.*

At the 1986 consultation I had the assignment of presenting a theological and ethical basis for eco-justice work in the context of the deepening crisis of ecology and justice that had become evident in our time. This presentation, which anticipated the theological-ethical work I did a little later for the Presbyterian Eco-Justice Task Force, was both biblically based and thoroughly contextual—maintaining that our understanding of the contemporary work and will of God depended significantly upon our reading of contemporary history. This does not mean that the witness in the biblical story now has to be corrected but that the story is still going on. In other words, God is in the eco-justice crisis, and our discernment of what this means is informed by the clues we get from the biblical story.

My talk was printed in the journal. The first section contains a number of references to current news that may make it seem dated now. I think, however, that these serve to underline the difficulty and the long-term character of the eco-justice journey. They show, for instance, that the scientific warnings about climate change were already available to the government and the public by the mid 1980s. Projections of global warming were less solidly established then; but the additional scientific modeling has mainly reinforced rather than changed the earlier findings. The nation has had ample time for an appropriate response. What stands in the way?

In 1986 the nation was still preoccupied with the Cold War, the arms race with the Soviet Union, and the alleged threat from the Sandinista regime in Nicaragua. In the 1990s, with the Cold War ended, the Sandinistas out of power, and the economy "booming," the priorities of public policy did not lead to a wiser and more compassionate treatment of vulnerable people and ecosystems, either at home or abroad, but rather to various "reforms" that treated them less caringly, often more harshly, even punitively. In Haiti, for example, after the many years of thwarted struggle for liberation and a better life, the plight of the people and the land is met with U.S. government indifference and held hostage to market ideology.

I believe my presentation at the 1986 consultation is the only one in which I have spoken of human beings as "co-creators" with

God. I do not disavow what I said then, but I recognize that the language of "co-creation" must be protected vigilantly from the corruptions of human arrogance and over-reaching pride. When we talk about taking care of creation or restoring it, we should know that we talk this way only because in taking care of ourselves we humans have failed to take care not to harm the rest of creation. Now to take care of creation means to reduce the human impact on it, so that by nature's resilience and restorative drive it may heal itself.

The theology expressed in this article is basic to my concept of the eco-justice task and journey. If God indeed is in the history of our own extraordinary time, people of faith may resonate with the affirmation that the Creator-Deliverer calls people into God's project of liberating earth as well as people from the powers that exploit and oppress the vulnerable.

Creation and Liberation as a Continuing Story

(The Egg: A Journal of Eco-Justice 7 [1], Spring 1987)

I. Earth and People: Dishonoring Their Claim

The love of earth and people is the eco-justice agenda—one agenda, because earth and people are one creation. To call it creation points to the Creator, the author, source, and sustainer of the creation, who has a purpose for it, who relates to it lovingly, wills its well-being, and influences and beckons it toward its destiny and fulfillment.

Do not confuse this idea of creation with the recurring furor over "creationism," which insists on taking the first chapter of Genesis as a literal account of what has been a process of billions of years, exceeding our comprehension, a process and drama still continuing. The idea of creation is too important to allow it to be discredited by a literal reading of Genesis 1. The earth and its people belong to their Creator. The love of earth and people begins with the Creator. The claim made by earth and people to be loved comes not from them alone but is at the same time the Creator's claim.

The future of the creation today is problematic because their claim to be loved has been shamefully dishonored. Pick up any week's periodical arrivals and find documentation of the dishonoring of the claim. The Fall 1986 issue of *The Amicus Journal* from the Natural Resources Defense Council warns that human beings are heedlessly upsetting on a planetary scale the ecological balances that determine temperature and climate. I refer to the build-up in the atmosphere of infrared absorptive gases, mainly carbon dioxide, resulting from the combustion of fossil fuels and the destruction of forests. Over the next three to five decades the continuation of current trends will lead to a warming of the earth that will have profound effects upon rainfall, agriculture, and the level of the oceans. Worldwide climatic conditions will be highly unstable for an indefinite period, with incalculable but devastating consequences for earth and people. Of course, if concerted measures were undertaken internationally soon to reduce dependence on fossil fuels and to reverse deforestation, the grim prospect could be changed. Governments, however, are not giving major attention to this matter.[1]

An article in *Time*, November 24, 1986, reports on the soaring numbers of homeless people. It makes a distinction between the old and the new homeless. The old homeless are predominantly the alcoholics, the mentally ill, the aged, some of whom (says *Time*) are on the streets by choice. "The new homeless," according to the reporters, "are the economically dispossessed . . . [including] blue-collar families who have been forced out of their apartments when their low-income housing is converted to condominiums; some hold jobs but cannot find or afford a place to live." The number of homeless people may be larger than at any time since the Great Depression, but federal funds for subsidized housing have been cut by 78 percent since 1980.[2]

And if you've followed *Doonesbury*, you've seen the air drop of millions of dollars for the *contras* juxtaposed to Alice, the elderly bag lady, who's being told there's still no housing available for her; and then some kids no longer getting lunch; and a bureaucrat explaining to a dejected farmer, "Sorry, Ed, we're going to have to repossess. There's just so much your government can afford to do for you." "Priorities" is the heading for this strip.[3]

In Cortland, New York, not far from where I live, city officials are trying to decide what to do about their water system, a part of which is threatened by contamination coming, allegedly, from the Smith Corona Company, the city's largest industry. The company is careful not to admit responsibility for the pollution, and the jobs it provides are centrally important to the city's economy.

And in Haiti, according to the December 1986 issue of *The Progressive*, the people, having overthrown their dictator the previous February, find themselves still hungry, ruled by a military junta, wondering what to do next to accomplish the revolution that would make it possible for them to work and to eat. The economy is in chaos. Much of the land is degraded from deforestation and erosion. Something like half or more of the potential work force has no employment. When Secretary Shultz visited in August, crowds jeered him and carried slogans saying, "Food Not Arms."[4]

II. The Crisis of Creation

Such items are not isolated, unusual problems. They reflect and document the crisis of creation. I use the word *crisis* advisedly, for our time is truly one in which the future hangs in the balance, with unresolved situations of momentous significance for good or ill, occasions of great danger and great opportunity.

The ancient flood story depicts a crisis of creation. It tells us that the earth, created good, had become corrupt because of the violence of the human creature. It was so rampant and lawless that it filled the earth until (we are told) "the Lord was sorry that he had made man . . . and it grieved him to his heart." (Gen. 6:6) God's judgment took the form of a massive flood. God's mercy was shown in the saving of a remnant, with whom God made a new beginning, based upon a covenant made not only with Noah and his family but with every living creature. "[The rainbow]," God told Noah, "is the sign of the covenant which I make between me and you and every living creature that is with you, for all future generations. . . ." (Gen. 9:12) "While the earth remains," God promised, "seed time and harvest, cold and heat, summer and winter, day and night, shall not cease." (Gen. 8:22)

Whatever the historical memory may have been that lay behind the flood story, there really is no precedent for the crisis that confronts us now. Quite simply, the future hangs in the balance because the violence of the human creature to the creation has been so destructive that the suffering, groaning earth desperately needs healing and restoration. The polluted air and water, the hills where the trees were cut down, the fields whose top soil has been eroded, the endangered species, and the hungry people are all victims whose affliction is deplorable because as the stuff of God's creation their value is intrinsic. The Creator loves them and desires their continuing health and integrity. But of course the crisis can be stated also in terms of the human prospect: the future hangs in the balance because the human creature's destructive impact undermines earth's capacity to provide the sustenance that people need. Human beings are making their own habitat unfit.

The flood story strikingly prefigures the present crisis. The flood covers the earth; our crisis is quite literally global. In the story the earth is imperiled because of the violence of men and women. The picture of the earth as "filled with violence" (Gen. 6:13) aptly expresses the degradation inflicted by people in our time upon fields and forests, streams and seas, natural cycles and underground minerals, animal life and human society. All have been damaged or depleted by the carelessness and greed embodied in technology, industry, warfare, and the exploding human population. In the story God promises never again to inflict massive destruction and makes a covenant, indicating providential care, with every living creature. In the present crisis Noah's descendants violate the spirit and the intention of that covenant. The consequences could be all-encompassing as in the ancient story. Our crisis is unprecedented because never before have human beings had it in their power to destroy the earth. They could do it all at once in a nuclear explosion. They could do it gradually over decades, undermining earth's fruitfulness, upsetting natural balances, and thus destroying the capacity of earth to carry them.

The human creature is at the center of the crisis. Of all creatures only the human plays a problematic role. Endowed with intelligence, memory, and freedom, he or she is uniquely fitted to participate intentionally in creation's fulfillment in accordance with the Creator's intent. But the human creature may either serve or violate that intent.

The 104th Psalm celebrates the Creator's provision of sustenance for all the creatures. "Thou makest springs gush forth . . . ; they give drink to every beast of the field." (Ps. 104:10f). "Thou dost cause the grass to grow for the cattle, and plants for man [and woman] to cultivate." (verse 14) The creatures "all look to thee, to give them their food in due season. When . . . thou openest thy hand, they are filled with good things." (verses 27f.) But "man [and woman go] forth to [their] work and to [their] labor until evening." (verse 23) The other creatures do what they do and are filled with good things because they are what they are within the realm of nature. But man and woman *work* and cultivate the plants to bring forth food.

Through work they participate in the care of creation. As human beings they are called to be cocreators, coworkers, with the Creator. They are called to participate in the building of communities of love and justice and cooperation, drawing carefully upon the sustenance of earth and sharing it equitably.

That in general terms is their God-intended role in the fulfillment of creation. The appropriate purpose of their freedom is to pursue the various tasks of cocreation that will express their particular talents, enrich their relationships with fellow workers, and maximize their contribution to the common good.

But human beings are free, also, to pursue what looks like their own advantage and security at the expense of the common good. They are free to assert dominance over persons weaker than themselves. They can reject the responsibility to care for creation. And so they have filled the earth with violence. Denying the limitations of their creaturehood, they relate pridefully, greedily, abusively to earth and people. Or escaping the responsibilities of freedom, they become indifferent, apathetic, willfully ignorant in the face of danger and opportunity. The cocreators, whether by creativity turned destructive or by creativity refused, have precipitated the crisis of creation.

III. The Liberation of Creation

I referred to Psalm 104, in which the psalmist praises the Creator for ordering things so well and providing so graciously and sufficiently for the well-being of the creatures. But the psalm ends on a discordant note. I used to wish the last verse could be edited out. Vehemently, bitterly the poet lashes out: "Let sinners be consumed from the earth, and let the wicked be no more." (verse 35) Why does he or she have to spoil a lovely picture of the harmony of creation by virtually cursing "the wicked"? The answer must be that the psalmist knows that the original, intended harmony has long since been broken. The earth is not the Garden of Eden; the time is "after the fall"; relationships and satisfactions are not as they are meant to be. Much later the Apostle Paul speaks of the "bondage" of the creation. ". . . the whole creation has been groaning in travail together until now." (Rom. 8:22) Despite the idyllic tone of most of the psalm, the psalmist senses that travail, cries out in pain against the disruption of harmony, and lashes out against the proud, the greedy, the careless, the violent, who oppress the creation, human and nonhuman, and subject it to bondage.

Because the creation is oppressed, the continuing work of the Creator is the work of liberation. Biblical faith is rooted in God's liberating activity. Moses was called to be God's agent of liberation.

"... behold, the cry of my people has come to me," said Jahweh, "and I have seen the oppression with which the Egyptians oppress them. Come, I will send you to Pharaoh that you may bring forth my people...." (Ex. 3:9f) Liberation from physical bondage and from spiritual bondage is the theme of the entire biblical story. There are various words for it: deliverance, salvation, redemption, justification. Always liberation is *out of* some kind of bondage, some kind of fouled up relationships that thwart the fulfillment of creation; and always it is *into* restored relationships under a renewed covenant within a covenant community of love and justice. Liberation or deliverance is necessary to the fulfillment of creation, and so the Creator becomes the Deliverer, and the Deliverer remains always the Creator. The work of the Creator-Deliverer is the deliverance of creation.

The deliverance or liberation of creation is, moreover, the distinctive and compelling task of our time for human cocreators. Four salient facts of our time reveal the crisis of creation and provide the starting point for the task of liberation. One, the totally unacceptable poverty and deprivation—and frequently also brutal repression—of the majority of the human family, who are denied their fair share of "good things," not because the sustenance available from nature is insufficient, but because the minority can and do take too much for themselves. Two, the deteriorating condition of natural systems and the depletion of mineral deposits, indicating that nature's vulnerability sets limits upon human behavior and that if these limits are not respected, as more and more people make greater and greater demands, the sustenance available in the future may no longer be sufficient. Three, the interdependence and interconnectedness that characterize not only the ecological realities but the social systems of the modern world, which mean that a global strategy is required for dealing simultaneously and wholistically with the problems presented by the first two facts. And four, the unprecedented potential for massive, ruinous destruction, which I have already cited. The task of liberation is to face up to these facts.

The liberation of creation is generally either neglected or short-circuited by theologians and ethicists—even by the contemporary theologians of liberation. We are deeply indebted to them for reminding us, in the context of contemporary social and economic realities, that God sides with the poor, the vulnerable, and the oppressed. They have given a renewed sense of self-worth and new hope for freedom to the victims of racial or ethnic prejudice and discrimination, to peasants and slum dwellers in Latin America and other Third World countries, and to women stifled by male domination in patriarchal culture. With the exception of Native American and some feminist theologians, however, they have given concentrated attention thus far only to the plight of human beings.

On the other hand, some of the new concern in Christian circles for the environment fails sufficiently to connect nature's plight with that of humans. Theologies of creation must not neglect the liberation of people. Creation includes humanity. Nature and the poor are co-victims of oppression. They will be liberated together or not at all.

The term eco-justice is not to be understood as in any sense turning away from concern for justice in the social order but rather as *combining* justice to people with justice to the rest of creation. It is not that we want the well-being of humankind *and* the well-being of nature, as though these represented two separate sets of concerns, but that we can't have either without the other. This realization is a major new insight of our time. Confronted by the crisis of creation, we know that justice must be understood as eco-justice and that eco-justice must be understood as retaining all that was meant by justice. We seek the restoration, protection, and well-being of earth and all people: eco-justice, the liberation of creation.

IV. A Continuing Story

Ralph Wendell Burhoe in a brilliant article in the collection called *Cry of the Environment* says that out of our human involvement in the flux and change of evolving systems "we can abstract a stable and universal rule: the highest value for all creatures is forever to seek and enact what our history requires."[5] Eco-justice, I believe, is what our history requires.

Seeking and enacting eco-justice means participating in what I call the continuing story, the story to which our history now brings us. From the standpoint of biblical faith it is the continuation of the biblical story—not a new story but the same story at the beginning of a new chapter. The chief actor is still the same—the One whom we know from the biblical story as the Creator-Deliverer of the world, the One who made heaven and earth and who executes justice for the oppressed.

The biblical story, focusing on the liberation of people, does not overlook nature. Paul, we observed, speaks of the creation as subjected to bondage. The prophet Hosea, condemning the people's faithlessness, tells us that "therefore the land mourns." (Hos. 4:3) He does not refer necessarily to environmental pollution but senses that when people go wrong somehow the land is implicated and affected, and he knows that the land will suffer if judgment comes in the form of conquest by a foreign power. Similarly, the biblical visions of *shalom* and of the fulfillment or consummation of creation and history include the healing of nature and the restoration of harmony. "For behold," says Jahweh, "I create new heavens and a new earth.... The wolf and the lamb shall feed together, the lion shall eat straw like the ox; and dust shall be the serpent's food. They shall not hurt or destroy in all my holy mountain." (Is. 65:17, 25)

In the continuing story the focus of attention expands to keep nature along with people at the center of concern. The abuse or oppression of nature occurring in our time makes this expanded focus an inescapable imperative. It simply will not do to point to the biblical story and argue that God's concern is people and not nature, or that God's special concern for people gives them any kind of license to abuse and despoil the earth. As the creatures who are cocreators, they have the Creator's permission and blessing to apply husbandry and technology to earth to increase and enhance its capacity for sustenance, but always with respect for nature's laws and systems, never in such a way as to flout those laws, ruin those systems, or deny the intrinsic worth of other creatures. What they were given no permission to do, however, they have increasingly done, overstepping the proper bounds of freedom. Not until our own time did the consequences become so intolerable as to make the expanded focus of liberation inescapable.

As always, the Creator-Deliverer executes justice for the oppressed, but now "the oppressed" means earth no less than people. We may venture then to state the key theological-ethical affirmation for guiding human participation in the continuing story: *the new thing that God does, declares, and commands is eco-justice.*

Those who participate faithfully in that story turn away from oppression and become agents of the liberation of creation. As cocreators they become codeliverers, protecting and restoring the vulnerable and the afflicted, both earth and people. Thereby they *get with* the Creator-Deliverer in the new chapter of the story, the momentous new era in the history of the world.

V. *The Leadership of the Churches?*

In 1978 Lester Brown of the Worldwatch Institute referred rather regretfully to the lack of religious leadership. "Unfortunately," he wrote, "... religious leaders and theologians sidestep the troublesome philosophical questions associated with ecological stresses, resource scarcities, and global poverty. To the extent they are prepared to deal with contemporary issues, many address symptoms of social problems rather than their causes." Nevertheless, Brown was not quite giving up hope for what he called "an interesting convergence between theology and ecology, one that holds out the prospect of church leaders and environmentalists joining hands and engaging in joint projects in public education and political action on theological-ecological causes."[6]

Perhaps that leadership and convergence, which did not emerge conspicuously at the end of the 1970s, can happen and gather momentum as the 1980s lead on into the 1990s. I believe everything I have been saying makes a case for why it ought to happen.

I want to conclude by suggesting six dimensions of what it might really mean for the churches to get serious about eco-justice as the new thing that the Creator-Deliverer does, declares, and commands. In each case I shall comment briefly on what the task entails, but time permits only a bare introduction to, or an overly glib summary of, what might be said.

The churches have, to begin with, a *theological task*, for which of course the theological seminaries have a special responsibility to equip the churches. If this task is not undertaken, the issues of eco-justice, such as acid rain, toxic pollution, and renewable energy sources, will continue to seem peripheral to the churches' essential mission. They will have to go on competing in a "laundry list" of more or less interesting optional topics, from which congregational study groups pick and choose, as they are moved by the whims or special interests of their more vocal members. This fall our project in Ithaca received a small check from a congregation with a note which said in effect: here's a contribution to get you off our backs, but please don't bother us again, because eco-justice just doesn't happen to be one of the things in which we're very interested. Obviously, when I met with some folks from that church, I failed to get them to see eco-justice as having any necessary and important connection with their faith and mission.

The task is to enable people to see the problems of environmental quality and the problems of socially/economically dispossessed people as dimensions of the one crisis of creation. It is to help them see such problems as evidence or instances of the salient realities of our time and to interpret those realities in the light of the biblical story. Since the Creator-Deliverer did not retire after the New Testament got written, theology cannot be meaningful today unless it is contextual. There is something wrong with sermons and mission statements that sound as though they could just as well have been prepared thirty or more years ago. If people are to think theologically about the present, they must be steeped in the biblical story, and they must look anew at the world as the arena in which the story continues. Otherwise they cannot hear the new things that God declares. If the churches begin to see the crisis of creation and to search there for God's work and will in our time, they may go beyond business as usual and undertake their proper part in the work of liberation.

Closely related to the theological task is the *prophetic task*. This task, in part, is to be critical, from the perspective of a faith that is both biblical and contextual, of that which thwarts the eco-justice agenda. This will entail exposing and challenging the assumptions and ideologies and nationalistic or cultural gods that get in the way of the new things that God declares.

Perhaps the most difficult and threatening part of the prophetic word for our time is the call for a fresh and thoroughgoing reconceptualization of economics in the light of ecological realities. Surely it is clear by now that indiscriminate, exponential economic growth has devastating effects on biological systems and natural resources. This kind of growth cannot be the key to overcoming poverty and hunger, and this realization radically changes anything but a very short-term strategy for economic justice. The good things of God's creation are to be obtained carefully and shared equitably. As cocreators and coworkers with the Creator, human beings are to make this happen through their work.[7] Only in this way can there be and continue to be enough for all. Economic arrangements must permit all to participate. No economy—no kind of *control*—is acceptable that turns any part of the human family into the economically dispossessed. This would be clear if we remembered that the root meaning of economics is the management or stewardship of a household. In the wisely, faithfully managed household all the members work together to obtain and enjoy a sustenance that is sufficient and sustainable.

Going beyond criticism, the prophetic task includes the envisioning of a future that could emerge—a just and sustainable global community, a restored environment, a world without hunger or warfare, a peace based upon the security of full participation in the life and work of one global household, in which the satisfactions of convivial community replace the hollow pleasures of excessive consumerism. The envisioning in some detail of what the liberation of creation would be like is instrumental to its realization.

The prophetic task leads into the constructive *ethical task* of delineating the values and norms appropriate to the liberation of creation, the enactment of eco-justice. This entails interpreting or translating the traditional norms of Christian faithfulness in terms distinctively relevant to our own extraordinary time. The claim of earth and people to be loved cannot be met in the present situation without sharing for the sake of *sufficiency*. Sufficiency is a norm to be approached from two directions. Those with too little require more to have enough. Those with more than an appropriate share of material things will be relinquishing some of them to move down toward that same standard of "enough" and thereby make it more possible for the needy to move up. Sufficiency goes hand in hand with *sustainability*, the norm that requires us to relate to the non-human creation with respect and care and maintain a life-supporting habitat for future generations. Sufficiency and sustainability are rooted in *solidarity*—the interconnectedness of created beings and the oneness of the human family within the whole; the central place of community in human fulfillment; the obligation to include everyone as full participant in the society and the economy and to stand with the oppressed and the excluded in their struggle for liberation and participation. The sustainable sufficiency must be for *all*.

In the fourth place, the churches have a *pastoral and practical task*: to be an open, welcoming, accepting, caring community of nurture, mutual support, celebration, and guidance, within which people are kept from feeling cornered, overwhelmed, or immobilized by the complex problems, impending dangers, and startling changes with which they have to cope. In such a community people may be helped to see, accept, and enjoy the simple, practical next steps that they can take in their personal and public lives to move in the direction of eco-justice. In the life of such a community people may appropriate the equipment of faith to take with them as they go out into their places of work, service, controversy, politics, and struggle, there to be cocreators and codeliverers with God in the world.

And then there is the *collaborative task*, as churches learn from, contribute to, and work with, secular organizations and movements that share their commitment to environmental wholeness and social/economic justice. This is the sort of thing Lester Brown was hoping for—church people, environmentalists, and (I would add) economic justice advocates, engaging in joint projects of education and action on theological-ecological-economic causes. The need for such collaborative work is one of the reasons for the convening of this consultation.

Finally, the churches have what I can only call their *evangelical task*. They can call their people to renewed faithfulness. They can proclaim the gospel of Jesus Christ, who tells us that we gain life by giving it away. They can show that the liberation of creation lies at the very core of what it means to live and act as the people of God in our time. And they can remind faithful people that they need not be anxious, because the chief Liberator is the Creator-Deliverer of the world, whose love for earth and people is steadfast, whose will-for-good is utterly trustworthy, whose grace is sufficient, and whose purpose, which is the fulfillment of creation, will in the end be accomplished.

That reminder, however, does not gloss over the seriousness of the present crisis. It does not underestimate the difficulty of transforming values and changing practices and policies soon enough to keep conditions from worsening. It affirms that there is meaning and joy in participating with the Creator-Deliverer in the continuing story of creation and liberation, even if in our lifetime defeats outweigh successes.

Robert L. Heilbroner, in a book which I regard as the most eloquent and moving challenge yet made from outside the church to the church on the future of the creation (even though he does not address it to the church), makes propositions that help to show what really is at stake in the evangelical task. First he asserts (with convincing evidence) that "the inescapable need to limit industrial growth" is "the central challenge" as humankind looks now to the future.[8] But he is deeply pessimistic: the challenge will not be met in time. This is because "the challenge to survival" still lies too far in the future, and "the inertial momentum of the present industrial order" is still too great.[9] He concludes: "The voluntary abandonment of the industrial mode of production would require a degree of self-abnegation on the part of its beneficiaries—managers and consumers alike—that would be without parallel in history."[10] He is convinced that it will not happen, and that therefore the world will pay a "fearful price."

The church claims that self-abnegation, self-denial, the losing of life for Christ's sake—and paradoxically finding it—is what the new life in Christ is all about. The gospel is a call to conversion, a fundamental change of heart. If it becomes responsive to the crisis of creation, the church will call privileged people to let go of present privileges, to love earth and people sacrificially, and in that way be involved eagerly and joyfully in the liberation of creation. Such a conversion on a mass scale is not to be expected. But where it happens it will make a difference.

Notes

1. George M. Woodwell, "Global Warming and What We Can Do About It," *Amicus Journal* 8 (2), Fall 1986, 8–15.

2. "Down and Out and Dispossessed," *Time*, November 24, 1986, 27f.

3. G. B. Trudeau, "Doonesbury," (Universal Press Syndicate), *Ithaca Journal*, Ithaca, New York, November 19, 1986.

4. Mark Lurlansky, "Haiti: The Revolution That Wasn't," *The Progressive*, December 1986, 24–27.

5. Ralph Wendell Burhoe, "Cosmic Evolutionary Creation and Christian God," in *Cry of the Environment: Rebuilding the Christian Creation Tradition,* Philip N. Joranson and Ken Butigan, eds. (Santa Fe, N.M.: Bear & Company, 1984), 241.

6. Lester R. Brown, *The Twenty-Ninth Day: Accommodating Human Needs and Numbers to the Earth's Resources* (New York: W. W. Norton, 1978), 315.

7. See Dorothee Soelle with Shirley A. Cloyes, *To Work and To Love: A Theology of Creation* (Philadelphia: Fortress Press, 1984), chs. 5–9 on work.

8. Robert L. Heilbroner, *An Inquiry into the Human Prospect* (New York: W. W. Norton, 1974), 54.

9. Ibid., 133.

10. Ibid., 135.

6

Teaching the Eco-Justice Ethic: The Parable of Billerica Dam

J. Ronald Engel

Editor's Notes

In this article J. Ronald Engel makes beautiful use of parable to illustrate the value of stories for drawing the American people into the struggle for eco-justice. This too was a talk delivered to the consultation, "For the Love of Earth and People: the Eco-Justice Agenda." The struggle, as he depicted it, has meaning and durability as a chapter in a shared religious and/or civic story that encompasses our heritage, our present, and our destiny.

In speaking of the biblical story as a continuing story, I had sought to recall people of biblical faith to their involvement in God's liberating activity in history. Ron Engel then applied the idea of participation in story to the civic community. To teach the eco-justice ethic, we need to recapture what is authentic and good in our democratic heritage, the commitment to "liberty and justice for all." We have to engage again in the unfinished American Revolution—against unjust power and the violation of human rights. We have to pick up once more and boldly extend the inclusion of nature's rights in the one struggle.

People will be empowered by "revolutionary parables of democratic faith." The journey to eco-justice is the making of a revolution—a revolution into reality, into eco-justice, the reality our society tries desperately to escape.

Teaching the Eco-Justice Ethic:
The Parable of the Billerica Dam

(*The Egg: A Journal of Eco-Justice* 7 [1], Spring 1987)

I. A River and a Dam

On the last day of August 1839, a Saturday, Henry David Thoreau, then twenty-two years of age, and his brother, John, twenty-four, set out in their home-made boat on the Concord River for a week's camping trip. Thoreau later wrote about the trip in his first book, *A Week on the Concord and Merrimack Rivers.*[1]

After passing out of Concord and floating by the first battleground of the Revolution, where in 1775 "once the embattled farmers stood, and fired the shot heard round the world," they drifted leisurely downstream for most of the afternoon, winding their way through the lush grassy meadows that lay on either side of the river, arriving near sundown at the outskirts of the Town of Billerica. Here, on a spit of land jutting into the river, they camped for the night—the first night of his life Thoreau spent out of doors.

As they sail along that afternoon, Thoreau observes with delight the rich diversity of fishes and plants that inhabit the river and its banks, and the occasional solitary fisherman who lingers by its shores. But when the two brothers come within the vicinity of Billerica a sudden shift in perception occurs. Three species of fish, salmon, shad, and alewives, Thoreau writes, "were formerly abundant here, and taken in weirs [nets] by the Indians, who taught this method to the whites, by whom they were used as food and as manure." Now, however, they are missing from the river because "the dam, and afterward the canal at Billerica . . . put an end to their migrations hitherward." There was a time, he recalls, still within memory of the eldest citizens, when the river overflowed with "miraculous draughts of fishes."

Thoreau's interest is especially attracted to the plight of the shad, who migrate each year up the river only to be met—"by the corporation with its dam." "Poor shad!" he writes, "where is thy redress? When nature gave thee instinct, gave she thee the heart to bear thy fate? Still wandering the sea in thy scaly armor to inquire humbly at the mouths of rivers if—man has perchance left them free for thee to enter. . . . Armed with no sword . . . but mere shad, armed only with innocence and a *just cause* . . . I for one am with thee, and who knows what may avail a crow-bar against that Billerica dam?"

Yet the shad are not the only ones oppressed by the dam. Thoreau goes on: "At length it would seem that the interests, not of the fishes only, but the men of Wayland, of Sudbury, of Concord, demand the leveling of that dam." For the dam has not only stopped the harvesting of fish for food and manure, but has flooded the meadows for many miles upstream. And in the heavily wooded Massachusetts countryside of 1839, natural meadows are a precious resource, essential to farmers for hay for their livestock. The farmers now stand idly "with scythes whet," vainly "waiting the subsiding of the waters...." "So many sources of wealth inaccessible!" Thoreau exclaims.

II. Stories of Eco-Justice

To achieve a world of eco-justice we will need a far-reaching political, social, and economic revolution. Not because eco-justice is a utopian ideal in the "real world" of contemporary economics and politics, but because eco-justice is the reality our society is so desperately seeking to escape. Think what it would mean for those communities we [at this consultation on our field trips] saw this afternoon if the natural environment were restored to health and every person had enough to live on and freedom to work at a worthwhile job. Eco-justice is so simple and so real that it staggers the mind!

If we are going to teach the ethic of eco-justice in ways that will empower the public to act on its behalf, we will need to tell stories about reality.

Jesus began the revolution that is Christianity by teaching parables of the Kingdom. For generations black Americans have maintained their struggle for political freedom by telling stories of spiritual liberation. According to John Adams, the real American Revolution took place in the hearts and minds of the people long before it happened on the battlefield. British loyalists failed because they had no story to match the sacred story of human rights. The power of the refugees who come into our churches for sanctuary from Central America is their testimony to reality through the stories they tell.

People know and act by stories. Our private lives are largely governed by the personal stories we understand ourselves to be living out. Our religious communities live or die on the basis of the redemptive reality of the stories they tell. This is no less true of the civic communities in which we participate: the stories that we live out as citizens. Our collective destiny is shaped by the public stories that we believe provide trustworthy clues to the meaning of our common world and direction for the future.

If we are going to teach a public ethic of eco-justice we will need public stories of eco-justice. Let us call them *public parables*—stories that have the capacity to communicate the religious and moral truth of our public world: the meaning of our love for earth and people as citizens, the reality of the ongoing struggle for eco-justice in the ongoing history of our civic communities.

Without them, all our pronouncements and programs are futile. Such stories alone will empower us as citizens to do the two most basic things: first, *to identify ourselves as members of civic communities*—inclusive of the natural communities with which we share common ground. And second, *to organize ourselves as civic communities*, by regaining control of our social, political, and economic institutions, and reinhabiting the land that sustains us.

It is evident that in today's world such public stories will be revolutionary parables of democratic faith: stories that carry forward the prophetic convictions of our biblical and religious heritage through the story of our shared secular struggle for "liberty and justice for all." Now I want to suggest that we have substantial resources in the progressive democratic traditions of the United States and other cultures of the world for liberating parables of eco-justice. Thoreau's story of Billerica Dam is one example.

III. A Continuing Revolution

Like the parable of the Good Samaritan, the story of Billerica Dam holds in tension two ways of being in the world: One the ordinary way, and the other, the way of the Kingdom—where the last are first and the least is the greatest. Also like the parables of Jesus, it is built upon a new and radical metaphor, in this case the root metaphor for all stories that teach the ethic of eco-justice.

The story begins in the world of ordinary experience. Thoreau and his brother, floating down the Concord River admiring the scenery, come upon Billerica Dam. It is an ordinary enough sight—ordinary until Thoreau shifts the point of view and we find ourselves looking at the scene through the eyes of lowly shad seeking a way up the river to spawn; through the eyes of elderly citizens who remember their own childhood when the fish ran free; through the eyes of farmers and oxen barred from cutting hay. Then *our* eyes are opened, and we see that *this* is the world that alone is worthy of our love; the world that *ought* to be fulfilled, indeed, in the most fundamental sense, the world that *is* and *will be*: Thy will be done on earth as well as heaven! Listen to this passage from Thoreau:

> Who hears the fishes when they cry? It will not be forgotten by some memory that we were contemporaries. Thou shalt ere long have thy way up the rivers, up all the rivers of the globe, if I am not mistaken. Yea, even thy dull watery dream shall be more than realized. If it were not so, but thou were to be overlooked at first and at last, then would not I take their heaven. . . . Keep a stiff fin then, and stem all the tides thou mayest meet.

This is the *truth* about the scene. The moral claims of shad and farmers and oxen that we did not know existed until a moment ago are the real world! And the "corporation and its dam" are world-denying. The parable bids us ask: How can this be? How can a corporation have the power to wreak such injustice upon the people and other living creatures who depend upon the Concord River running free?

We still have not identified the most powerful part of the story—the root metaphor by which Thoreau defines the real world. That metaphor is an analogy between the human struggle for liberation and nature's struggle to be free. Like the apostle Paul, Thoreau saw all creation groaning in travail (Rom. 8); unlike Paul, he was born in a nation young with liberty.

It is no accident that Thoreau begins his story by passing the revolutionary battlefield where "once the embattled farmers stood, and fired the shot heard round the world!" This is the assumed metaphorical reference for everything that follows. The shad, like the Concord farmers, have, as he says, a "just cause," and when Thoreau asks what might avail a crowbar against the Billerica Dam he is pointing to the need for continuing the revolution. The whole point of Thoreau's story—indeed, of all his writings, including *Walden, Civil Disobedience*, and his famous *Plea for Captain John Brown*, is to tell the public that the revolution of 1776 is not yet over; we have not yet achieved true economic and political self-government; the people and the land we love are oppressed still.

IV. Humanity and Earth, One Struggle

I believe that the most powerful tools we have available to us for teaching the ethic of eco-justice are stories built upon the analogy between human oppression and nature's oppression, between the human struggle for liberation and nature's struggle for fulfillment. All that we hope to say about the interdependence of people and the earth, economic justice and ecological responsibility, is ultimately rooted in this metaphor and its message that the struggle of humanity and the earth is one.

This is not a new metaphor in human history. It lies powerfully latent, occasionally explicit, in the biblical texts. "Let justice roll down like waters, and righteousness as a mighty stream," declares Amos. (5:23) "Then he showed me the river of the water of life, sparkling like crystal, flowing from the throne of God and of the Lamb down the middle of the city's street," prophesied the author of Revelation. (22:1f) A river running free and clear through the city! Is this not Thoreau's prophetic vision of the Concord River passing through Billerica?

But for those of us who live in the west and share in the traditions of European civilization its implications have only become clear in the modern era. Indeed, its *full* implications may only be clear for the first time to our generation.

The critical turning point was the eighteenth century: the age of human rights and the first democratic revolutions. William Wilberforce, the English reformer, after successfully leading the struggle to abolish slavery from the British Empire, sponsored the first bill to protect animals in the British Parliament. Movements for human rights and animal rights began at the same time. Thomas Paine declared that, if it had not been for tyrants, "the earth, in its natural, uncultivated state, was, and ever would have continued to be, the common property of the human race." The Declaration of Independence audaciously grounded the inalienable rights of persons in the laws of nature and nature's God.

By 1839, at least one American, Henry David Thoreau, grasped the full implications of the metaphor and made the crucial connection with the public story of democracy told by his countrymen. In the years since, as the means of human destruction have grown ever greater, and the extent of human willingness to deny the world has become ever more excruciatingly apparent, the profound truth of the analogy has also become increasingly evident, and its connection with democratic aspirations even stronger.

If you want to experience the power of the metaphor today, recall the movie of the Vietnam War, *The Deer Hunter*. It opens, you will remember, with a group of young Pittsburgh steel workers going on a hunting trip before shipping out to Vietnam. They kill a deer and bring it home draped over the roof of the car. After the terror of the Vietnam experience is over, one of the men returns to the mountains to hunt. In the climax of the story, he sees a magnificent stag, but this time is unable to pull the trigger of his gun.

Or listen to this short poem by Father Ernesto Cardenal, Minister of Culture, Republic of Nicaragua:

> We will restore our forests, rivers, lagoons.
> We will decontaminate Lake Managua.
> Not only humans longed for liberation.
> All ecology groaned for it also. The revolution
> Is also one of lakes, rivers, trees, animals.[2]

Or talk to Roy Brown, native of Puerto Rico, who leads the Puerto Rican band, *Aires Bucaneros,* which plays what are called "new songs," songs that seek to make a statement about contemporary society and are associated with the Puerto Rican movement for independence. Ask him about the song the group plays called *"Arboles,"* "Trees." He will tell you that the song tells about the importance of trees to the future of Puerto Rico, the purity of trees, how straight they are, how honest they are in their beauty, how human beings should be like that, take the side of the little guy, should—like trees—give shade. And he will also tell you about how the commercial radio stations in Puerto Rico refuse to play his songs because they are considered politically dangerous.

Or talk to the people of the Village of Reni in northern India. One day in 1970, so the famous story goes, the women of the village spontaneously began to hug the local trees, their precious source of firewood, stopping the New Delhi corporations—who were logging the forests for foreign export—dead in their tracks. The Andolan Chipko movement was born. Similar symbolic actions spread rapidly throughout the region in the wake of a grand procession that marched to the music of drums, bells, and cymbals for weeks from village to village. Eventually a twelve thousand square kilometer water shed was saved and an ambitious community-based development program began.

V. Return to Billerica

One afternoon a couple of weeks ago I found myself wondering what happened to the Billerica Dam.

To my surprise, I discovered that the Unitarian Universalist Association, with which I am affiliated, has a member church in

Billerica, in fact, the First Parish of Billerica. A call to the minister, Reverend Phil Larson, brought the suggestion that I call the church historian, a Dr. Charles Stearns.

From Charles Stearns I learned that the dam Thoreau saw had been rebuilt in 1835 by a Boston business concern in order to supply water to the Middlesex canal and divert trade from Newburyport to Boston. There were other dams that preceded this one; in fact, in the eighteenth century there was a series of legal suits filed by local farmers against the various corporations that built dams on the river. In 1725 one of these suits was actually won, and the dam was temporarily torn down. Ironically, Charles said, while the dam and canal are now preserved as a national historic landmark, the Concord River is so polluted by manufacturing plants upstream at Sudbury that his children would never think of the river for fishing, swimming, or boating. Charles suggested that I call Wayne Klug about the conservation battle going on in Billerica.

Wayne Klug, a local college teacher, was eager to talk. It seems that an old farm that abutted the river was privately sold recently to a developer who plans to turn it into a housing development for Boston commuters. The land is still a working farm and is crucial to the preservation of the river wetlands; it also includes the site on which Thoreau and his brother camped in 1839. Wayne said that his group had come straight up against the local power structure who considered private property to be "god." He also said that the battle had taught him the need to "revolutionize our priorities." But it was not the only battle fought in Billerica. "Call Helen Knight," he said.

Helen, a retired English teacher, led the "infamous group of five" (including a 6'5" construction foreman) in a successful battle to clean up the Billerica dump. She said she had never engaged in this kind of thing before, but she was outraged when—seven years ago now—her first complaints were brushed aside by the local Board of Health. The group discovered that the dump contained toxic materials that were contaminating the groundwater of Billerica and the Concord River, as well as making other threats to human health. The group fought hard to get the Attorney General of Massachusetts involved; now the site is on the Federal Super Fund list. The basic problem, she said, in addition to corruption, was the conviction of the local power structure that the dump owner could do anything he wished with his "private property." "I have become a very radical old lady," Helen Knight said.

VI. *Ethical Meaning in Public Tradition*

I want to conclude with a brief word to those of us who work directly with religious communities. If anyone has the responsibility to teach the ethic of eco-justice by telling stories of the shared struggle of humanity and nature for liberation, we do.

Why, then, should we hesitate to take the liberating stories of our civic communities with moral seriousness? Billerica is not unique. Go to any of the communities we visited today and we will find the same struggle and there will be something like the parable of Billerica Dam waiting to be told.

Those of us who visited the Passaic River project this afternoon certainly found this to be true, even to the point of listening to Grace George, a long-time resident of Patterson, New Jersey, tell stories of the magnificent rainbows that appear in the Great Falls at Patterson, the very falls that began the industrial revolution in the United States. Today the Passaic River is heavily polluted and the City of Patterson is in economic depression. Yet Grace George tells us the rainbow—the symbol of the original promise of the covenant of creation—is still present, a symbol now of the new covenant of free citizens to restore the environmental and social health of the region.

In the final analysis, it seems to me that our ability to teach the ethic of eco-justice to the public depends upon the assessment we make of the religious and ethical significance of our public traditions, in particular the civic tradition of participatory democracy. If we are unable to affirm important enough meanings in the stories of our civic communities to be shared and celebrated in our churches, we will always stand in a secondary rather than primary relationship to the contemporary struggle for eco-justice in the common life. If, on the other hand, we find such stories illuminating of the prophetic convictions of our biblical and religious heritage, in some cases expanding those meanings in new and revealing ways, we will find the inspiration to speak new words of judgment and hope.

VII. *The Parable Grows*

On the last day of August 1839, Henry David Thoreau, then twenty-two years of age, and his brother, John, twenty-four, set out in their home-made boat on the Concord River for a week's camping trip. . . .

One afternoon in 1980, a retired English teacher, who now describes herself as a very radical old lady. . . .

The parable grows.

"Such is the never failing beauty and accuracy of language," Thoreau wrote, describing the night he and his brother camped out at Billerica and lay awake listening to the sounds of the Concord River. "Language, the most perfect art in the world; *the chisel of a thousand years retouches it.*"

Notes

1. Henry David Thoreau, *A Week on the Concord and Merrimack Rivers* (New York: Hurst, 1920). There are of course earlier editions.

2. Ernesto Cardinal, from "Ecology," *Flights of Victory*, trans. Marc Zimmerman (Maryknoll, N.Y.: Orbis Books, 1985), 71.

Conclusion to Part I

The 1970s: The World Was Warned

In the decade of the 1970s the world was warned. The warnings were quite plentiful, and I need not offer comprehensive citations. However, I think immediately of ecologists such as Barry Commoner and Rachel Carson (who had spoken out in the 1960s); Aurelio Peccei and the Club of Rome, which fostered systems dynamics and analysis by Jay Forrester, Dennis and Donella Meadows, and others, using computer projections to examine the "world problematique"; theologians, including Joseph Sittler, Ian Barbour, Kenneth Cauthen, and Roger Shinn; and a few economists, notably E. F. Schumacher, Herman Daly, and Robert Heilbroner.[1]

In the 1970s the stark realities and extreme dimensions of the eco-justice crisis became painfully clear. On the one hand they showed the *injustice* of the rich-poor gap. Hunger and poverty were not new, and injustice was not new, but the dimensions of unnecessary poverty and the enormity of the disparity between the extremes of affluence and misery had become distinctively characteristic of the modern world. The spectacular achievements of science and technology, industry and agriculture, might have been applied to the responsible use and distribution of earth's abundance for the benefit of all. Modern civilization failed its historic opportunity.

On the other hand was the fact of *limits*—the limits imposed by nature upon human activities and human numbers, human use of technology and "capital" to exploit nature's bounty. The fact of limits hit the world of the 1970s as a radically new and shocking blow. The limits had always belonged to the order of nature, and history tells of localized civilizations that died from violating them. But in the 1970s, after many decades of exponential growth of population and production, came massive evidence on a global scale that nature was revolting against human assaults.

Theologically understood, the judgment upon injustice was and is God's judgment, and the violation of limits was and is the violation of God's ordering of creation. The eco-justice crisis had become the overarching reality of the century and the century to come, in which people of faith must seek to discern the contemporary activity of God as Creator and Deliverer. The crisis had become the context within which people of the covenant, continuing the biblical story, had to struggle with the meaning of faithfulness in our time.

Surely today faithfulness means that the unnecessary and therefore unjust and shameful fact of the chasm between rich and poor cannot be accepted and tolerated. The fact of ecological limits, on the other hand, must be accepted and respected. Acceptance of the second fact, however, makes it harder to refuse to accept the first. If I am privileged, I may have to relinquish privileges for the sake of equitable distribution on a finite planet. The realization of limits makes it easier for comfortable people to tolerate the discomforts of others, even as it becomes more likely that the poor and the oppressed will turn disruptive, violent, and revolutionary. But faithfulness requires solidarity and sharing. If the cries of the earth and the poor are heard sooner rather than later, and the movements of oppressed people for their own liberation are not thwarted by brutal power, advances can be made toward eco-justice.

The 1980s: An Accelerating Transition?

The warnings and new realizations of the 1970s would, I thought, make the 1980s the decade of the beginning of an intentional, long-term transition to a fundamentally changed world. The 1980s, I thought, might be the decade noted for the rise of a new social paradigm—a paradigm of realistic and workable ways for a society to relate to the natural order and shape the economic order.

A social paradigm is a generally held conception within a society of the way things are and the way society works. It consists of assumptions and attitudes that prevail quite generally without being called much into question. It includes values, norms, beliefs, habits, customary practices, and survival rules that have evolved over many years and passed from one generation to the next.

The industrial era paradigm conceives the mastery of nature and the expansion of the economy not only as desirable but as unending. It assumes an abundant and continuing supply of cheap natural resources together with natural "sinks" capable of absorbing the waste and poison of high-technology industry and agriculture. If problems arise, science and technology will solve them. The leading values are efficiency, productivity, and a rising level of production, consumption, and wealth measured in quantitative, monetary terms. The paradigm assumes that self-interest, operating as the chief motive of individual behavior and institutionalized in the economic order, will work out for society's "good."

That paradigm is obsolete. It is fundamentally incompatible with the new realizations of limits, the ancient imperatives of justice, the human need for community, and the biblical vision of *shalom*.

A new paradigm emerges, contradicting the old but not yet driving it out. The new paradigm builds the foundation for a society that can be sustainable and more just. The expectation of always having more gives way to a concept of material sufficiency in the satisfaction of basic needs. Resources are to be used frugally, and society makes a deliberate shift to dependence on the sustainable yield of those that are renewable. Nature is to be appreciated, used carefully, and cared for rather than dominated. The first priority is a sustainable sufficiency for all, with continuing human development and fulfillment measured by intellectual, aesthetic, moral, and spiritual criteria.

In 1982 I delivered a talk entitled "The Ecology of an Accelerating Transition" to a Social Ministry Institute sponsored by the Presbyterian Program Agency and the Presbytery of Utica (New York). I discussed a number of factors of understanding, motivation, and policy that needed to be strengthened, so that in their synergistic interaction they would be conducive to the transition to a more eco-just world. I spoke of the vision of an eco-just future, combined with the shock of the eco-justice crisis; of courageous leadership that could give voice to people's concerns and aspirations but also bring them to heightened consciousness and new purpose; of sacrificial engagement in the cause by some, but also of certain basic securities that would enable people to cope with the uncertainties and anxieties of change; and of the importance of a hope and a trust, in response to grace, bringing assurance of the meaningfulness and worthwhileness of engagement in the eco-justice journey and struggle, an engagement with the One who is still at work in history and nature as Creator and Deliverer.

That talk was printed in the September 1982 issue of *The Egg*. Introducing the issue, the editor, Sharon Lloyd, struck an upbeat, hopeful note. She pointed to my confidence that a transition to a more eco-just world was underway and increasing its pace, and to my excitement about the special, "kairotic" time so full not only of great danger but of great opportunity to influence the future for the better.

She also announced the forthcoming Eco-Justice conference, at Cornell, on a similar "transition" theme. The keynote speakers were to be Dennis and Donella Meadows, two of the authors of *The Limits to Growth*. They too had been expressing hope and excitement about the prospects for sustainability and justice. They could see a different, better world forming here and there in the midst of the old, destructive order.

An Obsolete Paradigm Entrenched

My speech and the 1982 conference seem now to have marked the high point in the feeling that we in the Eco-Justice Project had that the momentum of appropriate response to the eco-justice crisis had been gathering steam and would continue to accelerate. We were not blind then to the formidable obstacles in the way. But I think we underestimated the propensity and the capacity of political, academic, and church leaders and teachers to remain shortsighted and self-serving, and of powerful economic interests, including the major media, to downplay unwanted evidence, to disseminate misinformation, to tout the glories of an ever-expanding economy, and to exercise decisive power over governments. We underestimated, also, the inclination of the American people as a whole to shed their own disturbing new awareness, to find relief in false assurances, and to remain attached to the material excesses and seductive attractions of a consumption oriented society. We knew in 1982 that President Reagan had not simply shelved *The Global 2000 Report* to President Carter but had repudiated it. Nevertheless, it was hard for us to conclude, from this and other signs, that the momentum of transition was diminishing.

In 1982 I was too quick to see some of the economic problems of that day as indications that the economy was actually running into ecological limits. I cited "stagflation," the high unemployment combined with steep inflation. I pointed to high energy prices and said the age of cheap oil had gone forever. Of course it hadn't. Oil reserves—and the eagerness of oil producing countries to sell—had been underestimated.

By conventional assessment, the economy rebounded from the doldrums of the 1980s and early 1990s. President Clinton in his second term hailed the U.S. economy as "the strongest in the history of the world," ignoring the sustainability factor, the environmental destruction, and the gross inequalities. Vice President Gore, despite his remarkable 1992 book, *Earth in the Balance*, spent the rest of the decade as a gung-ho promoter of growth, globalization, and free trade. Despite the efforts of some cities to become "sustainable" and the changed world view of increasing numbers of people, the nation's major institutions and their spokespersons, including the policymakers and power brokers setting the nation's priorities, seemed to present a united front of commitment to the old, obsolete, and self-destructive paradigm.

Nevertheless, basic change will come, because the old paradigm is truly unsustainable. The tardiness of human societies to respond intentionally, intelligently, and vigorously to present perils and opportunities will mean that the pain and disruption of change will be shamefully worse than it needed to be. In the new century the folly of clinging to the old paradigm will finally become too devastatingly plain to be denied. The eco-just future, to which I believe we are led and commanded by the One who is author of life and source of meaning, will not be simply the culmination of gradual transition. Perhaps the idea of transition suggests a journey too steady and smooth for fundamental, revolutionary change. The necessary "ecology" of fundamental change may have to include the bitterness of breakdown to generate humility for a new beginning.

Notes

1. I shall cite a few of the books of the 1970s that greatly influenced me: Donella H. Meadows, Dennis L. Meadows, Jørgen Randers, and William W. Behrens III, *The Limits to Growth: A Report for the Club of Rome Project on the Predicament of Mankind* (New York: Universe Books, 1972); The Editors of *The Ecologist, Blueprint for Survival* (Boston: Haughton Mifflin, 1972); Joseph Sittler, *Essays on Nature and Grace* (Minneapolis, Minn.: Fortress Press, 1972); Ian Barbour, ed., *Western Man and Environmental Ethics* (Reading, Mass.: Addison-Wesley, 1973); Kenneth Cauthen, *Christian Biopolitics: A Credo and Strategy for the Future* (Nashville: Abbingdon Press, 1971); E. F. Schumacher, *Small Is Beautiful: Economics as If People Mattered* (New York: Harper & Row, 1973); Herman E. Daly, ed., *Toward a Steady-State Economy* (San Francisco: W. H. Freeman, 1973); and Robert L. Heilbroner, *An Inquiry into the Human Prospect* (New York: W. W. Norton, 1973).

Part II

Eco-Justice Issues

Over the fourteen years of its publication, *The Egg / Eco-Justice Quarterly* carried a wide range of articles dealing with the eco-justice issues. These all fitted our definition of an eco-justice issue: they required consideration of both ecology and justice. They could not be addressed realistically and responsibly without taking account of ecological facts and values, on the one hand, and fairness and equity to human and other beings, on the other hand.

Ecological facts have to do with the processes and cycles of nature, the interdependence of all kinds of beings (including the human kind) competing and cooperating, the fundamental dependence of humans upon a healthy biotic community for sustenance and survival, the limits that nature imposes upon human behavior, the vulnerability of natural systems and nonhuman creatures to human disruption and abuse, and nature's resilience and capacity for healing when humans give priority to working with nature instead of mastering it.

The value of the natural world is twofold. We humans value nature for our own sake, because we depend for our lives upon it. But nature makes claim upon us to be valued for its own sake. Nature understood as God's creation makes claim to be valued for the Creator's sake. At root it is the Creator's claim. The integrity of creation is to be respected and preserved. The nonhuman forms of life have a Creator-endowed right to their place and role in the evolutionary process without the uncaring human intervention that ruins their habitat and threatens or perpetrates their extinction.

Of course our human intervention in nature to meet our needs is unavoidable, but it is to be restrained and guided by respect and appreciation. Unless we care about nature because we acknowledge its intrinsic value, we shall not take sufficient care in appropriating its gifts. Unless our self-interested relationship to the created order is transcended by deeper ties of wonder, gratitude, kinship, and solidarity, we shall not have the wisdom over time even to serve our own self-interest.

The eco-justice norms and goals of sustainability and solidarity reflect and reinforce the twofold basis and motivation for protecting the creation, reducing the human impact, and fostering healing and renewal.

Eco-justice extends the concept of justice beyond the strictly human realm to all of nature, to animals and trees and undiscovered species, soils, seas, and landscapes, life-sustaining systems and myriad configurations of order, beauty, and enjoyment. Justice entails respecting their integrity, their claim to life and to wholeness. Justice means that our human claims are not all that count. Many times these are to be reduced or relinquished for the sake of our nonhuman companions, whose worth to ourselves defies calculation but whose claims in any case also count.

In the human realm justice requires fairness and equity and vitality in community—in communities at many levels, whose members cooperate for the common good, establishing reliable practices and structures to balance competing claims and ensure that every member may participate in the good of the community. In the context of the eco-justice crisis, the constant need to include the factor of sustainability in our judgments and calculations, and the massive, still widening chasm between affluence and poverty, the distinctive norms of justice for our time are sufficiency and participation. As I've noted (see Selection 2), these norms entail a sense and a standard of what is enough for a life reasonably secure and fulfilling, without extravagance and excess, made possible for all the members of a community. They all participate, according to their abilities and talents, in the decisions that affect their lives, the work needing to be done, and the enjoyment of a sustainable sufficiency.

With this necessarily general background on taking both ecology and justice into account, we move now to specific issues of eco-justice. The articles of Part II are representative of the journal's coverage of the major categories of eco-justice concern. These categories, of course, are not discrete. They overlap, and some articles might have been differently placed. For reasons of space, I have omitted additional articles that I wanted to include. Those that follow provide descriptions of the eco-justice journey, show the obstacles on the path, and flesh out the content of eco-justice as a destination.

Section A

Toxic Pollution and
Environmental Justice

Editor's Notes

In the summer of 1988 The Egg: A Journal of Eco-Justice *devoted an issue to "Pollution, Poverty and Power." In my editorial introduction I said:*

> *The assumption behind this issue is that the victims of pollution tend to be the poor, the powerless, the vulnerable. They are the factory and farm workers inadequately protected by the Occupational Safety and Health Administration. Their jobs are hazardous, but they cannot afford to lose them. They are the welfare mothers and children, the unemployed youth, the elderly poor, and the homeless, stuck in the blighted urban jungle. They cannot afford to move away. They are Blacks, Hispanics, Native Americans, and rural Appalachians who lack the clout to oppose the champions of relentless development and hard technology, or to insist that the incinerator and the landfill be put in someone else's backyard.*

I noted that the powerless in many places were organizing to gain and assert power, refusing to accept the role of victim. The spreading of pollution, moreover, was eroding the distinction between victim and non-victim. "We all will be hurt by pollution to some significant degree." Still, the great majority of the American people did not yet recognize emotionally that this was so. They had not experienced the ill effects sufficiently to shatter the complacency and denial to which "the politicians and merchants of endless expansion" wanted them to hold fast. But they could not really hide their eyes to what was happening to communities near and far. I suggested that "the crucial spiritual-ethical test in our time is whether we who are not yet hurt can stand and act in solidarity with those who already are."

We carried an article by Richard Grossman (author of Selection 3) entitled "The Saturation of the South." Grossman reported on his travels through eighty communities in eight southern states on a commission from the Interreligious Economic Crisis Organizing Network. He concluded, "The South is saturated with poisons and dominated by poisoners." The details of conditions and community organizing, of course, are not current, and space considerations precluded reprinting the entire article here. But in his portrayal of the problem as deeply rooted in the economic system as such and in the realities of power, Grossman paints a picture of the situation still continuing, in which corrections or improvements are spotty and tenuous, and vigilance and grassroots organizing remain essential.

On his travels Grossman "met people who physicians and worker-health experts say are experiencing the symptoms of common industrial practices and the products of science and industry." The list of ailments goes on and on, ranging from liver, kidney, and blood diseases to cancers and leukemias and to miscarriages, infertility, and birth defects, among much else.

More than half of U.S. petroleum refining and chemical production takes place along a four-hundred-mile stretch between Corpus Christi, Texas and Baton Rouge, Louisiana. Grossman reported:

> *I drove along the meandering Mississippi in southern Louisiana past sixty factories. My eyes, nose, and mouth burned the whole way. I drove in and out of small, poor, mostly unincorporated, minority communities that go right up to the companies' chain link fences. I . . . talked to people . . . who told of buried children, mass burials of livestock, buried friends and relatives dead at early ages of mysterious ailments becoming increasingly common. I was told . . . that the communities had no authority to collect taxes or oversee what these factories did. I was told that in 1986, eighteen petrochemical companies in just two parishes had legal permits to spew 196 million pounds of chemicals into the air.*

In Grossman's account of toxic pollution, unsafe disposal, and corporate and even government frustration of community efforts to obtain redress, he arrives at some telling conclusions about the power of the "poisoners" and their subordination of the safety and the health of workers and the public to their institutionalized interests.

> *If this destruction and poisoning were a once-in-a-blue-moon blunder, an oversight . . . a regrettable error, we could reason-*

ably expect that those "adults," firms, and agencies respon-
sible would be moving swiftly to stop the poisoning now, to
repair the harm, to treat the victims, to make restitution, and
to find safe ways to make the products the nation truly needs
and wants. But as people told me wherever I traveled, the
adults are stepping up production. Seeking more dumps.
Intensifying their intimidation of victims.

The adults . . . have responded thusly to questions and
complaints: they do not acknowledge what they have done and
continue to do; they choose not to install air and water moni-
toring; they choose not to conduct medical tests, even . . . when
disease clusters are well known; they choose not to see the liver
damage and the miscarriages or the streets across the South
which parents have named "Leukemia Alley."

. . . the people of the South face multiple economic and
*societal **injustices**, which are spreading poverty and dis-*
ease. These injustices exist because investment and produc-
tion decisions are being made by people whose institutional
values are hostile to life and nature, antithetical to justice
and democracy.

. . . The institutions—giants of finance, production,
marketing, advertising, research and development—operate
in pursuit of their production, control, and monetary goals.
They have convinced many that their goals and our goals are
one and the same. As insurance, they have held our jobs, our
economy, our communities, our national security, as hostage.

The point is not that the grassroots people's organizing never
has any successes, or that it never gets government to do what
government ought to do, but that it is continually struggling against
the enormous force of institutionalized private interest. The struggle
has to "break the power of the poisoners and impoverishers." This
will mean, among other things, "ending the nation's deafening
silence on management decision-making" and "increasing the power
of our communities in relation to the producers." Yes, we journey
on a rocky road toward eco-justice.

The journal frequently carried an "Action for Eco-Justice"
column. This covered various cases of grassroots organizing, action,
and coalition building for "environmental justice." Such mobiliza-
tions occurred quite often in the 1980s and still continue. Local
organizing begins in response to immediate experience and alarm.
Ordinary "nonexperts," horrified by perceived cancer clusters, for
example, or abnormally numerous miscarriages, compile the facts
and rally their friends and neighbors. Sometimes they get assistance
from local churches or existing environmental groups or from church
bodies or environmental organizations at the state or national level.

The Winter 1988–89 issue of the journal carried a column by Andrew Moore, "A Walk for Toxic Justice" in Louisiana. This walk demonstrated the breadth of the coalition building around environmental justice, which has continued to ebb and flow—involving a mixture of racial identities, environmentalists and church people, workers and labor unions, victims of pollution and those who stand and walk with them, sometimes with and sometimes without the support of local governments and state and national agencies for environmental protection.

The term "environmental justice" is used sometimes instead of "eco-justice" to cover the broad range of ecology and justice concerns. The Presbyterian Church (U.S.A.), for example, has an Office of Environmental Justice. "Environmental justice," however, came into wide use as a technical term for the justice concerns of poor and minority groups disproportionately affected by the siting and the operation of pollution-generating factories or such facilities as toxic waste incinerators and landfills of various kinds.

Indeed, the devastating impact of poisoned environments upon racial and ethnic communities has been such that environmental justice as a movement emerged and gathered momentum as a response to environmental racism. In Selection 7, "Toxic Pollution and Race," Charles Lee explains the particular vulnerability of racial/ethnic communities in being sited for toxic waste facilities and insufficiently protected from the toxics. He reports on the substantiation of this connection by the major study conducted by the Commission for Racial Justice of the United Church of Christ.

In our journal's "Action for Eco-Justice" column, Winter 1991–92, the late Jean Sindab, then the National Council of Churches' (N.C.C.) Program Director for Environmental and Economic Justice, reported on the challenge by people of color to environmental racism. It reached a high peak with the October 1991 First National People of Color Environmental Leadership Summit. The United Church of Christ Commission for Racial Justice sponsored this event, with N.C.C. support. To propel and undergird the environmental justice movement, the Summit issued a Call to Action together with Principles of Environmental Justice.

Environmental injustices, whether occurring in communities of color or elsewhere, result from the failure to take care—to take the necessary precautions to prevent contamination of the environment and harm to people. Over the past decade efforts have been made to get corporations to accept responsibility for environmental protection and to give a regular accounting of their stewardship. In Selection 8 J. Andy Smith tells the story of the "CERES Principles," originally called the "Valdez Principles" in the aftermath of the disastrous oil spill by the Exxon Valdez *into Prince William*

Sound, Alaska. The Principles set forth a code of environmentally responsible conduct, to which corporations pledge themselves.

The article appeared shortly after the Sun Oil Company (whose name is now officially Sunoco) had endorsed the CERES Principles. It was the first large, prominent company to do so. I asked Andy Smith to provide an update on developments in the CERES project.

"In the years since the endorsement," Smith reported, "Sunoco has forged a strong partnership with CERES, stimulating culture change on both sides. . . . The company has improved its environmental record substantially and saved millions of dollars in the process."

Smith gave a further update as follows:

One year after Sunoco endorsed, General Motors followed. Other large endorsing companies include APS (formerly Arizona Public Service), Bank of America, FleetBoston Financial, Baxter International, Bethlehem Steel, Coca Cola USA, H. B. Fuller, ITT Industries, Interface, PPL (formerly PP&L Resources), Polaroid, American Airlines, Consolidated Edison, Ford, Green Mountain Energy, Nike, United States Trust, and William McDonough and Partners. In addition, a number of smaller companies have made the commitment, including Ben & Jerry's, the Body Shop, Northeast Utilities, and the Timberland Company. The total of companies and organizations endorsing is now seventy-two. The CERES report, required by the Principles, has evolved into a benchmark for environmental reporting. The Global Reporting Initiative, an outgrowth of the CERES report, now brings together industry, government, accounting, environmental, and other groups around the world to address sustainability reporting. The guidelines, first released in the spring of 1999, include financial, social, and environmental data, but do not compromise rigorous measurement practices.

These are encouraging developments. They show an acceptance of responsibility by some corporations that Richard Grossman did not find in his travels through the South. The corporations named by Andrew Moore in "A Walk for Toxic Justice" are not included in Smith's list of CERES endorsers. But we may welcome, wherever it occurs, corporate responsibility that reduces pollution.

Corporate anti-pollution commitments, welcome as they are, do not remove major systemic obstacles to eco-justice: the undemocratic and dangerous concentrations of corporate power, the inability of capitalism and the market to foster equity, and the contradiction between sustainability and the growth imperative.

7

Toxic Pollution and Race

Charles Lee

(*The Egg: A Journal of Eco-Justice* 8 [2], Summer 1988)

In recent years, there has been unprecedented national concern over the problems of hazardous wastes and environmental pollution. Efforts to address this issue, however, have largely ignored the specific concerns of African Americans, Hispanic Americans, Asian Americans, Pacific Islanders, and Native Americans. Unfortunately, as the following examples illustrate, racial and ethnic Americans are far more likely to be unknowing victims of exposure to dangerous chemical substances.

- The nation's largest hazardous waste landfill, receiving wastes from forty-five states, is located in predominantly black and poor Sumter County, Alabama.

- The State of North Carolina is on the verge of permitting a regional chemical waste treatment plant along the Lumbee River, a predominantly black and Native American area. The nation's first commercial low level radioactive waste incinerator was also proposed for this area. [See Winter 1987–88 issue of *The Egg*.]

- The predominantly black and Hispanic south side of Chicago has perhaps the greatest concentration of hazardous waste sites in the nation.

93

- In Houston, Texas, six of the eight municipal incinerators and all five of the municipal landfills are located in predominantly black neighborhoods.

- Black residents of a west Dallas neighborhood, whose children suffered irreversible brain damage from exposure to lead pollutants from a nearby lead smelter, won a $20 million out-of-court settlement.

- Pesticide exposure among farm workers, predominantly Hispanic, causes more than three hundred thousand pesticide related illnesses per year. A great percentage of farm workers are women of child bearing age and children. This may be directly related to the emergence of a cancer cluster in McFarland, California.

- The Navajo community in Shiprock, New Mexico, where over one hundred million tons of uranium mill tailings flooded the Rio Puerco River, is one of numerous Native American communities near uranium mills and nuclear facilities.

- Three executives in Illinois were convicted of murder in the death of a worker from cyanide poisoning. This plant employed mostly Hispanic and Polish immigrants who spoke and read little English; the skull and crossbones warnings were erased from cyanide drums.

- Black workers are one and a half times more likely than other workers to be severely disabled from occupational injury and disease.

Historical Context

To understand the causes of these problems, it is important to view them in a historical context. Two threads of history explain the basis for the disproportionate impact of toxics on racial and ethnic communities. The first is the long history of oppression and exploitation of Africans, Latinos, Asians, and Native Americans. These have taken the form of genocide, chattel slavery, indentured servitude, and racial discrimination with respect to employment and residence. What we have today are the remnants of that sordid history of racism as well as new and institutionalized forms of that racism.

Most Americans probably have never heard of Gauley Creek, West Virginia. This is the site of the worst recorded occupational disaster in American history. During the 1930s, black workers from the deep south were employed by the New Kanawha Power Company, a subsidiary of the Union Carbide Corporation, for purposes of digging a tunnel. Over a two year period, approximately five hundred workers died and fifteen hundred were disabled from silicosis.

Strong men literally dropped dead on their feet from breathing air laden with microscopic pieces of silica. Men who came out for air were beaten back into the tunnel with ax handles. At subsequent Congressional hearings, New Kanawha's contractor said, "I knew I was going to kill these niggers, but I didn't know it was going to be this soon." An undertaker was hired to bury dead workers in unmarked graves; he agreed to do this at an extremely low price because he was assured that there would be a large number of deaths.

The other thread of history is the massive expansion of the petrochemical industry since World War II as the result of advances in organic chemistry and other sciences. Between 1940 and 1980, the production of synthetic organic compounds increased from less than ten billion pounds to over three hundred fifty billion pounds a year. Each year, approximately one thousand new compounds are added to the seventy thousand in use in 1980. This goes on outside a context of sufficient concern about their potential impact on the environment. As a result, we have thousands of abandoned and hazardous waste sites, millions of tons of waste produced each year, billions of pounds of pesticides being used in agriculture, and continuing reports regarding the link between these materials and illness.

Although this can in part be attributed to lack of knowledge, it cannot be left at that. For most of the problem chemicals and substances that we must deal with today, there is a history of suppression and distortion of information, deliberate attempts to continue the production and marketing of substances known or suspected of being a health threat, and the continued manufacture and sale of chemicals that have been banned or restricted in the United States, such as the export of certain pesticides to underdeveloped Third World countries.

The unwritten law governing corporate decision making about toxics seems to have been, "Do what you can get away with." It means that those communities which are poorer, less informed, less organized, and less politically influential become more likely targets for the location of hazardous facilities and abuse from polluters. As Barry Commoner has said, "There is a functional link between racism, poverty and powerlessness and the chemical industry's assault on the environment."

U.C.C. Commission for Racial Justice

The United Church of Christ Commission for Racial Justice became involved with these issues in 1982. The State of North Carolina sited a PCB disposal landfill in poor and predominantly black Warren County. As many of you know, this led to a civil disobedience campaign culminating in more than five hundred arrests. Subsequently the U.S. General Accounting Office studied the racial and socioeconomic characteristics of communities surrounding hazardous waste landfills in the southeast. It found that three out of four communities studied were predominantly black and poor.

After Warren County, Dr. Charles E. Cobb, the former Executive Director of the Commission for Racial Justice, saw the need to address these issues on a national basis. Since then the Commission has made these issues a programmatic priority. Recently the Commission completed and released its report, *Toxic Wastes and Race in the United States: A National Report on the Racial and Socio-Economic Characteristics of Communities with Hazardous Waste Sites*. This is the first comprehensive national study to document and demonstrate the disproportionate location of hazardous waste sites in racial and ethnic communities. Among the most significant findings are:

- Race consistently proved to be the most significant among factors tested in association with the location of commercial hazardous waste facilities.

- Communities with the highest number of commercial hazardous waste facilities had the greatest composition of racial and ethnic residents.

- More than fifteen million blacks and eight million Hispanics lived in communities with one or more uncontrolled toxic waste sites.

- Forty percent of the nation's total commercial hazardous waste landfill capacity was located in three predominantly black and Hispanic communities.

Conclusion

The Commission's report put the issue of toxics and race on the map. At this time, in our opinion, sufficient evidence of the impact of toxics on racial and ethnic communities has come to the fore to silence anyone who argues that there is no connection between pollution and race. At the same time, there is a great ferment of activity within racial and ethnic communities around toxic pollution problems. Concerned persons and policymakers who are cognizant of this hitherto unaddressed national problem must make this a priority concern.

8

Corporations and Community Accountability

J. Andy Smith III

(*The Egg: A Journal of Eco-Justice* 13 [2], Spring 1993)

In 1989 the Coalition for Environmentally Responsible Economics (CERES) announced the "Valdez Principles," a code of conduct for companies professing a commitment to environmental protection. They affirmed that "corporations have a responsibility for the environment, and must conduct all aspects of their business as responsible stewards of the environment by operating in a manner that protects the Earth," and that "corporations must not compromise the ability of future generations to sustain themselves." CERES imagined that many corporations would sign and complete an annual report on their performance. That fall a number of corporations received shareholder proposals for vote at their annual meetings asking them to report on their progress in implementing goals of the Principles.

Over the following three years, over two hundred corporations received proposals to sign the Principles or report their action for environmental protection. In 1992 this code of conduct was modified to incorporate suggestions from industry. The name was changed to the CERES Principles.

The work of shareholders and members of the CERES Coalition resulted in many environmental initiatives within industry—increased environmental reporting, public announcement of industry programs, adoption of environmental policies, and appointments of new executive leadership for the environment at the highest levels. Yet not one large publicly owned corporation rushed to endorse. Signatories included fifty-two companies, mostly small and only three publicly held.

The large corporations held firm to their position that industry did not need accountability to any group outside itself and government. Nevertheless, the vice president for environmental affairs of a large midwestern utility, American Electric Power, stated:

> The movement created by CERES and exemplified by the [CERES] Principles has had a powerful effect on American industry. At least partially in response to the Valdez oil spill and the creation of the [CERES] Principles, corporate America has adopted progressive environmental principles tailored to the unique circumstances of particular companies. A heightened consciousness of the need to be a responsible steward of the environment has been achieved from the CEO down through the entire corporation.

An Important Step

Finally, this February [1993], the SUN Company [hereafter called Sunoco, now its official name] announced that it would endorse the CERES Principles and that it was adopting a new policy on health, safety and environment that applied the CERES Principles to its own oil and gasoline business. In taking this giant step forward for public accountability, Sunoco broke ranks with other Fortune 500 companies. Sunoco chairman and president Robert Campbell stated that the company wanted to achieve new levels of environmental excellence. Campbell recognized the importance of building a relationship with a coalition like CERES, representing the wide public interest in a way no other environmental coalition did. He hailed the trust and spirit of cooperation that made the achievement possible.

The CERES Principles are unique in two important ways. First, they are the only environmental code sponsored by a coalition representing a cross section of the public. Other codes are from industry associations, like the Chemical Manufacturers Association, or industry-dominated groups, like the International Chamber of Commerce. Members of CERES include environmental groups like the Sierra Club, National Audubon Society, and the National Wildlife Federation; socially responsible investors and public pension funds like New York City, the State of California, and the Calvert Social Investment Fund; consumer groups like Coop America and the Public Interest Research Group; and churches represented in the Interfaith Center on Corporate Responsibility (ICCR). Second, the CERES Principles call for a standardized report on progress that is to be publicly available.

Sunoco's action provides a model that any corporation can follow. The introduction of the Sunoco policy states that the company "endorses the CERES Principles as a generic environmental code of conduct applicable to business behavior throughout the world." At the same time, Sunoco adapted the CERES Principles to its own needs in a way that the CERES board affirmed is "consistent with CERES goals." Sunoco also agreed to complete the annual CERES Report on its actions to implement the principles.

Sunoco Chairman Campbell stated that the company was committing to a new dimension of excellence in health, safety, and the environment. "This agreement can shorten the distance between environmental organizations and business," he said.

The act of endorsing the CERES Principles does not mean that Sunoco is a company without environmental problems or even that it has the best environmental record of companies in its industry. It does mean that Sunoco is making a commitment to improve its environmental performance and to be publicly accountable for that improvement.

Local Action

Community environmental groups have an important role to play in the CERES process. Once commitment to public accountability for environmental protection becomes corporation policy, community groups have a standard to which they can hold any company. Persons living near facilities are invited to have dialogue with the company about their concerns. The company, in turn, is committed to responding to those concerns in an accountable way.

Persons and groups interested in helping CERES and Sunoco and other companies achieve the goal of a cleaner environment can take a number of actions, including:

1. Write the Chairman and congratulate the company for endorsing the CERES Principles and for its commitment to

public accountability. (John G. Drosdick, Chairman, Chief Executive Officer and President, Sunoco, Ten Penn Center, 1801 Market Street, Philadelphia, PA 19103-1699; tel. 215/977-3000).

2. Apply for a SUNOCO credit card and let the company know why. (Call 1-800/278-6626.)

3. Start buying SUNOCO brand gas and let the company know that you are purchasing from Sunoco because they endorsed the CERES Principles.

4. If you are aware of specific environmental problems related to Sunoco operations, let the company know of your desire to work with them in resolving the problems.

5. Take actions similar to the above with other CERES endorsing companies. A current list is available on the CERES website at www.CERES.org.

6. Let other corporations in which you are a shareholder, neighbor or stakeholder know of the actions of Sunoco and other CERES companies and ask them to endorse the CERES Principles.

The CERES Principles

1. *Protection of the biosphere.* We will reduce and make continual progress toward eliminating any substance that may cause environmental damage to the air, water, or the earth or its inhabitants. We will safeguard all habitats affected by our operations and will protect open spaces and wilderness, while preserving biodiversity.

2. *Sustainable use of natural resources.* We will make sustainable use of renewable natural resources such as water, soils and forests. We will conserve nonrenewable natural resources through efficient use and careful planning.

3. *Reduction and disposal of wastes.* We will reduce and where possible eliminate waste through source reduction and recycling. All waste will be handled and disposed of through safe and responsible methods.

4. *Energy conservation.* We will conserve energy and improve the energy efficiency of our internal operations and of the

goods and services we sell. We will make every effort to use environmentally safe and sustainable energy sources.

5. *Risk reduction.* We will strive to minimize the environmental, health and safety risks to our employees and the communities where we operate by employing safe technologies and operating procedures, by maintaining safe facilities and by being prepared for emergencies.

6. *Safe products and services.* We will reduce and where possible eliminate the use, manufacture and sale of products or services that cause environmental damage or health or safety hazards. We will inform our customers of the environmental impacts of our products or services and try to correct unsafe use.

7. *Environmental restoration.* We will promptly and responsibly correct conditions we have caused that endanger health, safety or the environment. To the extent feasible, we will redress injuries we have caused to persons or damage we have caused to the environment and will restore the environment.

8. *Informing the public.* We will inform in a timely manner everyone who may be affected by conditions caused by our company that might endanger health, safety or the environment. We will regularly seek advice and counsel through dialogue with persons in communities near our facilities. We will not take any action against employees who report dangerous incidents or conditions to management or to appropriate authorities.

9. *Management commitment.* We will implement the Principles and sustain a process that ensures that the Board of Directors and Chief Executive Officer are fully informed about pertinent environmental issues and are fully responsible for environmental policy. In selecting our Board of Directors, we will consider demonstrated environmental commitment as a factor.

10. *Audits and reports.* We will conduct an annual self-evaluation of our progress in implementing these Principles. We will support the timely creation of generally accepted environmental audit procedures. We will annually complete the CERES Report, which will be made available to the public.

Disclaimer: These Principles establish an environmental ethic with criteria by which investors and others can assess the environmental performance of companies. Companies that sign these Principles pledge to go voluntarily beyond the requirements of the law. These Principles are not intended to create new legal liabilities, expand existing rights or obligations, waive legal defenses, or otherwise affect the legal position of any signatory company, and are not intended to be used against a signatory in any legal proceeding for any purpose.

Section B

Technology and Energy

Editor's Notes

Technology as we know it is based on science. In a May 1984 article, which I regretfully had to omit from this volume, the late Professor Bart Conta of Cornell's Department of Mechanical Engineering stressed how difficult it is "to appreciate how recently and suddenly this link has been forged." In the middle of the nineteenth century the linkage with science radically transformed the nature of technology.

Of course humankind had always used tools. People and communities invented and developed tools and techniques out of diverse situations to meet immediate needs. Conta says this was "organic or folk technology."

The transformation to "science-derived professional technology" took place very rapidly after 1850.

The dominant effect of this transformation has been to change the primary motivation of technology from responding to human needs and wants to responding to scientific possibilities. Instead of necessity being the mother of invention, invention has become the mother of necessity. The new motivation has also been described as the technological imperative—a term that implies a tendency to actually do whatever is feasible, regardless of the consequences.

As examples of determination by scientific possibility—"solutions looking for problems"—Conta cites the supersonic transport plane, the space program, the laser, and nuclear technology. Today he would not overlook genetic engineering. These have mixed consequences; they cannot shed their ambiguity.

Conta sees contemporary indications of an inversion—efforts at the grassroots level to turn technology back, to employ it in response to human aspirations for peace and justice and ecological wholeness. Among other examples, he cites intermediate or appropriate technology as promoted by E. F. Schumacher and Ivan Illich.

Selection 9, "Technology: Opportunity and Peril," by Roger L. Shinn is a new article (2001), although based on a Summer 1986 contribution to The Egg. *Shinn provides insightful clarification of technology's possibilities for both good and evil. He discusses four attitudes toward technology, each of which has deep roots in our culture and is laden with social consequences.*

He offers timely identification and treatment of four big issues facing society, in order to show the human and ethical meanings of technology. The first issue is weapons.

The collapse of the Soviet Union and the emergence of the United States as the world's unrivaled superpower by no means eliminated the threat and the fear of nuclear catastrophe. Russia and the United States still have their bombs; secret nuclear weaponry development may be going on elsewhere. In the search for a technical safeguard the United States looks again to the Strategic Defense Initiative ("Star Wars"), but the success of this anti-missile program appears far-fetched in the extreme. There will be no technical fix. Whatever tentative security still remains possible "requires social organization that incorporates ethical insight."

In dealing with ecology, the second big issue, Shinn uses the phenomenon of famine to show how domestic and international politics interacts with ecological factors and shapes how problems are addressed. The problems will not be solved by technology alone, but there will be no end to starvation without the skillful use of various technologies.

The third big issue is globalization, which in its modern form has been made possible by the technologies for the swift transmission of knowledge, skills, money, and production around the world. Shinn looks at the arguments of its advocates and its critics and calls for a "more nuanced inquiry into the vast changes that technology is bringing in our contemporary world."

Finally, in discussing selfhood, Shinn looks at medical technology, genes and DNA, and computers (artificial intelligence?) to frame some penetrating questions about what is happening to our understanding of the human self. To protect the integrity, the loving, and the freedom of real persons, we respond to all the dazzling technologies "with reverence before the mystery of selfhood" and wonder before the cherished gift of life.

The eco-justice issue of energy is coupled with that of technology in this section, because a viable energy future for the United

States and the world depends upon the further development and the widespread, ultimately universal introduction and use of renewable energy technologies that can free the world from dependence upon fossil fuels. Modern industrial civilization rests on an energy base that is finite and cannot be maintained indefinitely despite the herculean efforts of corporations and nations to deny that this is so. At some point in this twenty-first century they shall have to recognize reality, like it or not, ready or not.

Over the years The Egg/Eco-Justice Quarterly *carried many articles and action columns on energy—encouraging conservation and efficiency, advocating solar alternatives, rejecting nuclear power as too fraught with dangers, and relating the energy issue to a more responsible style of life.*

The facts and projections about climate change and global warming from the late 1980s into the new century gave a momentous new dimension to the issue of energy. The problems of assuring a supply of oil to maintain economic growth, desperately needed Third World development, a never-ceasing increase in automobile traffic, and all the consumables of the "good life" were overtaken by strong evidence that human beings by burning fossil fuels had already undermined dangerously the protective atmospheric mantle surrounding the earth. This posed a new, more urgent imperative for making energy technologies, energy research and development, and energy policy and practice respond to need rather than to other kinds of determinants.

These considerations lie behind Selection 10, "The Conundrum of Oil: Less Would Be Better." Since 1991, scientific research, computer modeling, factual reports, and political events have confirmed the thesis and argument of the article. The economic recession of 1990–91 gave way to a long period of sustained economic growth, generally hailed without qualification or irony as a good thing despite the fact that steady, substantial increase in fossil fuel consumption kept it going. At the 1992 Earth Summit the nations agreed to a nonbinding climate convention aimed at keeping carbon dioxide emissions in the year 2000 at no more than 1990 levels. The United States made no serious effort to achieve that goal. In 1999 a stronger but still inadequate protocol was forged in Kyoto, Japan. President Clinton did not submit it to a Senate uninclined to ratify it. Then President George W. Bush explicitly rejected it and proposed energy policies that put the priority on obtaining more oil. Whether or not he can open the Arctic National Wildlife Refuge for drilling, the efforts to find and get oil continue relentlessly, from Alaska to the tropical rainforests to the states newly independent after the Soviet breakup, despite grim implications for fragile lands, indigenous peoples, wildlife, and the atmosphere.

The determination to maintain as long as possible the fossil fuel base of industry, transportation, consumer goods, and overall growth stands in the way of vigorous and creative efforts to expand and realize the great potential of solar and hydrogen fuel cell technologies. The decisions about technology cannot be accounted for by the "technological imperative" alone or by any of the attitudes toward technology that may be found throughout the general public or in universities. We have to look also at the profit imperative, the control imperative, the growth imperative, and the blind-momentum imperative to keep burning an extraordinarily useful and convenient fuel as long as it can be gotten out of the ground despite all the reasons for not doing so.

Big capital dominates decisions about energy policy and energy technologies. It does this to serve its own interests, which take precedence over sustainability as well as justice and community. The oil, coal, and automobile companies have fiercely and deceptively resisted the findings and strong consensus of climate experts, and have opposed and blocked the commitments necessary to achieve large greenhouse gas reductions. Governments in turn have wrangled over whether these commitments can be made without infringing upon economic growth. Where power and shortsightedness determine decisions, it is not yet plain that economic growth is less important than ecological and social sustainability and the flourishing of life.

9

Technology: Opportunity and Peril

Roger L. Shinn

Bertrand Russell, although he enjoyed witty put-downs of religion, especially Christianity, occasionally spoke out in an almost theological style. In 1953 he wrote: "The human race has survived hitherto owing to ignorance and incompetence, but, given knowledge and competence, combined with folly, there can be no certainty of survival. Knowledge is power, but it is power for evil just as much as for good."[1]

The knowledge that may do us in is, of course, scientific-technological knowledge. Russell had in mind particularly nuclear weapons—not only these, but these above all. He wrote after the bombs that fell on Hiroshima and Nagasaki in 1945, but before the attacks on the World Trade Center and the Pentagon in 2001. These later events only confirm his worries.

Both those momentous actions exhibit the destructive power of technology, but in quite different ways. The first came as the result of a massive mobilization of technological and economic resources, orchestrated by government and directed toward the specific purpose that it accomplished. It was a hi-tech achievement on the grand scale. The second came from a small conspiracy, seizing upon existing technologies and using them for its purposes. The actors made no scientific advances; in some ways it was a low-tech enterprise. Their immediate weapons were box-cutters that could be bought casually for loose change. They had modest abilities as air

109

pilots, picked up at U.S. schools available to most people, where they learned to steer airplanes but scarcely bothered to learn the more advanced skills of take-offs and landings. But their targets were hi-tech: nerve centers of economic and military power. And their big weapons were normal passenger airplanes, products of hi-tech but routinely present throughout most of the world. A high technology society gave them the means of destruction, which they used with commonplace technology. Their havoc was far less than that of nuclear weapons, but it was more readily available and, in that sense, more frightening.

The perils that worried Bertrand Russell arose out of the wedding of advanced science and technology, on a scale far more powerful than in any past history. Throughout much of history science and technology have been quite different enterprises. Plato and Aristotle, for example, put a great gulf between theory and practice. They admired science, but thought technology to be below their dignity. When Heron of Alexandria built a steam engine at an unknown date, a little before or after the time of Christ, people enjoyed it as a curiosity but did not put it to practical use. When steam engines reappeared in the modern world, societies used them to transform landscapes and human life.

Why was there such a difference? Perhaps because the ancient world did not have an adequate metallurgy or technological infrastructure for really powerful steam engines. But behind that is a deep cultural and religious difference. A society built upon a firm, permanent class structure has little incentive to apply its science to technology. The scientists usually belong to the elite; they don't have to do the world's work. There is not much need to reduce the labor of slaves, since slaves exist for labor.

A religious faith centered in a carpenter had a different attitude toward work. The Benedictine monks, as Lynn White has said, were the first intellectuals to get dirt under their fingernails. They combined prayer and physical labor, theology and work, theory and practice. So it is not an accident that Christendom gradually brought about a wedding between science and technology.

That union became basic to the modern world. In the seventeenth century Francis Bacon announced the manifesto for technological societies: "Knowledge is power." The Industrial Revolution made that statement its credo; it overlooked Bacon's later declaration: "God almighty first planted a garden; and, indeed, it is the purest of human pleasures."[2] Eventually a U.S. Secretary of Defense would invent the slogan, "More bang for the buck," subordinating science, which loves knowledge for its own sake, to its practical consequences. That, of course, is a long way from the Benedictines, although in the labyrinthine channels of history it might not have been possible without them.

So now human beings wield the power that disturbed Bertrand Russell and today disturbs most of the world. Power is not evil. Neither Christian insight nor common sense despises power. Nobody wants to be powerless. The Apostle Paul wrote, "The kingdom of God does not consist in talk but in power" (I Cor. 4:20). But if the kingdom is power, that does not mean that power is the kingdom. Power can create or destroy.

I. Some Prevailing Attitudes Toward Technology

In a world so oriented to power as ours, it is useful to distinguish some attitudes toward technology. These run deep in our culture, rarely defined with any clarity, but often functioning unconsciously in individuals and societies, influencing attitudes, emotions, and ways of living. I shall distinguish four.

1. Messianism

To some, science and technology are the way to salvation. Science undermines dogmatism, advances knowledge, and liberates the human spirit. Technology removes pain and increases economic production. In 1916 John Dewey, then on the way to becoming America's most influential philosopher, made the dramatic declaration: "Wholesale permanent decays of civilization are impossible."[3] In past centuries those decays have happened; Oswald Spengler, Arnold Toynbee, and others have made massive studies of them. But scientific method and technology have changed the world. Whatever catastrophes might strike particular societies, Dewey, in a leap of faith, was sure that scientific method would repair the damage. Of course, he did not know of the future development of nuclear weapons or the perils of ecological exhaustion.

More recently John Naisbitt's briefly popular *Megatrends*[4] saw the coming of a pleasant world of decentralized power, with cooperation replacing hierarchy and information largely replacing industry. Fewer people, he said, will do sweaty work in fields and factories; more will work in air-conditioned comfort. Although he saw some of the perils of technology unknown to Dewey in 1916, he hardly noticed war, ecological hazards, and the increasing number of people throughout the world living in desperate poverty.

Such messianism rightly recognizes that science and technology can be used to solve problems. It overlooks fundamental human problems for which there is no technical fix. It turns a genuine but paradoxical human capability into a savior.

2. Demonry

If technology is not messianic, possibly it is demonic. This belief comes in two forms. The first form, echoing Marxism or a pseudo-Marxism, says that technology is basically an instrument of oppression. Here is one formulation of the belief: "Science is the product of economic conditions of society, and its social function is to benefit the ruling classes of society."[5] These words, surprisingly, were written by a distinguished scientist, James Conant, who was once chairman of the National Defense Research Committee, then president of Harvard University. He was not stating his own belief. He was telling teachers of science that they should inform their students that this is, in fact, a powerful belief in contemporary societies.

Advocates of this belief point out that 97 percent of the expenditures for research and development are in the developed nations and only 3 percent in the less developed countries, where about two-thirds of the world's people live (UNESCO data). If we expect technology to relieve poverty, we had better realize that, so far, most of it is increasing the gap between rich and poor. While technocrats luxuriate in the benefits of technology, others see it as an oppressive force.

The second form of the demonic understanding maintains that there are in technology, whether in rich or poor societies, capitalist or socialist economies, inherent fateful impulses. Their effect is to subordinate people to machines, creating a dehumanizing society.

Jaques Elul is the most eloquent representative of this opinion. He reifies "technique," which is not quite the same as technology, but is virtually the same in the contemporary world. He sees it as an enslaving power, for which "there is not even a beginning of a solution, no breach in the system of technical necessity."[6]

3. Neutrality

Perhaps technology is neither a savior nor a demon, but a neutral power, usable for good or bad. The surgeon's knife, which can save life, can be a weapon to destroy life. The laser that has been a blessing to human health can become part of a Star Wars scenario. Airplanes can deliver food to areas of famine or can drop bombs, and in Afghanistan in 2001 they did both (although in this case the food might be considered a weapon). The telephone, e-mail, and the internet operate with indifference to the message they carry. They are equally available to criminals and law enforcement officers, to terrorists and the International Red Cross, to pornographers and educators.

The judgment of neutrality shifts the ethical evaluation from the technique to its users. It is a convincing opinion in many cases. But not in all.

4. Ambivalence

In this opinion, technology is not always neutral. An intentionality, creative or destructive, is built into many technologies. Granted that the same knife might be an instrument of healing or of death, there is a difference between a switchblade and a surgeon's scalpel. The switchblade is not intended or often used for surgery, and the surgeon's scalpel is not intended or often used for murder. The instruments are not totally neutral. Something of human intention is part of their reason for being. Ivan Illich, when he describes anti-social effects of technology, sometimes sounds like Jaques Elul. But when he writes about *Tools of Conviviality*,[7] he shows an appreciation for some technologies that enrich life and human relations.

Some technologies are inherently beneficial. I have mentioned the elimination of smallpox. (It brings accompanying problems, as it contributes to the population explosion, but nobody wants to slow down the population explosion by unleashing smallpox.) Some technologies are inherently harmful. An example is bacterial warfare. In our time a large part of technological research is financed by military agencies.

In this complicated world the benign and malignant are often interrelated. The same biological research that leads to healing can lead to destruction. A scientist once told me that three-quarters of the research directed toward biological warfare at Fort Detrick (halted in 1969) might have been done at the National Institutes of Health. The researcher cannot know what will be the outcome of the research. But the further we move from basic research into its technological employment, the more we see the ethical distinction between the creative and the destructive.

II. Some Big Issues

I have distinguished four attitudes toward technology. Why bother with such distinctions? Because attitudes affect society. Each of these attitudes is part of a mindset that influences politics, personal choices of careers, and ways of spending money. The first welcomes technologies and seeks a technical fix for every problem. The second resists technological innovation. The third directs attention from technologies to their social context. The fourth urges evaluation of every technology, both in itself and in its social setting.

The human and ethical meanings of technology become clearer as we look at some of the big issues our society—and all societies—face. Here I am selecting four.

1. Weapons

The overwhelming peril to the word is the nuclear war that might destroy all civilization and bring nuclear winter to the northern hemisphere, possibly to the whole planet. War is an old story, but the massiveness of modern war is new. Technology makes the difference.

Technological messianists promise technical answers. This is the lure of the Strategic Defense Initiative, often called Star Wars. Skeptics call it a Maginot Line in the sky. For many scientists the claim is ludicrous: a technology that will be saturation-proof in repelling the thousands of weapons that can, on short notice, invade our atmosphere. Even its strongest advocates don't quite believe in it. At the peak of the Cold War, the U.S. Advanced Strategic Missiles program sought to design weapons to penetrate any strategic defense that the Soviet Union might develop in imitation of ours. That brought the possibility of another round in the escalation of weapons, as each side struggled to catch up and get a little ahead of anything the other side might do.

As early as 1964 Jerome Wiesner and Herbert York published the classic statement on the basic issues. They explained that they had spent most of their professional lives in work on military policy and weapons development. York had worked in the Eisenhower administration, Wiesner in the Kennedy administration. They described the simultaneous increase in weapons technology and decrease in national security. And they came to the momentous conclusion: *"It is our considered professional judgment that this dilemma has no technical solution."*[8] This did not lead them to despair. But it meant that they turned their attention to international agreements that, without ignoring technology, would look for social, political, and ethical answers to the problem. They saw no technical fix.

The end of the Cold War has brought some relaxation of fears of nuclear war on the grand scale. No sane national leaders want to unleash the war that would destroy themselves. But the last century has taught us that reliance on the sanity of national rulers is a precarious base of security. The world is at risk as far ahead as anybody can see. The late Alva Myrdal, the Swedish Nobel Laureate in peace, pointed out that even if all nuclear weapons were destroyed (an extremely unlikely event in her judgment), the knowledge of how to make them would remain. It is the destiny of our generation and those who follow us to live with a risk unknown throughout the past millennia of human life. Technology has important uses in moderating the risk; for example, the satellites ("eyes in the skies") that can prevent major violations of agreements. But no technological answer, no technical fix can assure safety. Security—that is, whatever tentative security vulnerable earthly beings can achieve—requires social organization that incorporates ethical insight.

There are more insidious hi-tech perils than nuclear weapons. One is cyber warfare. In a time when teenage pranksters can mess up communications networks, we can only imagine what skilled and determined terrorists might do to disrupt military and economic systems. Another peril is development of chemical and biological weapons. In March 1995 the Aum Shinrikyo cult released sarin, a nerve agent, into the Tokyo subway system, killing twelve people and sickening thousands. Soon after the catastrophe of September 11, 2001 came the sudden scare about deaths from anthrax. The press reported that Iraq had learned how to make thousands of gallons of anthrax, though not (so far) how to distribute it on a mass scale. These events led to speculations about the possible release of smallpox on vast populations, never immunized because medical scientists by 1977 had presumably, but not certainly, eliminated the threat of smallpox forever. Some countries have experimented with cholera and plague as weapons. Once again every technical fix will be welcome, but no technical fix offers permanent security.

2. Ecology

Recent decades have brought a new awareness of the ecological hazards of the contemporary world. Technologies for exploiting nature have brought dramatic perils. They are of three major kinds: (1) catastrophic accidents, of which the Soviet nuclear disaster at Chernobyl is an example; (2) the exhaustion of nonrenewable natural resources, due partly to increasing population and more to rising consumption; and (3) the saturation of the atmosphere, the earth's waters, and sometimes the soil with pollutants.

Catastrophes catch public attention. People get excited, then often forget until the next big scare. Exhaustion of resources and pollution, by contrast, are cumulative processes. No single day is decisive for a large society, even less for the world. But the process, unless checked, goes on relentlessly. Sometimes it grows exponentially, so that a slow process suddenly becomes swift, and the awareness may come too late to correct with acts that once would have been helpful.

There is occasional good news. Some lakes and rivers are cleaner than they were two or three decades ago. Worries about an energy crisis led to big increases in energy efficiency in the United States, but then prosperity and love of gas-guzzling vehicles, especially the SUV, put us back on wasteful, perilous pathways. Sometimes a modification of reckless activities gives the world more time to cope with the problems. But the problems persist on a global scale, and they are frightening. Even in the immediate present the dependence of the United States on oil imports has a decisive effect on foreign and military policy.

For a time it was often said that ecology was a hobby of the affluent and comfortable. In international gatherings, whether of the United Nations or scientists or the World Council of Churches, the wealthy societies warned against the population explosion and heedless economic growth, while the poor worried about poverty. Sometimes it seemed as though the rich, having achieved a comfortable lifestyle, were telling the poor to hold down their consumption. To victims of oppression it seemed that privileged liberals, bored with issues of civil rights and social injustice, had turned to a new, less demanding fad.

That talk is fading from conversation. Increasingly the world realizes that ecological troubles bring most pain to the poor, that ecology cannot be separated from issues of justice. One example among many is the famine in Ethiopia in the 1980s. A report prepared for the Senate Judiciary Subcommittee on Immigration and Refugee Policy[9] included these estimates of the Ethiopian famine: about a million people died in the famine, and about seven million were saved by international efforts involving governments and voluntary activities. Since then famines have come again, striking other societies.

The causes of famines, ecological and political, are intertwined. Frequently people, needing food and fuel, turn forests into deserts, initiating an agricultural crisis. Domestic and international politics usually interact with ecological factors at every stage. The suffering of Afghanistan at the beginning of the twenty-first century, a local phenomenon with worldwide reverberations, is a striking example of the relationships among war, social conflict, poverty, and starvation. Amartya Sen, a Nobel Laureate in economics, has argued that no democracy has ever suffered a famine—poverty and pain, but no famine. That brings the hope that social improvements can eliminate famine; but it is hard to introduce democracy into a society suffering from starvation and illiteracy. Permanent answers to starvation will require technologies in agriculture, medicine, transportation, communication, and restraint of population growth. There will be no technical fix; the political and social issues of justice are not solved by technology. But there will be no answers without skillful uses of technology.

Barry Commoner, although he has made fine contributions to contemporary ecological awareness, went too far in popularizing the slogan, "Nature knows best."[10] In dissenting, I do not mean that human contrivances are always better than nature. But nature's way of enabling human survival is to provide a high human birthrate, checked by high infant mortality, epidemic diseases, harsh climate, famine, and other perils. I prefer human ways, not of "conquering nature"—an absurd aim—but of modifying nature. I find wisdom in the biblical insight that God has invited us to "till and keep" the garden of earth (Gen. 2:15). Technology can help us in that task, if we avoid arrogance and misplaced confidence in the technical fix.

3. Globalization

Globalization is a word that did not even appear in dictionaries until the late twentieth century, then quickly became a buzz-word in popular controversies. It has many definitions, often depending on the polemical intent of the users. It derives from the fact that technology has made possible the swift movement of knowledge, skills, money, consumer products, and jobs around the world.

The advocates of globalization point to its benefits: medical skills extending life expectancy, access to education once reserved for elites, increased food production that in most areas has out-paced the population explosion, the reduction of narrow parochial-isms and prejudices, opportunities for travel and enrichment of transcultural enjoyments and understandings. Some argue that the sharing of values leads to democratization and advance of human rights. For a short time Marshall McLuhan's image of a "global village"[11] became popular.

The critics of globalization see it as a form of Western economic imperialism that enables hi-tech societies to exploit the mass of humankind. They also see a cultural imperialism once called Fordism, still called Cocacolonization, with the spread of fads in fast food, dress, skin piercing, music, and, even more menacing, terrorism. They see not a global village, but the erosion of village values as Western movies, television, and money surfeit the world.

Some of the institutions of globalization are the World Bank, the International Monetary Fund, the World Trade Organization, various world conferences on human rights, ecology, global warming, and population. Their advocates believe, sometimes innocently and sometimes craftily, that they benefit the world. They are amazed when organized protests, sometimes riots, disturb their meetings (as at the meeting of the World Trade Organization in Seattle in December 1999) or require postponement or relocation of other meetings.

One of the most thoughtful evaluations of globalization comes from Herman Daly, the more impressive because he was for a time an economist on the staff of that global institution, the World Bank. In globalization, he writes, "National boundaries become totally porous with respect to goods and capital, and even more porous with respect to people, who are simply viewed as cheap labor—or in some cases as cheap human capital. . . . Acceptance of globalization entails several serious consequences, namely standards-lowering competition, an increased tolerance of mergers and monopoly power, intense national specialization, and the excessive monopolization of knowledge as 'intellectual property' "[12] But rather than indulge in dogmatic opposition, he advocates "internationalization" rather than globalization. That means that arguments must rely less on slogans and more on nuanced inquiry into the vast changes that technology is bringing in our contemporary world.

4. Selfhood

Finally I ask what technology means to human self-understanding. Here technology shakes up not only the world around us but our inner selves and our sense of what it is to be human. Here I give three examples.

The first is medical technology. Its benefits are obvious. I, who write this, and some of you who read it would not be alive without the medical achievements of our generation. But here I ask what it means to our own selfhood.

Take, as an example, the shock that some people felt about the first heart transplants and uses of artificial hearts. In response, one surgeon commented that the heart is simply a pump. I think I understand that, and I can read it without blanching. But I'm sure the surgeon was not talking about the hearts that we celebrate on St. Valentine's Day or the heart of St. Augustine that is restless until it rests in God. He requires us to ask: At what point does the person become no more than an elaborate car—an assemblage of pumps, belts, energy mechanisms, and electric activities with no will of its own, a mechanism that we use and abuse at our caprice? And what happens to the real persons whom we love and to ourselves who love?

A second example is genetics. Genetic science, in contrast to genetic hunches and superstitions, began with the experiments of the Austrian monk, Gregor Mendel, in a monastery garden, first disclosed in 1865. Then it slumbered until the start of the twentieth century, when a series of dramatic discoveries brought a surge of knowledge. One high point was the discovery of the "double helix" by James Watson and Francis Crick, announced in 1953. That led to the mapping of the human genome and new powers to manipulate DNA, that amazing acid that constitutes genes and chromosomes of bacteria and mice and human beings. Already we benefit from new powers to correct and heal destructive diseases.

We also worry about the uses and potential uses of the manipulation of DNA. It enables parents to determine the sex of their offspring, usually by prevention of births of female infants. It makes possible cloning. There is much talk, some fanciful and some close to reality, about "babies made to order," perhaps to suit the prejudices and caprices of parents. It raises disturbing questions about the meaning of selfhood. It leads us to ask: Does the new genetics enhance human freedom to relieve menacing diseases or does it eliminate freedom by making our supposedly free acts the mechanical outcome of DNA molecules that don't have the slightest knowledge of what they are doing?

A third example is from the computer specialists who are trying to build an "artificial intelligence." Never mind that their schedules are far behind their predictions; they may catch up. Already their ambitions affect our self-awareness. One, who admires the accuracy and speed of his computers, as compared with the fumbling and fallible work of the human mind, describes the brain as simply a "bloody mass of organic matter." There lies a disturbing question. What shall we make of this miracle of a bloody mass of matter that can build computers, as computers cannot build human minds and spirits? How shall we respond to the bloody matter that is a person, capable of loving and dreaming, hoping, struggling, laughing, weeping, praying, and, yes, destroying?

Part of the response to genetics, as to all of the technologies mentioned in this essay, is reverence before the mystery of selfhood. Human life is filled with problems. Technology can solve some of them. But ultimately life is not a problem to be solved. It is a source of wonder, a gift to cherish.

Notes

1. Bertrand Russell, *The Impact of Science on Society* (New York: Simon and Schuster, 1953), 97.

2. Francis Bacon, "Of Heresies," 1597; "Of Gardens," 1625. Both sayings can be found in various translations from the Latin and in various editions.

3. John Dewey, "Progress," *International Journal of Ethics* 26 (1916), 314.

4. John Naisbitt, *Megatrends* (New York: Morrow, 1990).

5. James B. Conant, *On Understanding Science* (1947; Reprint, New York: New American Library, Mentor Books, 1951), 110.

6. Jaques Elul, *The Technological Society*, trans. John Wilkinson (New York: Random House, Vintage Books, 1964; first French ed. 1954), xxxi.

7. Ivan Illich, *Tools of Conviviality* (New York: Harper & Row, 1973).

8. Jerome B. Wiesner and Herbert F. York, "National Security and the Nuclear Test Ban," *Scientific American* 211 (4) (October 1964), 28. Emphasis in original.

9. *New York Times*, April 28, 1986, national ed., 2.

10. Barry Commoner, *The Closing Circle* (New York: Knopf, 1972), 41.

11. Marshall McLuhan, *The Gutenberg Galaxy* (Toronto: University of Toronto Press, 1962).

12. Herman E. Daly, "Globalization and Its Discontents," *Philosophy and Public Policy Quarterly* 21 (2/3) (Spring/Summer 2001), 17.

10

The Conundrum of Oil:
Less Would Be Better

William E. Gibson

(*The Egg: An Eco-Justice Quarterly* 11 [2], Summer 1991)

In a "Hi and Lois" cartoon that came out several years ago, the son Chip says to his father, "Dad, I heard in school that in twenty years we won't have any gas for our cars. Isn't anybody worried?" Hi answers, "I guess our leaders think it's too far in the future to think about." "That stinks!" says Chip. "It's not too far in *my* future."

Chip is worried that the world will run out of gas—that when he grows up, his place in the car culture (to which as a typical American adolescent he eagerly looks forward) will be cut short.

Running out of Oil?

A lot of people in the early 1980s, still sobered by the shock of the 1973–74 OPEC (Organization of Petroleum Exporting Countries) oil embargo and by the sharp hike in oil prices in the mid 1970s and again at the end of the decade, worried about the "energy crisis." The realization had hit them that the world's supply of petroleum was finite and nonrenewable, and that foreign lands held most of what was left. So there was much talk and writing about energy conservation and the dawn of the solar age. Amory Lovins came on the scene with amazing but convincing reports on the energy savings achievable by using more efficient technologies and relating energy sources and means of delivery more appropriately to end-use requirements. Many of us insisted that the so-called soft energy path was the one to follow, because (we said) the day of cheap energy was gone forever, and nuclear energy entailed unacceptable risks.

This analysis, I still believe, was essentially correct, but off the mark with respect to short-term developments. By the middle of the 1980s petroleum prices had fallen as sharply as they had risen. The oil-producing countries were anxious to sell their product, and cheap energy did come back. Some critics charged that the recent energy crisis, with its allegedly short supplies and its soaring prices, had been largely contrived by "big oil" in its own interest. Still, there was no denying that most of the world's petroleum reserves lay in the Middle East. OPEC nations had demonstrated their power, and they might do so again.

In 1986 a report came from Carrying Capacity, Inc. on three years of research by the Complex Systems Research Center at the University of New Hampshire.[1] The report revealed that three-fourths of U.S. oil in the lower forty-eight states had already been extracted and used. Production from the Alaskan fields would peak within a few years. Sometime between 1995 and 2005 it would become uneconomical to search for new oil in the United States, because the energy obtained would no longer exceed the energy spent in drilling and pumping. Old wells would continue to be pumped for awhile, but by 2020 the United States would be virtually out of oil and dependence on foreign sources would be complete. Those sources, according to the report, would last only another two or three decades—to 2040 or 2050.

Of course, such a scenario must be imprecise. Well before supplies were exhausted, prices would skyrocket. Massive chain reactions would be set off throughout the global economy. If the world is to have a smooth transition to a time "beyond oil," policy must be so directed without additional delay. In any event, the shift, smooth or convulsive, to a different energy base is something that today's young people and even people not so young will live to see. Obviously it is not too far in the future to demand not only thought but action. Chip may have to discover that life can be good without cars.

U.S. policy seems based on denial that any of this is so. Access to oil, however, is seen as all-important. For that we have just fought a war [1991] with Iraq.

Global Warming: How Much? How Fast?

The energy crisis has been overtaken by the threat of global warming. Oil, like the other fossil fuels, emits carbon dioxide when burned. CO_2 accounts for at least half of the "greenhouse effect"—the buildup of gases in the upper atmosphere that trap heat from the sun and keep it from escaping out to space, so that the temperature at the earth's surface rises. The earth's atmospheric mantle has always functioned as a major determinant of temperature—as one of many contributors to the conditions that make life on this planet possible. Global warming results from an *anthropogenic* intensification of this natural function: human agency begins now to change the climate of the earth. We thought we had a problem of too little oil to maintain industrial civilization. The far greater problem is that the energy base of our civilization jeopardizes our own and other life. The world burns too much oil for its own good.

Over seven hundred scientists from more than one hundred countries at the Second World Climate Conference, in November 1990, issued a statement declaring that the scientific and economic uncertainties related to the phenomenon of climate change must not be used as excuses for postponing strong societal responses to the dangers that threaten the planet.[2] Admittedly, study and research should continue to focus on the complex factors determining climate and on the probable and possible consequences of the continuing generation of greenhouse gases by modern production and consumption. But the scientific consensus affirms that we know enough already to justify vigorous, concerted action to slow and limit the buildup of these gases.

The findings of meteorologists, climatologists, biologists, and other scientists, as collected and confirmed with increasing clarity over the past half dozen years and brought together in last fall's World Climate Conference, present a peril-laden picture.[3] If, as projections now suggest, the global mean temperature increases by something like 5 degrees F. in less than one hundred years, that will constitute an extraordinarily rapid alteration of climate. It will be completely unprecedented in that human agency will have caused it. It will overwhelm any changes or variations that might have occurred naturally apart from the human impact. Its effects will not be uniform around the globe, for temperature increase will be minor at the equator but will be more than average in upper latitudes. Humans, animals, forests, watersheds—indeed all natural and social systems—will face enormous problems of adjustment. Some will not survive.

Weather patterns will be increasingly erratic and unpredictable. Heat waves, droughts, storms, and hurricanes will all be more severe. (Are the recent cyclones in Bangladesh an indication of global warming?)

In upper latitudes the winters will be shorter and wetter, the summers longer and drier. Effects on agriculture will be uneven, as some major cropland areas revert to grassland or even desert, and others, closer to the poles, are opened up. The most severe effects and most painful adjustment requirements will hit areas already highly vulnerable. Many of these will be in impoverished countries that for some years now have been falling behind in the effort to make food production keep pace with population growth.

Forests will be under increasing stress, as rapid climate change outstrips their ability to adapt. Timber zones, like agriculture, will tend to shift pole-ward. Fires will likely be more frequent and destructive. Burning and decaying forests will emit huge amounts of CO_2. Forest losses, with accompanying loss of wildlife habitat, will compound the massive problems of tropical forest destruction and species extinction already causing great alarm.

The sea level will rise as the water warms. The melting of polar ice caps may add to the increase. Low islands, coastal plains and cities, and river deltas will suffer periodic flooding, exacerbated by the increasing severity of storms and in some cases will become untillable or uninhabitable. Water supplies will be contaminated, wetlands ruined. Cities such as Miami, New Orleans, Shanghai, and Cairo will have to make huge investments, if they can, in dikes and sea walls. Tens of millions of people will become environmental refugees.

If we knew that the consequences of present trends would prove to be only half as severe as the foregoing scenario suggests, the world would still have ample cause for strong, prompt, national and international measures to reduce the pace and degree of the climate change to be precipitated by human impact. It is too late to forestall it altogether, or to turn back the change that may well have already begun. But there is much that can be done to answer in the world's favor the questions of how much change will take place and how fast it will occur.

Responding to the Threat

The measures that should be undertaken are essentially the same as those advocated ten years ago, even fifteen years ago, as appropriate responses to the energy crisis as then perceived. The most immediate payoff will come from using less energy—by developing and employing more efficient technologies, so that we accomplish the same amount of work with less expenditure of fuel. At the same time, most Americans should be conserving energy by simply not doing some of the unnecessary and wasteful things that characterize their lifestyle in the consumer society that now prevails. That lifestyle may be transformed into one more responsible and fulfilling—by buying less, driving less, sharing more, and enhancing the quality of life by nurturing community, enjoying nature, working for the common good, and organizing and advocating for justice and sustainability.

Another set of measures has to do with policies and practices to accelerate the inevitable transition away from fossil fuels to the various nonpolluting, renewable sources of solar energy.

The difference after fifteen years is that we respond now, not just to a grim prospect of running out of oil, but to the much grimmer prospect of global warming from burning the oil and coal still available. The problem is not too little oil, but too much. Because it is there, our society is still bent on burning it. Because it is there, policies of conservation are not put in place. The transition to the solar age is resisted and delayed. The political decision makers dominating policy in Washington have, in effect, extended their denial of the necessity of that transition to include denial of the peril of global warming.

Obstacles to Response

The obstacles to urgently needed steps to curb CO_2 emissions do not, of course, consist solely in the obstinacy of politicians oblivious to the evidence of planetary danger or else coldly unconcerned about the kind of planet they are leaving to their children. As I have argued elsewhere, the destruction of the protective functions of the earth's atmospheric mantle

> . . . exemplifies the damaging, often unforeseen effects of modern civilization's essential thrust. I refer to an anthropocentric, nature-conquering, growth-oriented, consumption-emphasizing paradigm for relating to the world and understanding the meaning of life. It has succeeded spectacularly in overcoming want for a portion of the human family (while perpetuating it for the rest), but its inherently destructive and unjust tendencies are rendering it obsolete. Global warming was not intended, but it is the consequence of a relentless,

ever more forceful pursuit of material security and affluence. It challenges us to a fundamental critique of Western philosophical assumptions and economic institutions.[4]

Delegates to the 1990 World Convocation on Justice, Peace and the Integrity of Creation, convened by the World Council of Churches, called upon their churches "to lead in the indispensable reversal of the thinking which supports unlimited energy consumption and economic growth."[5] If this could happen, it would be an enormous contribution to the curbing of the greenhouse effect. Despite cogent criticisms from many quarters, however, the ideology of economic growth, as measured by gross national product, remains virtually unassailable. Vigorous growth is the almost unquestioned measure of the health of a nation's economy. Almost daily we get figures and speculation in the news pertaining to "recovery" from the [1990–92] recession. It goes without saying that recovery means the resumption of economic growth. And though welcome progress was made in the 1980s in reducing the expenditure of energy per unit of economic output, it remains patently impossible to minimize the greenhouse effect while maximizing growth.

Despite growing environmental awareness and concern, it remains excruciatingly difficult to crack the dilemma posed by the contradictory goals of ecological sustainability and endless economic growth. The existing economic system cannot accommodate the radical kind of conservation that goes beyond efficiency to a foregoing of unnecessary consumption and energy expenditure. Such a refusal to use resources for things not needed would impose upon the workers who make those things the inability to obtain what they really need.

Less Would Be Better

We should welcome as a step in the right direction the efforts of European nations to cut CO_2 emissions without curbing economic growth. The Bush Administration adamantly refuses thus far to follow their lead by setting specific targets for emission reductions. The explicit reason given is that this cannot be done without threatening economic growth. The prospect of a strong international treaty to accelerate a united effort to limit global warming, a treaty that was to be ready for signing at the 1992 UN Conference on Environment and Development, remains dim.

At some point the people of this and other countries, with leadership (not yet provided) by universities, churches, and even governments, will have to face the choice between environmental deterioration, with accompanying societal breakdown, and a deliberate, step-by-step restructuring of national and global economies according to the criteria of ecological sustainability and participation by all in good work and sufficient sustenance. The second alternative constitutes the most essential and formidable prerequisite to a viable future. We are still only at the preliminary stage of consciousness-raising, whereby people come to see that the present dilemma is intolerable and unnecessary.

This issue of oil, in the radically new context of climate change, poses a dramatic test of whether the world can take a significant step now toward sustainability and justice. Not sustainable development, which under the obsolete but still prevailing paradigm is a contradiction in terms, but sustainable sufficiency for all. The administration responds to the test by going to war and seeking more oil. The linchpin of its newly unveiled energy strategy is to drill for oil in the Arctic National Wildlife Refuge. Every individual and organization that knows better can say *no* to this. Less oil would indeed be better.

Notes

1. John Gever et al., *Beyond Oil: The Threat to Food and Fuel in Coming Decades* (Cambridge, Mass.: Ballinger, 1986).

2. *International Environmental Reporter*, November 7, 1990, 455.

3. Sources for the summary information in the following paragraphs include Reports to the Intergovernmental Panel on Climate Change from IPCC Working Groups I and II, June 1990; United Nations Environment Programme, *UNEP Brief No. 1*, "The Changing Atmosphere"; and Lester R. Brown et al., *State of the World* Reports 1986 through 1990 (New York: W. W. Norton).

4. William E. Gibson, "Global Warming as a Theological-Ethical Concern," Dieter T. Hessel, ed., *After Nature's Revolt: Eco-Justice and Theology* (Minneapolis, Minn.: Fortress Press, 1992), 114.

5. *Now Is the Time: Final Documents and Other Texts from the World Convocation on Justice, Peace and the Integrity of Creation, Seoul, 1990* (Geneva, Switzerland: World Council of Churches, 1990), 31.

Section C

Creatures, Systems, and Sense of Place

Editor's Notes

In the emphasis of eco-justice on sustainability as a value and a goal we have sought consistently to go beyond anthropocentrism—that is, not only to value nature for the sake of human beings, but to recognize and honor the claim of myriad and diverse creatures to be valued for their own sake, and to respect the integrity of natural systems simply because they are the ordering of the earth and all life. This is a basic and general starting point, self-evident to persons and communities attuned to the natural order, and affirmed in faith by those who see the world as the creation of One who willed and cherishes it.

This valuation of all that is has been obscured, undermined, and often destroyed by a civilization carried away by the idea of the superiority of humans and focused inordinately on mastering nature for human purposes of security, ease, and control. Today it requires reaffirmation, prompted by shock at the damage from human mastery and by a search for a more authentic place and role for humankind within the whole.

What does our human honoring of the nonhuman mean in practice? What does it mean for our relations to animals, plants, and natural systems? What does it mean for the way we relate to the wild realm that does not belong to human culture? What does it mean for ethics? People are the only creatures that have to think about the moral issues in relating to their own and other kind. The responsibility to choose and act rightly constitutes a major qualitative factor in identifying what "human" means. Ethics has largely confined itself to human personal and social relationships. Now with the reaffirmation of the value and integrity of the whole natural order, ethics has to give special attention to the responsibilities of human creatures to nature and other creatures.

Selection 11, "Duties to Animals, Plants, Species, and Eco-systems: Challenges for Christians," makes it clear that these duties are not a simple matter of extending Christian ethics of justice, compassion, and neighbor love to our nonhuman neighbors. Holmes Rolston III tells us that the prime orientation for the human treatment of wild animals is to let them go free. This is not the same thing as showing compassion toward individual animals. The forces of nature drive for the preservation of the species. Humans have a duty not to disrupt the ecosystemic processes essential to the diverse kinds of animals and plants. And in a country where most of the land has been settled for human purposes, Rolston has a particular concern that the remaining wildlands and wildlife continue free from human violation.

Within their settlements comprising most of the land, humans remain under the claim to respect the order, beauty, and integrity of the community of nonhuman life, including elements of wildness, within which their own community is set. But this respect needs nurturing, and has in turn to be expressed in particular places. The care of a place has roots in love for that place. The Fall 1994 issue of Eco-Justice Quarterly *carried articles on the significance of place. In one entitled "Fidelity to Place" Allen D. MacNeill (who chaired the Eco-Justice Coordinating Council) observes that faithfulness to a particular location is foreign to the American psyche. In Europe and America for two centuries the major institutions—governmental, military, economic, academic, and ecclesiastical—have induced a kind of forced migration. To make one's way in any of these, one must expect to move, perhaps repeatedly. To want to stay in a certain place is a sign of weakness. But MacNeill maintains:*

> *To turn aside our blind and suicidal rush toward ecological disaster, we must all learn fidelity to place. To do so will involve expanding our concept of fidelity. There are four domains of fidelity, only two of which most people are aware of. They are, in order of increasing inclusiveness: fidelity to self, fidelity to others, fidelity to place, and fidelity to the whole. . . . Americans and other western peoples recognize fidelity to self, sometimes profess fidelity to others, but rarely if ever even comprehend fidelity to place or to the whole. Indeed, market economics is founded on fidelity to self, excluding all other considerations.*
>
> *The boundaries between ourselves and other people, between ourselves and our ecosystems, even between ourselves and the biosphere are highly permeable and not static. We are quite literally one family of interconnected members.*

Fidelity to place is fidelity to self. Ultimately, we must learn fidelity to the whole, to the pattern that connects it all, to the mystery of creation, and to that which creates.

Let yourself love where you are. Pledging fidelity to a place is just like a marriage; you learn to love it each day, despite the bad days and the illnesses and the little hurts. You become addicted to a place, so much so that leaving it, even temporarily, causes you pain, and returning great joy.

Defend your place, as you would your lover or your children. Destruction of a place is quite literally the slaughter of the innocents; if you will not protect and defend the air, water, soil, and living things of your place, who will?

The article printed here in full as Selection 12 is an interview of George Tinker, an Osage Indian and a professor of theology, conducted by Sabine O'Hara who edited the issue of the journal in which it appeared. Tinker conveys eloquently what "rootedness in spaciality or place" means to Native Americans. This rootedness has a much more formative role in Indian identity and self-understanding than does time or history as conceived in Western culture. Where time is a factor in Native American culture, it is cyclical and has to do, not with "progress," but with maintaining harmony and balance. Tinker goes on to explain how spacial rootedness expresses itself in acquiring knowledge, the organization and leadership of community life, and the inclusion of all living things in the circle of creation, whether they be two-legged, four-legged, winged, or growing from the ground.

11

Duties to Animals, Plants, Species, and Ecosystems: Challenges for Christians

Holmes Rolston III

(*The Egg: An Eco-Justice Quarterly* 13 [3], Summer 1993)

(Essentially the same article also appeared in *The Annual of the Society of Christian Ethics 1993,* and is used here by permission.)

Christianity is a religion for people; its ethical genius lies in redeeming persons in their interpersonal relations. The great commandments are to love God and neighbor; the Golden Rule is do to others as you would have others do to you. "Neighbors" and "others" include the victim left helpless by thieves, aided by the Good Samaritan, or a brother forgiven seventy times seven. Animals do not sin, nor do they need repentance, rebirth, forgiveness; they are not alienated from God; we do not exhort them to love neighbors. So perhaps Christianity cannot inform environmental ethics.

Yet God created the fauna and flora and pronounced them to be very good. Humans have responsible "dominion": "Behold I establish my covenant with you and your descendants after you, and with every living creature that is with you, the birds, the cattle, and every beast of the earth with you" (Genesis 9:5). In modern

133

terms, the covenant is both ecumenical and ecological. "A righteous man has regard for the life of his beast" (Proverbs 12:10). The ox that treads out the grain is not to be muzzled (Deuteronomy 15:4). That begins to suggest environmental ethics.

Jesus calls to repentance, declaring, "My kingdom is not of this world." That first suggests no environmental ethics at all. But then we realize that he was teaching in the imperial Roman world, and that "this" refers to the fallen world of the culture he came to redeem, to false trust in politics and economics, in armies and kings. God loves the created "world," and in the landscape surrounding him Jesus finds ample evidence of the presence of God. He teaches that the power organically manifest in the growing grain and the flowers of the field is continuous with the power spiritually manifest in the kingdom he announces. That shows an ontological bond between nature and spirit.

The following sections lay out some general compass directions Christians can follow toward a provisional environmental ethics. They highlight biblical insights, regarding our duties to animals, plants, species, and ecosystems. But adherents will also need further guidance, from outside the Christian faith, before they can determine routes of travel more completely.

I. Duties to Animals

Just to treat animals like people is not very discriminating; in some ways they are our cousins, in other ways not. The world cheered in the fall of 1988 when we rescued two gray whales from the winter ice off Point Barrow, Alaska. The whales were stranded for three weeks several miles from open water, rising to breathe through small, shrinking holes in the ice. Chain saws cut pathways and a Russian icebreaker broke open a route to the sea. A polar bear, coming to eat the whales, was chased away. When television showed suffering whales sticking their heads out of the ice, trying to breathe, everybody wanted to help. But was that really the right thing to do?

Maybe it was too much money spent, a million dollars that could have been used better to save the whales—or to save people. Maybe money is not the only or even the principal consideration. Maybe our compassion overwhelmed us. Maybe we need help thinking through our duties to wildlife. Consider a less expensive case, no big media event.

One February morning in 1983 a bison fell through the ice into the Yellowstone River, and, struggling to escape, succeeded only in enlarging the hole. Toward dusk a party of snowmobilers looped a rope around the animal's horns and, pulling, nearly saved it. But darkness came and the rescuers abandoned their attempt. That night, temperatures fell to 20 below; in the morning the bison was dead, with ice refrozen around it. Coyotes and ravens ate the exposed part of the carcass. After the spring thaw, a grizzly bear was seen feeding on the rest, a bit of rope still attached to the horns.

The snowmobilers were disobeying park authorities who had ordered them not to rescue it. One of the snowmobilers was troubled by the callous attitude. A drowning human would have been saved at once; so would a drowning horse. The Bible commends getting an ox out of a ditch, even if this means breaking the Sabbath (Luke 14:5). It was as vital to the struggling bison as to any person to get out; the poor thing was freezing to death. A park ranger replied that the incident was natural and the bison should be left to its fate.

That seems so inhumane, contrary to everything we are taught in Christianity about being kind, doing to others as we would have them do to us, or respecting the right to life. Isn't it cruel to let nature take its course? The snowmobilers thought so. One contacted radio commentator Paul Harvey, who made three national broadcasts attacking park service indifference. Harvey said, "The reason Jesus came to earth was to keep nature from taking its course." Was the Yellowstone ethic too callous, inhumane?

The national park ethic emphasizes that a simple extension of compassion from human, and Christian, ethics to wildlife does not appreciate their wildness. Perhaps we are beginning to see the trouble with rescuing those whales. Or maybe we are carrying this let-nature-take-its-course ethic to extremes. Has ethics here somehow gone wild in the bad sense, blinded by a philosophy of false respect for cruel nature?

The rescue of individual animals is humane enough and does not seem to have any detrimental effects, but that may not be the end of moral considerations, which ought to act on principles that can be universalized. Perhaps it brings these duties into clearer focus to consider populations, herds with hundreds of animals. In the winter of 1981–82, the bighorn sheep of Yellowstone caught pinkeye (conjunctivitis). On craggy slopes, partial blindness can be fatal. A sheep misses a jump, feeds poorly, and is soon injured and starving. More than three hundred bighorns, over 60 percent of the herd, perished. Wildlife veterinarians wanted to treat the disease, as they would have in any domestic herd, but, again, the Yellowstone ethicists left them to suffer, seemingly not respecting their life.

Their decision was that their disease was natural, and should be left to run its course. A Christian may protest, "Where's the mercy? Where is the good shepherd caring humanely for his sheep?" But perhaps mercy and humanity are not the criteria for decision here.

The ethic of compassion must be set in a bigger picture of animal welfare, recognizing the function of pain in the wild. The Yellowstone ethicists knew that intrinsic pain is a bad thing in humans or in sheep, but pain in ecosystems is instrumental pain through which the sheep are naturally selected for a more satisfactory adaptive fit. To have interfered in the interests of the blinded sheep would have weakened the species. Simply to ask whether they suffer is not enough. We must ask whether they suffer with a beneficial effect on the wild population. As a result of the park ethic, those sheep that were genetically more fit, able to cope with the disease, survived; and this coping is now coded in the survivors. Caring for these sheep does not mean bringing them safely into the fold; it means caring that they stay wild and free.

What we *ought* to do depends on what *is*. The *is* of nature differs significantly from the *is* of culture, even when similar suffering is present in both. We ought not to treat the bison as we would a person, because a bison in a wild ecosystem is not a person in a culture. Pain in any culture ought to be relieved where it can be with an interest in the welfare of the sufferers. But pain in the wild ought not to be relieved if and when it interrupts the ecosystemic processes on which the welfare of these animals depends.

In God, animals are born free. "Who has let the wild ass go free? . . . He ranges the mountain as his pasture, and he searches after every green thing" (Job 39:5–8). Letting wild animals "go free" provides a general orientation for their ethical treatment, not mercy or compassion.

II. Duties to Plants

Trees might not seem something that we can be directly ethical about. Where people have a stake in their trees, people count them as fuel, timber, watershed, shade trees, scenery. What counts for people does count morally. But there is more to it than that. How to count trees collectively, as forests, is a critical issue in environmental policy today. The larger issue is an appropriate respect for forests, not simply for what they are for people, but for what they are in themselves.

John Mumma, regional forester in charge of fifteen national forests in Montana, northern Idaho, and parts of Washington and the Dakotas, was recently forced to resign for his refusal to cut as much timber as was ordered. "I am in shock at what's happening on the national forests," he told a Congressional committee[1] In November 1989 sixty-five U.S. Forest Service Supervisors complained to the Federal Chief F. Dale Robertson that "The emphasis of national forest programs does not reflect the land stewardship values embodied in forest plans, Forest Service employees and the public."[2] Protesting especially the cutting of trees, this and related internal Forest Service memos received national attention on the ABC TV news show "Prime Time Live."

The old-growth timber controversy is the principal public issue in the Pacific Northwest. Indeed, some environmentalists count the value of cathedral old-growth trees so highly that they will spike these trees, lest they be cut. They are willing to risk civil disobedience, protesting that the Forest Service is itself disobeying the law, and citing as evidence the mounting dissension within the ranks of the Forest Service itself. Several thousand foresters have joined a protest organization, the Association of Forest Service Employees for Environmental Ethics. And the Society of American Foresters, by a three to one vote, just revised its canon of ethics, to include a land ethic that "demonstrates our respect for the land."[3] That is, if you like, an ecosystem ethic, to which we will be turning, but it all began with the cutting of trees, and a growing conviction that what people do to forests is a moral matter.

Is all this outside the province of Christian ethics? It can seem so; nothing about Christianity gives one any expertise in forestry, any more than elsewhere in botany or zoology. Trying to make trees moral objects seems strange. They do not suffer pains and pleasures, so we cannot be compassionate toward them. Trees are not valuers with preferences to be satisfied or frustrated, so we cannot practice the golden rule on them.

These are, we might say, just resource questions, about which Christians can say that resources should be justly and charitably used, and little more. The Society of American Foresters say, in their new code of ethics, "Stewardship of the land is the corner stone of the forestry profession,"[4] and Christians entirely concur, because they believe in the stewardship of everything. But after that, they have nothing more to say about making this forest ethic operational. Or is there more to be said?

Religious persons have often thought that there is something sublime, even sacred about trees. "The groves were God's first temples."[5] "The trees of the Lord are watered abundantly; the cedars of Lebanon which God planted" (Psalm 104:16). With forests, America is even more of a promised land than is Palestine. John Muir exclaimed, "The forests of America, however slighted by man, must have been a great delight to God; for they were the best God ever planted."[6] Such forests are a church as surely as a commodity. The forest is where trees pierce the sky, like cathedral spires. Light filters down, as through stained glass. The forest canopy is lofty, over our heads. In common with churches, forests invite us to transcend the human world and to experience a comprehensive, embracing realm.

Forests can serve as a more provocative, perennial sign of the transcendent realm than many of the traditional, often outworn, symbols devised by the churches. Such experiences Christians should welcome and seek to preserve. Muir continued, "The clearest way into the universe is through a forest wilderness."[7] That, some Christians say, is excessive. The clearest way into the universe is through Jesus Christ. Still, Jesus of Nazareth, at times, retreated into the wilderness when he wanted to get things clear.

Being among the archetypes, a forest is about as near to ultimacy as we can come in the natural world—a vast scene of sprouting, budding, flowering, fruiting, passing away, passing life on. The planet has produced forests wherever soil and climate permit, and has done so for many millions of years. Mountaintop experiences, the wind in the pines, solitude in a sequoia grove, autumn leaves, the forest vista—these generate experiences of "a motion and spirit that impels . . . and rolls through all things."[8] A forest wilderness is a sacred space that elicits cosmic questions, differently than town. Christians have a particular interest in preserving wild places as sanctuaries for religious experiences, both for Christians and for others inspired there.

III. Duties to Species

Some of the animals and plants in these forests are endangered species, forcing us to a new level of ethics and theology. When the U.S. Congress lamented the loss of species, Congress declared that species have "esthetic, ecological, educational, historical, recreational and scientific value to the nation and its people."[9] Religious value is missing from this list. Perhaps Congress would have overstepped its authority to declare that species carry religious value. But for many Americans this is the most important value. Christians and Jews will add that these species are also of value to God. Congress could not say that. But defending the freedom of religion, guaranteed in the Constitution, Congress might well have insisted that the species of plants and animals on our landscape ought to be conserved because such life is of religious value to the nation and its people.

Though God's name does not appear in the Endangered Species Act itself, it does occur in connection with the Act. The protection Congress authorized for species is quite strong, in principle at least. Interpreting the Act, the U.S. Supreme Court insisted "that Congress intended endangered species to be afforded the highest of priorities."[10] Since economic values are not among the listed criteria either but must sometimes be considered, Congress in 1978 amendments authorized a high-level, interagency committee to evaluate difficult cases. This committee may permit human development at the cost of extinction of species. In the legislation, this committee is given the rather nondescript name, "The Endangered Species Committee," but almost at once it was nicknamed "the God Committee." The name mixes jest with theological insight and reveals that religious value is implicitly lurking in the Act. Any who decide to destroy species take, fearfully, the prerogative of God.

In practical conservation of biodiversity on landscapes—concerned with habitat, breeding populations, DDT in food chains, or minimum water flows to maintain fish species—it might first seem that God is the ultimate irrelevancy. Yet, when one is conserving life, ultimacy is always nearby. The practical urgency of on-the-ground conservation is based in a deeper respect for life. Extinction is forever; and, when danger is ultimate, absolutes become relevant. The motivation to save endangered species can and ought to be pragmatic, economic, political, and scientific; deeper down it is moral, philosophical, and religious.

The Bible records the first Endangered Species Project—Noah and his ark! That story is quaint and archaic, as much parable as history, teaching how God wills for each species on earth to continue, despite the disruptions introduced by humans. Although individual animals perish catastrophically, God intends to conserve species. On the ark, the species come through. After the flood, God reestablishes "the covenant which I make between me and you and every living creature that is with you, for all future generations" (Genesis 9:12–13). Humans are to repopulate the earth, but *not* at threat to the species; rather, the "bloodlines"—today we say genetic species—must be protected at threat of divine reckoning (Genesis 9:1–7).

As with the treatment of animals before, we may first think that the endangered species question is easy. Noah settles that; we should save all endangered species. But, once again, the going gets tough in actual decisions, and sensitivity to life at the species level can sometimes make environmental ethics seem callous.

A top carnivore is missing from most American landscapes, and we are wondering whether we ought to restore that majestic animal, the gray wolf. One place the wolf does remain is in Minnesota where there are about twelve hundred wolves. We ought to respect the integrity of this species in that ecosystem. But there are also twelve thousand livestock ranches scattered through the wolves' territory, or, to phrase it the other way around, the wolves are scattered through the properties of thousands of ranchers. That works surprisingly well, but each year problem wolves begin to kill livestock on forty to fifty of these ranches. A controller inspects the kill, and if a wolf is guilty, it is trapped and destroyed. About thirty to forty wolves each year are killed in this mitigation.

Here it seems that if we are to have wolves, we must kill wolves. We ought to do both. This time we have to consider the interests of the ranchers, their cattle, and perhaps of those consumers who will eat the cows. But the integrity of the wolf population too is served by removing those animals who turn from their natural prey to domestic animals. Aldo Leopold wrote that in his trigger-happy youth, he thought that the only good wolf was a dead wolf, until he shot one once and reached it in time "to watch a fierce green fire dying in her eyes."[11] Here in order to keep that fire going in the species, we have, sadly, to put it out in individuals who lose that wildness and turn to killing cattle. We ought to restore that fierce green gaze on our landscape, where and as we can, even if in the resulting confrontation of people and wildlife, we sometimes have to kill. Sometimes in environmental ethics, there are no easy choices. But we are encouraged to think that God loves the predators too, because in the wilderness "the young lions roar for their prey, seeking their food from God" (Psalm 104:21).

In the spring of 1984 a sow grizzly and her three cubs walked across the ice of Yellowstone Lake to Frank Island, two miles from shore. They stayed several days to feast on two elk carcasses, when the ice bridge melted. Soon afterward, they were starving on an island too small to support them. These stranded bears would be left to starve—if nature took its course. The mother could swim to the mainland, but she is not going to without her cubs. This time the Yellowstone ethicists promptly rescued the grizzlies and released them on the mainland, in order to protect an endangered species. They were not rescuing individual bears so much as saving the species. They thought that humans had already and elsewhere imperiled the grizzly, and that they ought to save this form of life. A breeding mother and three cubs was a significant portion of the breeding population. The bears were not saved lest they suffer, but lest the species be imperiled.

Duties to wildlife are not simply at the level of individuals; they are also to species. Species are what they are where they are. We have a duty to conserve wildness, and species in their wild ecosystems, not just individual animal welfare. In Genesis, the "days" (events) of creation are a series of divine imperatives that empower earth with vitality. "And God said, 'Let the earth put forth vegetation.' . . . 'Let the earth bring forth living things according to their kinds' " (Genesis 1:11, 24). "Let the waters bring forth swarms of living creatures" (Genesis 1:20). "Swarms" is, if you wish, the biblical word for biodiversity.

A prolific earth generates teeming life, urged by God. The Spirit of God broods, animating the earth, and earth gives birth. As we would now say, earth speciates. When Jesus looks out over the fields of Galilee, he recalls how "the earth produces of itself" (Mark 4:28, Greek: "automatically" or spontaneously). God reviews this display of life, finds it "very good," and bids it continue. "Be fruitful and multiply and fill the waters in the seas, and let birds multiply on the earth" (Genesis 1:22). In current scientific vocabulary, there is dispersal, conservation by survival over generations, and niche saturation up to carrying capacity. Adam's first task was to name this swarm of creatures.

The Endangered Species Act and the God Committee are contemporary events; it can be jarring to set them beside the archaic stories of Genesis with their aboriginal truths. The Noah story is antiquated genre, but the Noah threat is imminent today, and still lies at the foundations. The story is a myth teaching a perennial reverence for life. If there is a word of God here, lingering out of the primordial past, it is "Keep them alive with you" (Genesis 6:19).

Indeed, these primitive stories sometimes exceed the recent legislation in their depth of insight. Noah is not told to save just those species that are of "esthetic, ecological, educational, historical, recreational and scientific value" to people. He is commanded to save them all. These swarms of species are often useful to humans, and on the ark clean species were given more protection than others. But Noah was not simply conserving global stock. The Noah story teaches sensitivity to forms of life and the biological and theological forces producing them. What is required is not human prudence but principled responsibility to the biospheric earth, to God.

Biology and theology are not always easy disciplines to join. One conviction they do share is that the earth is prolific. Seen from the side of biology, this is called speciation, biodiversity, selective pressures for adapted fit, maximizing offspring in the next generation, niche diversification, species packing, and carrying capacity. Seen from the side of theology, this trend toward diversity is a good thing, a godly thing. This fertility is sacred. Endangered species raise the "God" question because they are one place we come near the ultimacy in biological life. In biological perspective, genesis is "of itself," spontaneous, autonomous; and biologists find nature to be prolific, even before the God question is raised. Afterward, theologians wish to add that in such a prolific world, explanations may not be over until one detects God in, with, and under it all.

IV. Duties to Ecosystems

All peoples dwell on promised lands that are gifts of God to be used with justice and charity—without impoverishing them of native species. Which brings up two tensions in land ethics: (1) Are humans using their land resources intelligently, retaining enough ecosystem health not to degrade the resource? (2) Ought humans to manage land as nothing but resource for themselves and neighbors, or ought humans rather to see the integrity of ecosystems as a moral issue, loving the whole biotic community? The one view is, historically, that of Gifford Pinchot, who founded the U.S. Forest Service. The other view is, historically, that of John Muir, recently judged, in a poll, to be the most influential Californian ever. The one view, on the contemporary scene, is that of the "wise use" movement, which seeks to maximize the human goods obtainable from the landscape; the other is that of the Sierra Club, continuing the legacy of its founder, who wished to bring humans into harmony with a world that is valuable penultimately as a resource because it is ultimately valuable as it is in itself.

Consider wilderness designation. About 96 percent of the contiguous United States is developed, farmed, grazed, timbered, designated for multiple use. Only about two percent has been designated as wilderness; another two percent might be suitable for wilderness or semi-wild status—cut-over forests that have reverted to the wild or areas as yet little developed. The wise use people say absolutely no more wilderness, and they would like to open up much that we have already designated; the environmentalists press hard for more wilderness. The wise use people say that the Endangered Species Act, if not repealed, should be revised to decide whether to save species on an economic cost-benefit calculus. Environmentalists want the Act strengthened; they want ecosystem conservation as the basis of endangered species preservation.

Does Christianity have much to say about this? Since Palestine was chiefly treasured as a land flowing with milk and honey, should Christians want ecosystem management for multiple uses, maximized to enrich the human condition—more milk and more honey? But then again, members of the faith community are nowhere taught to be maximal consumers; they ought to know when to say, enough, and to become interested rather in conserving the natural values on the landscape, optimizing the mix of values in both nature and culture.

Humans need, in differing degrees, elements of the natural to make and keep life human. But do we want land health only for our human excellence? The Catholic Bishops seem to say so: "The web of life is one. Our mistreatment of the natural world diminishes our own dignity and sacredness, not only because we are destroying resources that future generations of humans need, but because we are engaging in actions that contradict what it means to be human."[12] Yes, that seems right.

But wait a minute! I make a large donation to the Fund for the Whales and another to the Nature Conservancy. Being asked what motivated my charity, is it to augment my dignity, to affirm what it means to be human? It would seem that Christians, caring for creation, ought to think and do better. They might, instead, have concern for the integrity of creation, and forget their self-image and dignity. Doesn't Christian ethics worry about those who make charitable gifts only in order to cultivate their excellence of character?

We ought to conserve in nature those radical regenerative processes that conserve life. From this perspective, Christians can join with Aldo Leopold and his land ethic. "A thing is right when it tends to preserve the integrity, stability, and beauty of the biotic community. It is wrong when it tends otherwise."[13] That does not put human dignity or wise use first, though it can hardly result in undignified humans or unwise use. Those who wish to reside in a promised land must promise to preserve its integrity, stability, and beauty. "That land is a community is the basic concept of ecology, but that land is to be loved and respected is an extension of ethics."[14] If so, we cannot inherit our promised lands until we extend Christian ethics into ecology. "The land which you are going over to possess is a land of hills and valleys, which drinks water by the rain from heaven, a land which the Lord your God cares for; the eyes of the Lord your God are always upon it, from the beginning of the year to the end of the year" (Deut.11:11–12).

When J.B.S. Haldane, in conversation with some theologians, was asked what he had concluded from his long studies in biology about the divine character, he replied that God had an inordinate fondness for beetles, having made so many of them. But species counts are only one indication of diversity, and perhaps the fuller response is that God must have loved life, God animated such a prolific earth. Haldane went on to say that the marks of biological nature were its "beauty," "tragedy," and "inexhaustible queerness."[15]

This beauty approaches the sublime; the tragedy of perpetual perishing is perpetually redeemed with the renewal of life, and the inexhaustible queerness recomposes as the numinous. If anything at all on earth is sacred, it must be this enthralling creativity that characterizes our home planet. If anywhere, here is the brooding Spirit of God. If there is any holy ground, this is it.

Notes

1. Paul Schneider, "When a Whistle Blows in the Forest . . . ," *Audubon,* January/February 1992.

2. The internal forest supervisor memos are printed in *High Country News* 22 (4) (February 26, 1990): 10–11.

3. Ray Craig, "Land Ethic Canon Proposal: A Report from the Task Force," *Journal of Forestry* 90 (1992), 40–41.

4. Craig, op. cit.

5. William Cullen Bryant, *A Forest Hymn*, 1825.

6. John Muir, *Our National Parks* (Boston: Houghton Mifflin, 1901), 331.

7. Linnie Marsh Wolfe, ed., *John of the Mountains: The Unpublished Journals of John Muir* (Boston: Houghton Mifflin, 1938), 313.

8. William Wordsworth, *Lines Composed a Few Miles Above Tintern Abbey*, 1798.

9. *Endangered Species Act of 1973*, sec. 2a 87 Stat. 884.

10. *TVA v. Hill,* 437 U.S. 153 (1978), at 174.

11. Aldo Leopold, *A Sand County Almanac* (Oxford: Oxford University Press, 1968), 130.

12. Roman Catholic Bishops, "Renewing the Earth: An Invitation to Reflection on the Environment in the Light of Catholic Social Teaching," Origins: CNS Documentary Service 21 (1991): 426.

13. Aldo Leopold, op. cit., 224 f.

14. Ibid., Foreword.

15. J. B. S. Haldane, *The Causes of Evolution* (Ithaca, N.Y.: Cornell University Press, 1932, 1966), 167–69.

12

Of Place, Creation, and Relations

George E. Tinker
(as Interviewed by Sabine O'Hara)

(*Eco-Justice Quarterly* 14 [2], Spring 1994)

O'Hara: Professor Tinker, you have written extensively about the differences between your own tradition's understanding of history and that of the Western tradition. Would you outline what those differences are?

Tinker: First of all, I would insist that history as a field of study and discipline is an invention of the European intellectual tradition. History in the sense that the West has understood it for maybe two hundred years has not, until recently, existed for Indian people, and it is imposed on us. Of course, Indian people understand the past; we tell stories of the past and pass on traditions that way. But the past is not as formative for us as it is for European peoples, and by "European peoples" I mean to include the American people as well. Our worlds are framed by a rootedness in spatiality or place much more than by time. Where time is a factor it's always cyclical time. Even one's lifetime is considered a cycle of existence. The universe goes on when someone dies; and when a new baby is born, the cycle begins over again. I like to insist, for instance, that notions of temporal progression in modern economics have to be replaced with a dynamic stasis in order to satisfy American Indian cultural values. The important thing is not progress or advancement but maintaining harmony and balance in the universe around us.

O'Hara: So place takes on a very important meaning for you.

Tinker: Yes, when I say that sense of place is important to Indian people, I mean a spatial rootedness. It is there in all of our ceremonies, in village architecture, in stories that are told and symbols that are used to convey meaning to people. For example, the simple and well known symbol of the medicine wheel, a circle with a cross inscribed in it, is a spatial symbol. It doesn't talk about eschatology. Rather it articulates the wholeness of creation. There are countless, polyvalent ways of describing what that circle means or interpreting it. The cross that is inscribed in it can be understood as marking the cardinal directions—East, South, West and North—and each of those directions will encompass some part of creation. So by the time you've gone around the circle you have included all of creation, the wholeness of creation.

O'Hara: It sounds to me as if this understanding of place and belonging also has important implications for your relationships to creation and to the resources given in creation, as well as to others within the human community.

Tinker: If we are spatially configured, where we are is important. Where the Creator put an Indian nation is critical, so that every tribe has stories about how they ended up where they were. They might be stories of emergence, for instance. The Hunka emerged out of Earth somewhere in Missouri. So then Missouri belongs at the center of the universe, or did at least until we were moved to Kansas and then Oklahoma. So it is not a matter of our owning Missouri, it's a matter of our belonging in Missouri and living in relationship with the land in that place and sharing that land with others, namely all the four-leggeds, the wingeds, and all the living moving things that live in that place as well.

If we live in some sort of dynamic stasis of harmony and balance, then there have to be rituals, ceremonies that enable us, for instance, to eat without harming the relationship of balance in that place. This means there have to be prayers and offerings of reciprocation whenever we harvest grain or corn, kill an animal for food or pick medicines. Nothing can be picked randomly but everything has to be done in a way to preserve the balance of all around us.

O'Hara: This kind of balance would require a deep understanding of the place where you are and the ecosystems in that place.

Tinker: When the Osages moved to Oklahoma, prayers with the pipe seemed to have ended at that time. I have often wondered about that because the pipe is so critically, fundamentally important to Indian people and to Osages. One elder explained it to me this way. When we moved to Oklahoma, he said, we no longer knew the land. We no longer could go out with confidence and pick the tobaccos because the land was different, the plants were different. We just gave in to the missionaries at that point and decided to follow a new way. Now this is not entirely the case. There are traditional ways left among the Osages, and the pipe is now coming back. But for roughly a century there were not plentiful prayer pipes in use among those Osages. Which is to say that, in fact, you have to know the land where you are.

O'Hara: What are the ways in which you have traditionally acquired that knowledge? It seems to me that to "know the land" requires a different kind of knowledge from the universally applicable knowledge which Western learning emphasizes.

Tinker: With Western systems of taxonomy, categories of cognition, and structures and modes of discourse, one can generate very powerful ways of knowing. That system generates a particular kind of knowing that indeed can exercise a great deal of control over one's environment. And Western philosophy, as many have argued, has been given over to controlling nature for many centuries now. In the Indian world learning is not done by learning category schemes, but by watching and observing. I can tell you a story that may illustrate what I'm saying.

When I was younger and more inclined to teach my students a little about Indian spirituality, I agreed (rather foolishly, I might add) to do a spiritual retreat. The day before the retreat itself began, about five of us climbed up a mountain in Colorado, looking for an appropriate place to have our prayers. When we found the place, I and one of my students, a Navajo, conducted blessing ceremonies to bless the spot where we would pray and to invite spiritual entities. We took a little bit of sage and burned it, using an eagle feather to spread the smoke around that area to bless the people and bless the land and all its inhabitants. As we came down from that spot the Anglo students, three of them, were so impressed that they kept utter silence about halfway down the mountain. Then it got to a point where one of them just couldn't restrain himself anymore. He had to ask the Western question. The student started off by saying, "That was beautiful," and after a long pause and more silence, he chimed in, "What did it mean?" The meaning question is always prevalent for Euroamericans. How are we going to categorize it? How are we going to explain this so it can become part of our world? If we can't explain it, it can't be a part of our world. As I thought about it, I was a little stunned. Finally I gave some answer. I made it up. For about a minute and a half I compared it to incense in the Old Testament as a physical expression of prayer and so on and so forth. Then I looked at the student and said, "There, I told you more about it than anybody has ever told me about the ceremony, more than I've ever told my own kids or anyone else."

You see, my children understand the ceremony. They know what to do when it happens. They understand its sacredness, so that explaining the ceremony isn't an important part of the Indian learning system. Rather, our young are expected to watch the elders in everything that they do, whether it is planting corn or telling stories or conducting a ceremony of prayer. They learn by watching. They learn by watching the relationship between their elders and the earth and the different people in the community.

O'Hara: The way you have just described knowledge reminds me somewhat of the distinction between abstract and concrete knowledge that feminism, particularly eco-feminism, has described. Do you see similarities?

Tinker: I think there are similarities and differences. In the Indian world we understand the difference between maleness and femaleness, and we also understand the different gifts that come with that, the different gifts that women have and men have. But we also know that there is a male and a female inside each one of us, that the world is constructed as constant reciprocation between maleness and femaleness. That's why God is called on quite often (I use the word God loosely here) as grandfather and as grandmother. Many times when I speak, feminists will want to claim me as a part of their mother earth goddess spirituality. And I say no, no, no, there has to be a balance between the male and female. There has to be both or things are out of balance, out of kilter. So I think there is something in maleness and femaleness that would generate perhaps different ways of seeing the world, different ways of understanding the world around us. Maybe we could call it male thinking and female thinking or indigenous thinking and industrial thinking. But I think that gets overdone a bit, because in our experience in the Indian world much of the colonial paternalism we experience comes from both the white men and the white women.

O'Hara: So how do you see your understanding of place and connectedness influence your own structures of relating, particularly with respect to socioeconomic structure? What kinds of things are socially respected or rewarded?

Tinker: As Indian people, at least in the plains culture, we see ourselves as part of the circle. There is no head of the line, no hierarchical or pyramidic structure. A man may be a chief, but he is simply a leader among peers and has no special rights as a chief other than the *responsibility* of bringing people together to make and implement decisions. Certainly the accumulation of power and wealth is not socially rewarded in the Indian world. One's status is not measured by what one accumulates. Rather, one's status is measured on the basis of one's contribution to the community. Therefore the giveaway becomes an important part of Indian life. In my own tribe in the old days the Council of Old Ones was the advisory body to the whole village. One did not get to be on the Council of Old Ones simply by growing old. Accordingly, we distinguish today between elders and the elderly. To be named to the Council, one needed to have achieved four things in life: demonstrable intelligence; morality (not in terms of sexuality, but of contributions to the community and how one has functioned in one's lifetime within the community); bravery in war (which for us always involves the sacred, so that the thirteen war honors of the Osage would have been earned by this person or, if she is a woman, by her husband); and finally, three times in one's lifetime one would have had to give away everything she or he owns. When appointed to the Council of Old Ones this becomes the occasion for a fourth giveaway.

The point is twofold: one's status depends upon the generosity and willingness to humble oneself in the community to the point of not having anything. Secondly, the community can't function in this kind of a system unless it has the will and resources to then take care of the family which has given everything away. There is a total relationship of interdependence. When someone is appointed or elected chief the same thing pertains. That relationship of interdependency is foremost, so that being a chief is a position of responsibility for helping to maintain the harmony and balance, the interdependence, among those in the community. It is never merely a position of power or privilege.

O'Hara: You mentioned the bravery of war as being sacred to your people. Would you say some more about that?

Tinker: Yes, I need to, because Hollywood has done a job in terms of depicting Indian war-making. We saw most recently in "The Last of the Mohicans" that violence was not put into any political context whatsoever. In every Indian community that I know, it is important to consecrate the lives of all people who may be lost in war-making. The sacredness of life is so pronounced in our consciousness that we cannot just engage in any random killing. In my own tribe, for instance, the Osage nation, it took eleven days to go to war, eleven days of ceremony and prayer, eleven days to think better about the need to go to war, eleven days to consecrate the lives of those who would be lost, including one's enemies. That's a long time to prepare for war, when posturing here can result in devastating air strikes overnight, as in the case of Iraq. Even when Osages finally completed the eleven days of ceremonial preparation (one day for the Council to meet, six days for the chief to complete the fasting Rite of Vigil, and four days of ceremony among the whole tribe) the war itself might last only a few days. It may include only one encounter with the enemy and that encounter may or may not result in physical combat. In fact, the whole war may consist of the two sides' standing on opposite sides of a creek shouting epithets at one another.

The reason for making war was not to accumulate honors and glory, but to maintain territorial boundaries. There is much overlap between neighboring tribes in terms of hunting ground, but for each tribe there is a heartland that your enemy may not enter into unless he is coming on an official visit into your village. When those boundaries—and they're moveable, they're not permanent forever—are violated, then there would be a reason for war. But, in fact, if a tribe had grown smaller the boundaries of the heartland would actually be adjusted as well. In any case it is in no way the most honored act to kill an enemy, but rather that act which is most honored is touching an enemy. It is showing the bravery to get close enough to a living enemy and touching him in battle and then withdrawing.

O'Hara: It seems to me that the term *mitakuye oyasin*, which I've seen you refer to in several of your writings, expresses well the relationships you have described between the land, its creatures and its people as understood by your people.

Tinker: The term *mitakuye oyasin* means "for all my relatives." If we go back to the image of the circle, the circle is a representation of *mitakuye oyasin*. It's a symbolic representation of all my relatives, and those include not just blood relatives but all the two-leggeds—black, red, yellow, and white. That is one way to go around the circle—black, red, yellow, and white. Some people like to say that this represents the colors of two-leggeds in the world. But then you go around the circle again and the relatives include two-leggeds, four-leggeds, wingeds, and the living, moving things. The circle includes all living things, so that one can't pick corn recklessly because corn is a cousin, and one can't kill a buffalo without making prayers because the buffalo is a cousin, and you can't kill your enemy recklessly because your enemies are cousins too.

O'Hara: Thank you so much for your insights.

Section D

Hunger and Agriculture

Editor's Notes

Hunger is the quintessential eco-justice issue, the one that most obviously and inescapably demands attention to both earth and people, the earth's fruitfulness and the people's participation in sufficient sustenance. There is no more basic necessity than food, and there is no food that does not come from earth. The capacity of the earth to satisfy human hunger depends upon the intricate functioning of ecological systems, and the capacity of human beings to satisfy their hunger depends upon careful gathering, cultivating, harvesting, and sharing. For all to be filled and hunger prevented, earth's yields have to be sufficient and sustainable, and human communities have to fashion participatory economies that aim at sustainable sufficiency.

The Eco-Justice Project and Network originated in, and in part because of, the anti-hunger movement of the 1970s. Spurred by widespread reports and horrifying pictures of malnourished and starving children and adults, the major church denominations instituted and funded programs to address world hunger. When campus ministry funds for the Eco-Justice Project dried up, hunger funds kept it going. The most generous grants came from the United Methodist Board of Discipleship and the Presbyterian Hunger Program. These came with a particular interest in the work that Eco-Justice did on lifestyle assessment. The grant-making committees recognized the incongruity between wretched hunger, domestic as well as global, and the overconsumption and political complacency of comfortable Americans.

The Eco-Justice Conference of October 1984 took the theme "Why Hunger in '84? Ten Years after the World Food Conference." Prof. Larry Rasmussen delivered the keynote address on "The

Persistence of Hunger: Ecological, Economic and Ethical Dimensions," printed here as Selection 13. A decade and one-half later, his talk remains on target with respect to hunger's continuing persistence.

The "meteoric shower of facts," which Rasmussen cites from an Oxfam America compilation, could be revised to fit the current situation. More people today have access to safe drinking water, and some countries have made improvements in sanitation, although these improvements leave great numbers unreached. Some of the potentially cultivable land has been brought under cultivation. But the basic thrust of the facts is distressingly the same or even worse. On every continent water tables are falling, primarily as a result of overpumping for irrigation. Many countries, including the two largest, China and India, depend on irrigation for most of their food. With the further globalization of the economy, many developing countries have become less self-reliant in food production. The pressure to increase exports in order to import necessities has consequences that include the further displacement of subsistence farmers and the acceleration of soil erosion and deforestation. The warming of the planet makes weather patterns more erratic.

The facts at the turn of the century underscore the analytical and ethical relevance of the 1984 presentation to the persisting problem. Poverty is still the chief cause of hunger. The human causes of poverty are still many and complex, firmly rooted in the global economic system and the ever greater concentrations of wealth and capital. The system itself thwarts the journey to eco-justice.

The second article in this section, Selection 14, gives some details of the operative effects of the modern economic system on agriculture. In "Let My People Farm," the late Donald Q. Innis, who was a professor of geography with extensive firsthand experience in the agriculture of many countries, explains how profit-driven, fossil fuel based, mechanized and chemicalized farming overrides the experience and skills of traditional farmers, excludes many of them from the land, degrades the soil, keeps poor people hungry, and jeopardizes future food sufficiency. Advocating particularly for intercropping, he maintains that traditional, site-specific methods on small farms can equal or exceed the yields of modern agriculture, while preserving soil fertility.

Innis's advocacy is in line with a current emphasis on community-based sustainable agricultural development, in which aid personnel work as partners with indigenous farmers to help them achieve their own goals pertaining to enhanced productivity, better nutrition, and long-term protection of the land. The critical question is whether this way of farming can withstand the onslaught of big, expanding, export-oriented corporate agriculture.

13

The Persistence of Hunger: Ecological, Economic, and Ethical Dimensions

Larry L. Rasmussen

(*The Egg 4* [4], December 1984)

I. Wrapping Our Minds Around Hunger

Your conference announcement begins with this paragraph:

> Ten years after Rome [the World Food Conference], four years after the Presidential Commission on World Hunger, we have useful international mechanisms for combating hunger, but the sum total of suffering from malnutrition and poverty may well be greater than in 1974. Has the anti-hunger movement lost momentum? Is this because the poor are lazy, or because the comfortable lack compassion, or because the claims of *justice* are more formidable and far-reaching than most people have acknowledged? What *systemic* changes are necessary? Why are they so difficult?

This conference could be very short. Those questions *do* have some ready answers. Yes, the anti-hunger movement has lost some

157

momentum, though it has also gained some institutional footage. Some of the poor are lazy. Most are not. Many overwork. Lack of compassion is *the* disease of the routinely affluent, yet few people, the comfortable included, can stomach starving human beings. Yes, the claims of justice are more formidable and far-reaching than most people have acknowledged. They have always been so. Many systemic changes are necessary, some of which we recognize with some clarity, some of which we have yet to discover. (As Pogo once remarked on a related subject: "We've got faults we haven't even used yet.") The known, required systemic changes are difficult for a whole bevy of reasons!

But I trust you did not assemble here from many places, only now to return, your hats full of succinct answers to the conference questions.

I do not mean to make light of any of this. Indeed, I chose that paragraph as an opening because I think it is precise. It reports just where we are and what kinds of questions must be addressed. I salute you for the kind of concern and commitment your topic and your presence signal.

I have puzzled and pondered much about the most helpful approach to such a complex as hunger represents. There are political, scientific, demographic, ecological, and economic dimensions. There are also dimensions of moral commitment and character, of human will and imagination, indeed elements of religious conviction and vision. There are local manifestations of hunger, and an awful global reach as well. Hunger is both problem and symptom, both tragedy and a result of human choice, a manifestation of both fickle nature and corrupt society. It is a place of the stark terror of life and sometimes the occasion of gentle beauty—when caring for one another's most elemental needs happens and hunger is assuaged. Hunger is obviously and most importantly a matter of the body. But it also has institutional and far-reaching systemic reality. (Indeed, the great new fact about hunger is that it is endemically systemic rather than an episodic matter of weather.) Hunger is awesomely physical. But food and eating and drinking, and the living and dying bundled up with them, have always been profoundly spiritual and social as well. Fasting has been a rite of both religious purification and social protest; and feasting has been the most universal way of celebrating the many miracles, and the sheer "giftedness," of life itself.

So when hunger is the subject, with it comes most of life—and much of death. Wrapping our minds around it can hardly be a modest effort! *We* may be modest, but the reality we are trying to understand is not. Indeed, the subject of your conference calls to mind another of Pogo's observations: "We are, dear friends, faced with insurmountable opportunities."

Faced with such insurmountable opportunities, I have picked and pruned and exercised near-arbitrariness in the choice of subjects. I am grateful that tomorrow's schedule will complement and supplement tonight's modest beginning.

The assigned topic is clear—"[reasons for] the persistence of hunger." I am also clear that I am to do a broad brush sketch of the hunger complex that will let your knowledge and experience fill in the details, details I do not have command of, details no *one* of us holds entirely, but details which we do hold together. None of us is as wise as all of us.

To do this sketch I will use a framework I sometimes employ as a teacher of ethics. In ethics we say there are three elements required for adequately addressing a social problem such as hunger. I will use these three elements to organize reflections on hunger's persistence. Otherwise I fear our grasp of the situation will be not unlike Edna St. Vincent Millay's testimony.

> Upon this gifted age, in its dark hour
> Rains from the sky a meteoric shower
> Of facts . . . they lie unquestioned, uncombined.[1]

We can combine and question by realizing that any credible stand on a major human issue such as hunger, and the implementation of that stand, entails at least these three elements.

- There is *conceptual adequacy*, the way in which the issue-at-hand is approached, analyzed, and deliberated. *How* we think about hunger, and how we do *not* think about it, is critical to our response.

- *Social prerequisites* must be in place, or created. Thinking well is in vain if there are deficient institutional forms and policies for enacting decisions or, indeed, for making them in the first place. Even if our ethical stands are conceptually sound, without the "earthen vessels" of systems, institutions and policies our stands on hunger would be too short-lived to matter much.

- The *moral character* of people is the third element. Sound investigation and grasp of hunger issues, and accessible forums for public action, are impotent if the kinds of people who will venture morally sensitive actions on weighty matters are not present, or their numbers are too few. To adapt an idea from physics: a kind of critical mass of moral character and conviction is necessary if an issue as deep and wide as hunger is to be effectively addressed. Without sufficient moral commitment, nothing will happen.

We can take each of these elements in turn.

II. Conceptualizing the Problem

Conceptual adequacy encompasses several different subjects. I will include the following, you may well add others: a) the factual realities of hunger; b) a normative perspective or vision from which to respond to those realities.

Now we must take each of *these* elements in turn. I have this image of building scaffolding around the Statue of Liberty so thick we can no longer see what it is we're repairing and we wind up trying to penetrate the scaffolding. Our "statue" is the hunger issue and we're about to discuss two subjects under one of the three elements involved in approaching the issue! But let's plunge ahead and hope that when we've finished we have a good map or grid rather than a good maze!

A. The Factual Realities of Hunger

Details are no doubt important, but the broad outlines and the most basic and intractable of the brute facts are clear and known. They remain the repugnant reality we face, whatever details inhabit the innards of that reality.

More than one billion people in the world are chronically undernourished. Between seven hundred and eight hundred million people live on incomes insufficient to adequately secure the basic necessities of life.

Fifteen to twenty million people die each year of hunger-related causes, including diseases brought on by lowered resistance due to malnutrition. Three out of every four of these . . . are children. Over 40 percent of all deaths in poor countries occur among children under five years old.

At least a hundred thousand children in Asia and Africa go blind each year from vitamin A deficiency caused by inadequate diet. More than five hundred million people in poor countries suffer from chronic anemia due to inadequate diet.

In wealthy countries, twelve to fifteen out of every thousand newborn infants die before their first birthday. In poor countries, one hundred out of every thousand newborns die before their first birthday.

One out of every four human beings . . . has no access to safe drinking water. In the forty lowest income countries, fewer than 30 percent of the people have access to safe drinking water.

In Britain, there is one doctor for every 880 people. Nigeria has one doctor for every 44,620 people, while Ethiopia has one doctor for every 73,000 people.

In eighty-three countries of the world, three percent of the land owners control almost 80 percent of the land.

Less than 60 percent of the world's cultivable land is currently under cultivation. Less than 20 percent of the potentially cultivable land in Africa and Asia is under cultivation. Most of that land is controlled by large land owners or is open country.

The price of one military tank could provide classrooms for thirty thousand students, or improved storage facilities for one hundred thousand tons of rice.

What the world spends in half a day on military purposes could finance the entire malaria eradication program of the World Health Organization.

In the wealthy countries, 20– 25 percent of the average family's income is spent on food. In most poor countries, the average rural poor family must spend as much as 75–80 percent of its income on food.

Every day, the world produces two pounds of grain for every man, woman, and child on earth. That is enough to provide everyone three thousand calories a day, well above the recommended daily minimum of twenty-three hundred calories.

The rich countries, including the United States, western Europe, Japan and Australia, consume 70 percent of the world's food grains. Most of that is used to feed beef and dairy cattle.

North Americans spend more on chewing gum, tobacco and alcoholic beverages each year than the entire annual budgets of many poor countries.[2]

This is only part of the "meteoric shower of facts" on hunger that fall to earth as a truly acid rain. Let me simplify them immensely, and at the same time say *why* the empirics of hunger make it such an intractable reality. From the facts given you may have noted that weather was not included. It could be, it should be. There are terrible crop failures now, especially in East Africa where famine stalks the land, ironically like the grim reaper. But adding a weather report won't fundamentally alter the major conclusion consistently drawn since the World Food Conference a decade ago:[3] the basic cause of world hunger is poverty, and the basic cause of poverty is human. Let me say it in the terms of your conference topic: the persistence of hunger is the persistence of poverty; the solution to poverty will simultaneously be the solution to hunger. I think Lappe and Collins, in *Food First!*, have told us the truth: hunger *per se* is not as fated or circumstantial as we thought. Enough food is produced virtually everywhere to sustain the people of that region. But poverty is entrenched in a thousand human ways, and hunger and its diseases ravage the poor.[4] Those are the brute facts, rendered conceptually easy and "practically" extremely difficult.

We cannot ignore the blizzard of facts. And we must not push aside the fundamental cause of ongoing hunger. But the statisticians aren't the best communicators, even of the empirics of hunger. The poets of the poor are. I include a portion of "The Great Tablecloth" by Pablo Neruda.

> The peasant in the field ate
> his poor quota of bread,
> he was alone, it was late,
> he was surrounded by wheat,
> but he had no more bread;
> he ate it with grim teeth,
> looking at it with hard eyes....
>
> Eating alone is a disappointment,
> but not eating matters more,

is hollow and green, has thorns
like a chain of fish hooks
trailing from the heart,
clawing at your insides. . . .

Let us sit down soon to eat
with all those who haven't eaten;
let us spread great tablecloths,
put salt in the lakes of the world,
set up planetary bakeries,
tables with strawberries in snow,
and a plate like the moon itself
from which we can all eat.

For now I ask no more
than the justice of eating.[5]

B. *The Moral Vision*

"[No] more than the justice of eating" leads into the second topic for thinking rightly about hunger—the normative perspective, the vision from which we respond to these brute facts. The facts alone never tell us how to respond, hard as they may kick. The facts interact with moral norms and deep convictions and commitments. That interaction sets the direction of response. Without compelling moral norms and commitments, the facts will simply lie dumb, unquestioned and uncombined.

I will sketch a normative response, shared by Jew, Christian, and many others as well, including good secular humanists. My religious reference is Judeo-Christian simply because I know it best and because it is the reference point for many here.

It bears remembering that for Jews, the people of the Passover Seder, the central ritual act is the sharing of food. It bears remembering that for Christians, the people of the Lord's Table, the central ritual act is also the sharing of food. And it bears remembering that for both Jews and Christians, the liturgical sharing is done with *a hope for all* creation and *a commitment to* the breaking of bread in abundance for and with *all*. If I may quote the French Jesuit, Gustave Martelet:

To involve human food and drink symbolically in a meal of love implies at the very least that in real life we have done nothing to deprive others of them; and, even further, that we are doing or have done . . . everything that is humanly and Christianly necessary and possible to ensure that these elementary supplies are produced in sufficient quantity and shared equitably. If this were not done, to take the bread and wine and offer them to the Lord would become intolerably false, since we would be seeking to give God with one hand what we were unjustly withholding from [people] with the other.[6]

In a frightful telescoping of Judeo-Christian moral tradition, let me add to the liturgical vision some core concepts that are, in fact, a part of it.

Creation is the theological word for *all things together in their relationship to God.* Had you interviewed Hebrews about the meaning of creation, they would have pointed to land, livestock, commerce, health, family, tools, table, governing institutions, village and city and countryside, patterns of social relationships and social traffic, rocks, trees and wild animals, sun, moon, and stars, even those cursed enemies—all things, except God the Creator.

This is a unitary vision. Creation, for all its fecund diversity, is one, human and nonhuman together, organic and inorganic, natural, social and cultural, ancestors, contemporaries, and posterity, the whole ball of atoms.

This unity of creation is important so that you will understand the sense of *"neighbor"* in Judeo-Christian perspective. It is a universal term. All are neighbors. Jesus voices the radical reach of this when he construes the enemy as neighbor and instructs his followers to treat all neighbors with a regard equal to the regard they accord themselves and their closest compatriots. Near and far, friend and foe, present and future creatures, all are neighbors. In H. Richard Niebuhr's phrase, the neighbor is "all that participates in being."

Justice is the third key notion. While the vision of creation is that harmonious, abundant, secure life together, as neighbors all, the actual experience of the world is creation broken, laced with deep discord, stirred by profound need and want—that meteoric shower of brute facts on hunger, for example. Fissures of suffering, pain and violation rend nature, psyche and society every bit as much as joy, ecstasy and satisfaction surface. Our ancestors in the faith knew this. From it emerged their notion of justice. It is not quite the same as Anglo-American notions. Those traditions have emphasized justice as either liberty or equality, or some combination thereof. Justice as liberty means guaranteeing the widest range of individual choice commensurate with such choice for others. Justice as equality means guaranteeing a comparative allotment of goods, services and opportunities at a humane level for the largest number possible. You ought to note that neither of these truly includes eco-justice, since the assumption is that the sphere of justice is populated by humans only and concerns human welfare alone. Instead, biblically, *justice is the rendering*, amid limited resources and the conditions of brokenness, of *whatever is required for the fullest possible flourishing of creation.*

Community is the last term to introduce. In the most basic sense, the primary unit of reality is the whole creation in God! But that's rather awesome in its reach, and our experience of it, as a totality, is more mystical and religious than it is everyday and ordinary. Our most common community experience is of *partial* community only. And that is the point. Some are always outside of the range of our mercy and the reach of our resources. Reigning policies, institutions, benefits, and privileges always exclude some and include others. Some are sated while others starve.

Let's see the stark reality, and the normative vision, in the round. Creation is one, though diseased, corrupted, awry, a friend to terror. All are neighbors, with something like an equal claim to the requisites for life in their niches of creation; yet the requisites for life for millions of neighbors go unmet. Justice is securing those requisites for nature and society. And where does justice begin? Wherever community is flawed. And community is flawed wherever some are left out, marginalized, cut off from life's bounty and love's ways, excluded from all those pilgrimages that will end at the messianic banquet. When community is whole, creation is cured. Then God's hopes are realized and there is rejoicing in heaven.

In sum: 1) Thinking about hunger means an unflinching honesty about the empirical reality of hunger. Basically it is suffering rooted in debilitating poverty, which kills cells and souls alike. It is the lot of almost unimaginable numbers of our neighbors. 2) Sound thinking about hunger is also responding to this massive blotch on creation with a certain mindset of convictions and commitments. Those are centered in a planetary vision of inseparable kinship with all creatures, great and small. The malnourished and starving are our co-siblings in creation. Justice is their due, and life together (community) is the goal for us all.

Yet empirical analysis and a moral vision are insufficient, though they are certainly vital and necessary. We must talk now of social requisites.

III. Social Requisites to Addressing Hunger

In our scheme of the three elements of a credible response to hunger, I listed social requisites as a reference to the systems, institutions and policies needed for addressing hunger satisfactorily, in other words, as pieces of a working strategy. But the assigned topic is the *persistence* of hunger and in that connection I must instead say something of what systemic, institutional and policy impediments already exist that stand in the way of addressing hunger, or are already in place as pieces which sometimes aid, sometimes hinder, solutions to poverty and hunger.

We could do worse than simply listing these impediments. You can and will do something with the list, beyond what I am able to do in the course of the conference. I intend no ranking in this list. In fact, the following all interact so as to constitute rather perverse evidence for the ecologist's observation that "all things are connected" so that "you can never do merely one thing."

We have asserted that poverty is the *basic* cause of hunger. But poverty is itself not a single thing or a simple thing and is not generated by only one kind of economic or other arrangements. Nor is poverty the *only* cause of hunger, even though it is basic. All this qualification makes the list a little like a spider's web. Locating the center—poverty—will let you trace the rest, but the center does not of itself indicate just where the strands will lead and where they are anchored:

- The continuation of historically unprecedented population growth.

- Resource abuse, inadequate land and water care.

- The complexity, and political difficulty, of agrarian reform.

- The colonial legacy of dependency, often continued as neocolonialist international trade relationships.

- Low status for agricultural development and other aspects of rural development, in contrast with priority given to urban, industrial development.

- The military budget as a strain and drain on national resources, for nonproductive ends.

- The force of traditions which impede new methods and technologies that might aid agricultural production and conservation.

- The inequality of wealth and income distribution, which skews markets to overconsumption in some quarters and poverty in others, both within nations and between them.

- Geographical and climatic factors.

- Political and economic oppression that brakes reform and sometimes drives people from the land into refugee status.

- Educational materials and systems that fail to understand hunger, or to communicate it effectively when it is understood.

- Inadequate food reserves for bridging times when hunger is temporary and circumstantial.

- Foreign aid that has exacerbated problems rather than solved them and that has been targeted to the less needy rather than the more needy.

- Inadequate political will on the part of people with the power to affect hunger reality; differently said, the moral apathy of affluence.

- The relative lack of institutions—international, national, and local—which amplify the voice of the poor and hungry and advocate on their behalf.

Any of these is itself a conference topic. Together they are rather overwhelming, if not to the intellect, certainly to any planning and action for alternative social arrangements. And this list is only partial! Nonetheless, the list does carry some explanatory power for understanding the persistence of hunger. It also makes clear that both the causes and the solutions to hunger are multiple and heavily institutional.

IV. Moral Character

Understanding the complexity of hunger and the corollary complexity of solutions to it will avail not at all if no one is moved to respond. Even the presence of a moral vision will tally zero if persons are not present who are ready to act upon that vision. This is to state the obvious. But the obvious fact is sometimes the most important one. And sometimes the obvious isn't even so obvious— until the obviously needed factor is obviously absent.

Let me pass along Langdon Gilkey's experience and reflections. In 1943 he and fifteen hundred other foreigners were interred by the Japanese in Northern China. The Japanese controlled the borders of the camp but left the fifteen hundred strangers to decide among themselves how to organize their own mini-society. Gilkey says the most important contributions to this society-in-the making in the first months were practical skills, technical genius, and administrative cunning. People with know-how and people who were creative problem-solvers were the VIP's. Gilkey, a budding theologian, decided that religious and philosophical reflection as well as moral inquiry were interesting but that they were not essential to society. Society needed a pragmatic spirit and technological skills. That would suffice. So he wrote in his journal:

> ... Humanity's ingenuity in dealing with difficult problems was unlimited, making irrelevant those so-called "deeper issues" of ... spiritual life with which religion and philosophy pretended to deal.

Gilkey was himself soon given an important moral task. He was placed in charge of housing. From that he learned something else. I must quote at length.

> Gradually, however, as I encountered more and more unexpected problems in my work in housing, I began to realize that [my] confident attitude toward things simply did not fit the realities of camp life. It was not that our material crises seemed any less urgent, or that our minds were any less capable of dealing with them. Rather, new sorts of problems kept arising that improved know-how could not resolve. For over and over what we can only call "moral" or "spiritual" difficulties continually cropped up. Crises occurred that involved not a breakdown of techniques, but a breakdown in character, showing the need for more moral integrity and self-sacrifice. The trouble with my new humanism, I found myself deciding, was not its confidence in human science and technology. It was rather its naïve and unrealistic faith in the rationality and goodness of [those] who wielded these instruments. If ... courage and integrity ... were evidenced in every facet of camp life, equally apparent was the intense difficulty all of us experienced in being fair-minded, not to say just or generous, under the hard pressure of our rough and trying existence.
>
> But most important of all, what became increasingly plain was that these crises of the soul were not of such a character as to disturb merely the prim and the straight-laced in our midst. On a critical level equal to an outbreak of dysentery or a stoppage of our bread supply, these moral breakdowns were so serious that they threatened the very existence of our community. It became increasingly evident to me that unless these inward crises

could be resolved, the entire microcosmic civilization which we had so painstakingly established to feed and care for us would not live much longer. I began to see that without moral health, a community is as helpless and lost as it is without material supplies and services.

This was the deepest lesson I learned from this experience. Since that time, both in studies and in observation generally, it has seemed to me to be a truth validated over and over in the life of every human society, great or small.[7]

"...[The] entire microcosmic civilization which we had so painstakingly established *to feed and care for us* would not live much longer... without moral health." Let me state that in positive terms, and include it in a summary statement.

Hunger is as persistent as poverty. It is equally complex and entrenched. Yet poverty has often, indeed continuously, been addressed positively, effectively, even if not finally, though that dream still lures us. It can also be the case, and has been, for hunger. It has been and can be addressed continuously, positively, effectively, and hopefully even with some finality. Abolishing most hunger requires sound analysis and hard thinking. Wrong action often follows from wrong understanding, and right action from right understanding. Abolishing most hunger also needs the pull of a compelling moral vision as well as the push of intolerable facts. Changing hundreds of institutional and policy patterns, large and small, is clearly, utterly necessary. So is the sometimes slow, sometimes sudden, transformation of moral character, the steady nurture of moral health among the young, middle-aged, and old.

All of this carries one important implication for strategy, given both the persistence of hunger and the three elements of a credible response. Let me put the implication in personal terms: I have never met anyone, young or old, educated or not, simple or sophisticated, contemplative or aggressive, of whatever race, sex, or creed, and gifted with whatever natural or acquired skills, who did not have *some* piece of *some* part in the ached-for answer to hunger. Each of you has a piece.

Notes

1. Edna St. Vincent Millay, from "Sonnet 137," *Collected Poems* (New York: Harper and Row, 1956), 697.

2. These data are from Oxfam America's "Facts for Action." Provided by the Hunger Program of the American Lutheran Church in a mailing in the summer, 1984.

3. Henry Kissinger, then Secretary of State, addressed the 1974 Rome World Food Conference. He said: "The profound promise of our era is that for the first time we may have the technical capacity to free mankind from the scourge of hunger. Therefore, today we must proclaim a bold objective—that within a decade no child will go to bed hungry, that no family will fear for the next day's bread, and that no human being's future and capacities will be stunted by malnutrition." A decade has passed and we have the hoped-for capacity. Yet millions of children go to bed hungry. Evidently Kissinger failed to take account of the relationship of technical capacity to the economic and political reality of wealth and poverty. The Kissinger quotation is from the helpful collection: William Byron, ed., *The Causes of World Hunger* (Mahwah, N.J.: Paulist Press, 1982), 2.

4. Frances Moore Lappe and Joseph Collins, *Food First: Beyond the Myth of Scarcity* (New York: Bantam Books, 1979).

5. Pablo Neruda, from "The Great Tablecloth," *Poems English and Spanish*, trans. Alastair Reid (New York: Farrar, Straus and Geroux, 1974), 44–47.

6. *The Risen Christ and the Eucharistic World* (New York: Seabury, 1976), 183.

7. *Shantung Compound* (New York: Harper and Row, 1966), 75–76.

14

Let My People Farm

Donald Q. Innis

(*The Egg: A Journal of Eco-Justice* 8 [1], Spring 1988)

Modern commercial, mechanized farming is designed to make a profit. "Old-fashioned" farming, using hand tools or animal power, was designed to supply people with food and work. The modern land ownership system often allows a person or corporation to own much more land than can be used. Traditional ideas of land ownership in most parts of the world held that anyone willing to work could have land. In the modern world, the type of ownership that produces the most profit per farmer also turns out to exclude many people from the land. Much land in the modern world is commercially owned but is farmed inefficiently from an ecological point of view or is not farmed at all because the market is flooded with food that is too much for the middle class to consume but too expensive for the poor to buy.

Poor, hungry people are not allowed to use commercially owned land because they would not produce a profit for the big land owner. Keeping land out of production and out of the hands of small farmers tends to keep prices and profits higher than would otherwise be the case. Poor people in urban slums and rural communities do not have the money to provide a large market for commercially produced foods. In the modern world, therefore, most farm products are grown by middle-class or rich farmers and are sold to middle-class or rich people. The millions of poor who can neither sell nor buy seem to have become irrelevant.

Modern educated people have been told that big machines are the best way to farm because they cut labor costs. They also learn that very little can be spent on soil enrichment and conservation because that would increase costs. They are saddened and puzzled when they realize that so many people have inadequate food, even though modern agriculture draws heavily on nonrenewable resources of fuels, fertilizers, and other farm chemicals. People today seem convinced that farmers must strip the soil of nutrients because there are so many poor people needing to be fed.

All this destructive and profitable modern agricultural activity does not help most poor people. Thousands of children and adults die every day because they don't have the money to buy the food which is stored and even rotting in warehouses all over the world. Countries like India, Pakistan, and the Philippines export food while thousands of their own citizens starve. Modern educated people have their attention directed to the "population problem" instead of the fact that people are denied access to land. Frances Moore Lappe and her coworkers have shown that the world produces some three thousand calories of food a day for every person on earth. So why are people hungry? Is it because some people eat more than their share, while believing that those who starve have only themselves to blame because they had too many children?

Investigating the Old Ways

Since most modern agriculture is not providing a continuous supply of food to the poor and is severely damaging the earth's capacity to produce, some researchers have begun to look for other ways of doing things. For many years, Third World methods were neglected because it was assumed that modern agriculture *must* be better than the traditional. This attitude is an example of the arrogance of the modern world. Scientists and modern farmers have gone into many poor countries with the message that they can improve agriculture even though they have never tested the efficiency of the traditional agriculture they propose to replace.

Good Farmers, a book by geographer Gene Wilken, gives many excellent examples of the ways in which Central American traditional farmers manage their resources. Many traditional small farmers produce food for their families and grow commercial crops at the same time in the same field. They carefully classify their soil according to their own system (often quite unaware that soil scientists have classified the same soils in modern ways). The traditional farmers have developed methods of soil treatment, such as adding organic matter, green manuring, applying silt from rivers and lakes, terracing, intercropping, and crop rotation, that maintain the productivity of the soil. Where necessary they have developed hand or animal powered methods for irrigation or draining the land.

F.H. King's book, *Farmers of Forty Centuries*, analyzes traditional Chinese agriculture. Since King was head of the U.S. Soil Survey, his enthusiasm for traditional methods should affect the thinking of those who are trying to understand the best way to keep up the productivity of the world's soil. In addition to many other techniques such as composting, the Chinese have always recognized the importance of returning the nutrients in human waste to the soil. There are scholars who feel that the persistence of Chinese civilization for four thousand years without a collapse is at least partly due to the traditional understanding of the soil and its needs.

Paul Richards is an anthropologist who studies West African traditional agriculture. His book, *Indigenous Agricultural Revolution*, contains many amazing examples of modern methods that have done a great deal of harm to the people and soils of West Africa. In one example, modern methods were introduced on an emergency basis during World War II but proved so much less productive than traditional methods that the old ways had to be restored even before the war was over.

In addition to these books, many research articles on traditional agriculture are being published. Soil scientists in Nigeria have been especially open to the suggestion that traditional small farmers know what they are doing. For decades, Nigerian agricultural extension agents and researchers had almost no success in persuading traditional farmers to adopt modern, more profitable methods of farming. The farmers have persisted, for instance, in the intercropping of pearl millet, sorghum and cowpeas in the same field, making it difficult for the extension agents to calculate fertilizer requirements or to recommend machine labor on the fields.

"Old-Fashioned" Intercropping

West African intercropping is an outstanding example of a traditional approach that modern ways cannot match. Take the millet/sorghum/cowpea combination of Nigeria. Pearl millet is drought-resistant and can grow in poor soils before the heart of the rainy season. A few weeks after it is planted and weeds have begun to flourish, farmers efficiently interplant sorghum and do their weeding simultaneously. Cowpeas are planted just before the millet harvest to reduce erosion. After the millet harvest, the sorghum, no longer shaded by a taller plant, rapidly begins to recover from the effects of competition with the millet. Experiments have shown that the total yield with intercropping, as described here, can produce twice the yield of sorghum grown alone.

Farmers use the differing lengths of the vegetative cycles of the three crops to maximize the efficiency of their labor and to conserve the soil. The harvesting of intercrops can be done by family labor since the work is spread over many days, whereas the harvesting of a single crop, all ripening at once, is better suited to machines. Intercropping helps provide a balanced diet for a family over a long period, whereas a monocrop tends to need a commercial market and often needs to be sold for cash to pay for machines, fuels, and fertilizers.

Intercropping is superior to monocropping because of its more efficient use of environmental resources in space and time. The existence of more leaves and root systems throughout the growing season makes better use of light, water, and nutrients. Sowing one crop under another (relay cropping) helps protect the soil from erosion and loss of nutrients, since the extra root systems capture some nutrients that would otherwise be lost by soil erosion and leaching. These recaptured nutrients contribute to a greater total harvest and also produce more organic matter by returning nutrients to upper parts of the soil when leaves, stems and roots decay. Intercropping reduces attacks by disease and insects, since they cannot spread as easily to the species of their choice when other plants are interposed. Weeds are suppressed for much of the growing season, because the extra crops utilize light, water, and nutrients that would otherwise be available to weeds.

A Nigerian experiment with intercropped legumes and maize produced the amazing result that total yields were 50–100 percent higher *and fewer nutrients were removed from the soil than were removed by monocropped maize.* The apparent explanation is that two sets of roots retrieve more nutrients, which would otherwise have been lost to erosion and leaching, than were utilized by the one crop. When fertilizers are applied, intercropping retrieves more of their nutrients than does monocropping, so less fertilizer needs to be used.

Intercropping combined with the use of locally bred species can decrease risk by providing resistance to disasters such as drought. An experiment in Burkina Faso showed that even when 80 percent of a local sorghum variety was killed by drought, the remaining plants compensated by growing extra stems (tillers) and seed heads. These adjustments more than made up for the disaster; the overall yield was higher than in a nondrought year. When drought occurs near the end of the growing season, intercropped sorghum survives better than monocropped, because there are only half as many plants to share the available moisture and there is less leaf area from which water could be lost.

A Word to the Thoroughly Modern

The profit motive of modern, science-based, cost-effective agriculture ensures that money will not be spent on soil maintenance because the profit would be compromised. Modern agriculture will do only a few of the things that must be done to keep the earth's soils fertile for an indefinite period, even into the time when nonrenewable resources have long since been used up. The interactions between plant roots and soil nutrients, soil flora and fauna, soil acidity and water supply are infinitely complicated. It is not economic for modern farmers with big fields to study all these things and make different soil treatment adjustments in different parts of a field. For the soil's future and the future of humanity, a more detailed supervision of the soil is required.

The argument of this paper is that small farmers through much of human time have known how to deal with these numerous factors at once and have kept large areas of the earth's farmland useable. It must be admitted that in many areas they failed to keep the land useable, but it seems clear that modern methods fail much faster. The traditional small farmer who understands the best of the old ways and has not learned to seek a quick profit deals successfully with a great many variables and is willing to make small-scale adjustments that would be uneconomical for a big modern farmer.

One conclusion, therefore, is that small farmers should be allowed access to land, on the condition that they look after it. Where small farmers still control good land and have not been driven onto stony hillsides, they should be allowed to remain, to feed themselves, keep up soil fertility, stop the flow of landless people to the cities, and produce some crops for sale.

So a new (old) interpretation of the world's agricultural problems seems possible. For persons of good will who are interested in finding the best ways to employ and feed the world's people, there are wonderful opportunities ahead. An agricultural system that has been developed and tested for thousands of years is available. There is no point in continuing to try to replace traditional agriculture with new methods that are already failing. Modern methods work even less well in the tropics than in temperate lands. There is mounting evidence that modern farm methods either cannot solve the problems of insects, disease, soil acidification, erosion, leaching, unemployment, malnourishment, starvation, vanishing micronutrients, and dependence on nonrenewable resources, *or* they *will* not because the solutions are deemed uneconomical. Over the centuries, small-farmer culture and agriculture have come to deal with these problems.

Explaining the tremendous accomplishment of the traditional farmer to modern people is a problem that remains. Traditional farmers can't use part of their income to manipulate the media of television, radio, newspapers, or even schools. Many tractor, fertilizer, and insecticide companies do have the money to advertise and editorialize because they are willing to destroy the earth's resources to make a profit. It will not be easy to make people realize that land needs to be in the hands of those who will preserve it for the indefinite future.

It might be fun to imagine what could be written by people who do come to this realization. The World Bank or any foundation or research establishment could be proud of a press release like the following imaginary example: "A type of spreading cowpea has been developed which will protect the soil from erosion with eight thousand plants per hectare instead of the seventy thousands now recommended. Sorghum varieties have been developed that send up new shoots if neighboring plants fail to sprout. This means that a self-adjusting form of agriculture has been developed in which some plants automatically extend into empty space in the field. This system assures that sunlight, water, and nutrients are used at maximum capacity and that soil is protected from erosion, many nutrients are no longer lost through leaching, and less labor is required. This intercropping system can often double the yields compared to other systems, other things being equal. When applied carefully and thoughtfully, it can produce a balanced diet for all people as long as the planet survives." Surely some ancient Africans should get a symbolic Nobel Prize.

References

Mesanobee Fukuoka, *The Natural Way of Farming: The Theory and Practice of Green Philosophy* (Tokyo: Japan Publications, 1987).

Donald Q. Innis, *Togo Journal*, (Geneseo, N.Y.: Intercropping Associates).

Frances Moore Lappe and Joseph Collins, *World Hunger: Twelve Myths* (San Francisco: Food First/Grove Press, 1986).

Section E

Population and Women's Concerns

Editor's Notes

The human species does not have a unique exemption from the ecological laws that maintain the essential balances of nature. Despite all our technologies, the capacity of the earth to carry the human enterprise cannot be extended indefinitely. It almost certainly has been breached already; the present global population is unsustainable over the long run. The danger from overpopulation is real and demands universal acknowledgment and response.

If I had entitled a section simply "Population," it would have included some of the particular perspectives of women on the issue of human numbers and the extent to which their spectacular increase over the past two centuries constituted an obstacle to an eco-just future. But the concern of women regarding the still huge and persistent growth of the human population can by no means be separated from women's other concerns.

Many women, especially in poor/developing countries, are loathe to admit population as a "problem" until it is put into the context of their basic concern to have a secure livelihood for themselves and their families. And that concern encompasses their appreciation of the necessity to maintain the natural resource base upon which their livelihood depends. It encompasses, also, their desire and demand for enhancement of the respect and the scope accorded to their role as women who shoulder the responsibility of drawing upon nature for sustenance and making it cover, sufficiently and sustainably, the requirements of their families.

In Selection 15, "Forging Common Ground on Population Issues," Carol Holst asserts at the outset the gravity of the population factor in "our species' dilemma." But this poses an issue on which a human consensus, urgently needed, remains extremely difficult to achieve. The 1992 Earth Summit could not rise to the occasion, because of the sharp "North-South" split over where to pin the prime responsibility for environmental degradation—Southern birth rates or Northern overconsumption.

Holst vigorously maintains that the issue of justice belongs at the center of concern about population. She calls for environmental organizations to show as much concern for endangered people as for endangered species. And she asks the movement for equitable distribution to embrace environmental justice. Common ground on population requires insisting on the connections. "We the affluent must take responsibility for the environmental destruction caused by a consumption-oriented way of life before we can realistically focus on the responsibilities of the deprived and oppressed."

In a Fall 1992 article (not included here) Paul R. and Ann H. Ehrlich declare the United States to be "The Most Overpopulated Nation" in terms of its environmental impact. They offer an equation. The total impact (I) is a product of the number of people (P) times the level of per capita consumption, or affluence (A), and the impact of the technology (T) used for each unit of consumption. Thus, I=PxAxT. The Ehrlichs call for a large reduction of U.S. population and for a concerted population policy to achieve this.

Selection 16 consists of excerpts from a number of articles, so that this volume may include these additional "Voices of Women on Environment, Population and Development."

Peggy Antrobus in "Women's Declaration on Environment and Development" expresses the findings of DAWN (Development Alternatives With Women For a New Era), based in Fiji. The central concern of poor women around the world for health and a basic, sustainable livelihood is exacerbated by the macroeconomic policies of governments, including "structural adjustment."

Karen Rindge, speaking from her participation in the people's Global Forum, which took place alongside the official Earth Summit in Rio, reports that none of the speakers at the women's conference acknowledged a direct link between population and environment. Like Holst, Rindge sees the need for a broad concept of the population issue.

Bernadine McRipley took part in the 1994 International Conference on Population and Development in Cairo. "It is not realistic," she writes "to seek to curb female fertility . . . in developing countries, without also making changes in development policies and in the production and consumption practices of privileged classes and nations." Women, traditionally undervalued, must become equal partners with men.

Helen Locklear, a Native American, offers the important reminder that it is not only human well-being that is at stake. All beings are related in one web of life.

Elizabeth Dodson Gray holds that the power to "name" reality is the power to shape it to serve the interests of the namer. For thousands of years the naming has been done by men, in patriarchal culture. Many women, she says, feel that if women had been doing the naming, they would have named a very different relationship between humankind and the natural context.

Over many centuries women have acquired great skills in the management and care of limited natural resources essential to human survival. They have found that cooperation toward this end proves more efficient than competition. These points are stressed by Joan Martin-Brown, another "voice," in "Women and the Environment," a Winter 1992–93 article not reprinted. As women receive recognition, respect, and attention at the center of development that really aims to be sustainable, they will have opportunity for more and better "naming."

The distinctive contributions of women are indispensable to the eco-justice journey. If, however, some succumb to the temptation to assert their right to prove their mettle with men in the brutal game of domination and control, they forsake the role for which the voices raised here are pleading. Naming indeed is power. The corruptions of power are a critical factor in the struggle for eco-justice. Women and men will have to join together in a new naming that respects the integrity of the whole earth community and seriously affirms the solidarity of the human family.

15

Forging Common Ground
on Population Issues

Carol Holst

(*The Egg: An Eco-Justice Quarterly* 12 [4], Fall 1992)

The projected doubling of the world's population in the not-distant future will greatly impede our efforts to preserve the integrity of God's creation. It cannot be overlooked in any thorough analysis of our species' dilemma. Working toward solutions to the global population-environment crisis requires forging an unusual degree of common ground, a process that gained small headway at the June 1992 Earth Summit (United Nations Conference on Environment and Development [UNCED]) in Brazil. Although it was considerably diluted, the final wording in the Rio Declaration does promote the need for "appropriate demographic policies."

I do not think that population ground was actually lost at UNCED, because the conference brought together nearly all the divergent views that need to be reconciled if human beings are to develop a universal, responsible reproductive ethic. The following sections summarize some of the points in major areas of dissension.

Multicultural Issues

The Earth Summit recorded in historic proportion the "North vs. South" character of sustainable development discussions. Since 80

183

percent of global environmental degradation is caused by the over-consumption and technological damage of Northern industrialized nations, Southern developing countries with high population growth rates maintained that they could not accept strong language connecting population and environment. When the North refused to acknowledge that it needed to support economic redistribution and make lifestyle changes, the South blocked specific population language altogether. Clearly, that impasse was precipitated by the inflexibility and shortsightedness of (most particularly) the U.S. administration in failing to recognize a moral obligation to cease the ruinous exploitation of the earth and many of its peoples.

The essential but often missing contribution of justice considerations is evident not only in population discussions, but also in many efforts to deal with environmental concerns. We see this in global dialogues and also in national and local struggles.

From the aftermath of Los Angeles riots to the results of the Earth Summit, it is clear that the gap between privileged and disadvantaged people in the world is one of the greatest obstacles to creating an environmentally sustainable future. If we are to overcome it, environmental organizations need to demonstrate emphatically that they care as much about endangered people as about other endangered species. This means protesting the "institutionalized looting" that characterizes much of modern society and the relations between Northern and Southern countries.

The concern for equitable distribution must entail support for "environmental justice." Impetus and inspiration for environmental justice as a movement [and for its eventual incorporation into Environmental Protection Agency policy] came from the 1987 study issued by the Commission for Racial Justice of the United Church of Christ. This study concludes: "Although socioeconomic status plays an important role in the location of commercial hazardous waste facilities, race is the leading factor."[1] All population-environment organizations lobbying for increased family planning funds need also to lobby enthusiastically for an end to the racist placement of toxic waste dumps, both here and abroad. As long as we tolerate a government of, by and for the privileged, it is unlikely that we shall arrive at sufficient common ground on population issues.

Another important multicultural dimension is the prevalence of elitist language, which must be altered. Whoever originated the terms "First World" and "Third World" did nothing to further the dialogue of planetary survival. To replace the latter Tom Sine uses "Two-Thirds World," a more accurate and dignified description.[2]

Also, I have yet to meet a person of color who prefers being referred to as a "minority." In California we are learning to use the term "emerging majority." The faster we make language shifts, the less likely some people of color will think they need to increase demographically to survive and build a sociopolitical system that treats everyone fairly.

The population community is fortunate that, despite all of the above, the final wording in UNCED's Agenda 21 calls for governments to "implement as a matter of urgency, measures to ensure that women and men, without bias of gender, have the right to decide freely and responsibly on the number and spacing of their children, to have access to the information, education and means, as appropriate, to enable them to exercise this right in keeping with their freedom, dignity, and personally held values." Agenda 21 estimates that funding for this purpose should double from $4.5 billion a year to $9 billion by the year 2000.

Religious Responses to Population Issues

During UNCED a "Summit of Parliamentarians and Spiritual Leaders," which included the Dalai Lama, acknowledged population growth as part of the complex of problems, saying: "It is our unanimous opinion that the problems of poverty, population growth and environmental degradation are inextricably intertwined, and that these problems can only be solved by global action at the international and national levels, guided by principles of equity."

It is undeniable, however, that the Roman Catholic Church continues to raise formidable obstacles to limiting global population growth. Explicit references to birth control were deleted from Earth Summit documents because of pressure from the Vatican, supported by Argentina and Ireland, and by fundamentalist Muslims.

Lewis Regenstein of the Interfaith Council for the Protection of Animals and Nature, affiliated with the Humane Society of the United States, writes that Catholic opposition to modern contraceptive methods "exacerbates the urgent problem of human overpopulation, which is causing environmental degradation, human misery, and massive poverty and starvation . . . around the globe."[3]

Nevertheless, Pope John Paul II stated in 1988 (*Sollicitudo Rei Sociallis*, No. 25), as well as in 1980 (*Familiaris Consortio*, Article 31): "[The Catholic Church] also recognizes the serious problem of population growth in the form it has taken in many parts of the world and its moral implication."[4] Then on November 14,

1991, the National Conference of Catholic Bishops (in the United States) approved a policy statement on the environmental crisis that belatedly refers to population growth as a contributing factor. The bishops urge continued use of the rhythm method to ease population pressures.

As an alternative, the Ministry for Population Concerns is a continent-wide interfaith network supporting voluntary global population stabilization through increased contraceptive availability. Four national faith groups currently participate and have issued study guides and/or resolutions on the subject: Evangelical Lutheran Church in America (Office for Environmental Stewardship, Office for Studies), United Church of Christ Network for Environmental and Economic Responsibility, Unitarian Universalist Association, and Friends Committee on Unity with Nature. In addition, many local congregations of these and other communions in thirty-five states, Guam, and Canada take part in the advocacy network, strengthened by the participation of Clergy and Laity Concerned.[5]

An encouraging new step in the religious response to population growth is the publication of Susan Power Bratton's book, *Six Billion and More: Human Population Regulation and Christian Ethics*. She urges the development of a Christian contraceptive ethic, interpreting Genesis 1:28 as follows:

> Although set in the imperative, "be fruitful and increase" is actually, as the Genesis texts clearly indicate, a blessing, and it is a blessing shared with the animals. . . . While the blessing does impart generative power and fertility, its intent is reproduction in balance, springing joyfully forth to produce the well-being God continues to weave into the entire created universe. . . . Human population growth has no mandate to damage or desecrate the cosmos.[6]

The most outstanding example to date of forging common religious ground on population issues came from the "Mission to Washington" of the Joint Appeal by Religion and Science for the Environment. Involving leaders of the National Council of Churches and its member communions, the World Council of Churches, National Baptist Churches, seminaries and rabbinical associations of all four branches of Jewish life, and the National Conference of Catholic Bishops Committee on Science and Human Values, the Joint Appeal declared on May 12, 1992, that environmental justice includes limiting population growth: "We believe there is a need for concerted efforts to stabilize world population by humane, responsible, and voluntary means consistent with our differing values."

Women's Concerns

When the Vatican prevented clear birth control language from appearing in official UNCED documents, Bella Abzug led a massive protest on behalf of feminists who see access to contraceptives as liberation for women. They were countered, however, by other feminists, especially the Brazilian Women's Coalition, who were "outraged by the suggestion that women's fertility rates (euphemistically called population pressures) are to blame" for environmental degradation.

Central to any meaningful consensus on population will be the unequivocal declaration by the population community that the greatest "blame" for the ecological crisis lies with the selfish and abusive behavior patterns of industrialized countries. We the affluent must take responsibility for the environmental destruction caused by a consumption-oriented way of life before we can realistically focus on the responsibilities of the deprived and oppressed.

Concurrently with the Earth Summit, nongovernmental organizations (NGOs) held a Global Forum, which formulated an NGO Treaty on Population, Environment and Development. The opening sentences declare: "Women's empowerment to control their own lives is the foundation for all action linking population, environment and development. We reject and denounce the concept of control of women's bodies by governments and international institutions. We reject and denounce forced sterilization, the misuse of women as subjects for experimental contraceptives, and the denial of women's free choice. We affirm and support women's health and reproductive rights and their freedom to control their own bodies. We demand the empowerment of women, half of the world's population, to exercise free choice and the right to control their fertility and to plan their families."

It is no accident that forced sterilization and the abuse of women are denounced before women's right to plan their families is affirmed. The sooner we in the rich world adopt and promote the same set of priorities, the sooner voluntary family planning programs grounded in commitment to justice will be accepted globally.

Despite all these considerations there remains a basic difference between the reproductive *rights* movement, concerned with women's and men's freedom to choose their parental roles, and the reproductive *responsibilities* movement, concerned with raising consciousness regarding the universally important small family goal. Perhaps as the environmental crisis continues to deepen and the danger to God's kingdom on earth becomes increasingly evident, these positions will flow together. Both are based, after all, on vastly strengthening women's rights, education, and opportunities around the world.

Notes

1. Robert Bullard et al., *We Speak for Ourselves: Social Justice and Race and Environment* (Washington, D.C.: Panos Institute, 1990).

2. Tom Sine, *Wild Hope* (Dallas, Tex.: Word, 1991).

3. Lewis Regenstein, *Replenish the Earth* (New York: Crossroad, 1991), 127.

4. Sean McDonagh, S.S.C., *The Greening of the Church* (Maryknoll, N.Y.: Orbis Books, 1990), 59.

5. As part of the Center for Religion, Ethics and Social Policy, the Ministry for Population Concerns made the transition in 1996 into Seeds of Simplicity, which is the first national nonprofit membership program for the general public centered on voluntary simplicity. In raising the joys of self-examined living instead of the pursuit of material goods, Seeds of Simplicity's work in our affluent society goes to the depths of the population issue, as this article explains.

6. Susan Power Bratton, *Six Billion and More: Human Population Regulation and Christian Ethics* (Louisville, Ky.: Westminster/John Knox, 1992), 43.

16

Voices of Women on Environment, Population, and Development: Excerpts from Several Issues of the Journal

1. From

Women and Naming

Elizabeth Dodson Gray

(The Egg: An Eco-Justice Quarterly 13 [1], Winter 1992–93)

For thousands of years of recorded time men have "named" and shaped the culture from their point of view—from the standing point of the male body and male life experience, just as Adam named the animals in Genesis. Naming is power. To name reality is to shape it into a form which serves the interests of the namer.

So both women and nature have lived *within* the myths, symbols and categories of thought in what I have called "Adam's world." Sometimes that male naming has said, "Women are closer to nature, while men are *above* nature in a transcendence based in religion or rationality or science." Such "naming" has justified male control of both women and nature.

Today we are living in a turning point of human history. The power to name is being claimed by the ancient silent partner in the human species—the woman.

Slowly, as if awakening from a long sleep, women are shaking the film of male concepts from our eyes and looking into life as if seeing it "for the first bright time."

Today as our ecological disasters accumulate and male-controlled cultures seem intent upon continuing high-risk ecological brinkmanship, many are trying to understand "What went wrong." Women wonder if these social diagnoses will name every "-ism" in our mental closet from socialism to industrialism to capitalism to consumerism—and never mention the "-ism" of male privilege and the pervasive ranking of diversity—in society, in science, in religion—known as patriarchy.

Many women feel sure that if we had been doing the naming, we would have named a very different relationship between humankind and our natural context, our web of life, our "home." And with that different naming, we know we would have shaped a very different patterning of human activities upon this planet earth.

Women still find unfamiliar the role of being the namer. But more and more we are compelled by events to find within ourselves this power of naming, to call it forth within us, to take our individual feelings and shape them into words, words never uttered before but words that we know come out of the reality of women's lives.

As we awaken to our precarious ecological situation, women around the world become eco-justice activists, especially as the risking of the planet's ecosystems impinges on our own ability to maintain our lives and feed our children. From Love Canal to the Chipco movement women are mobilizing.

2. From

Women's Declaration on the Environment and Development

Grassroots Women's Perspectives

Peggy Antrobus

(The Egg: An Eco-Justice Quarterly 13 [1], Winter 1992–93)

Issues of health and livelihoods were central concerns [at an Inter-regional Workshop conducted by Development Alternatives With

Women For a New Era (DAWN) in 1991]. But a consideration of the health and livelihoods of poor women takes us immediately to the macroeconomic policies of their governments. Since the 1980s these policies—a package of measures entitled Structural Adjustment—have been influenced by multilateral institutions like the International Monetary Fund and the World Bank. Formulated in the context of the debt crisis of the 1980s, they are designed to cut domestic consumption and to increase exports, so that international debts incurred in the 1960s can be repaid. In the process they have exerted increased pressure on the poor—especially on poor women—and the natural resource base, as governments have intensified the exploitation of the country's natural resources.

The experiences of poor women reflect the common pressures on basic survival resulting from inequitable social, political and economic systems. Their views of environmental degradation are shaped by their conditions of life. The case studies which informed our analysis illustrate the diversity of their specific concerns. Thus in Africa women identified food security and desertification as pressing problems. Asian women saw increasing poverty, deforestation, loss of biodiversity, and natural disasters as central to their crisis. Pacific women saw nuclear testing as the primary threat to their environment. For Latin Americans, increasing poverty, the absence of clean air, safe water, and sanitation, and the imbalance of land settlements were central to the concerns of poor urban women. Caribbean women experienced growing poverty, negative environmental impacts of tourism, natural disasters, and the overuse of pesticides and fertilizers.

However, the common thread which links all these wide-ranging environmental problems is the search for sustainable livelihoods. Women across the world have recognized the failure of global and national policies to address that need. An analysis of these policies shows that they not only undermine livelihoods but also create and exacerbate environmental hazards and degradation. In short, the major causes of environmental degradation are the same ones that cause the degradation of human and social environments.

A widely held myth is that population growth is responsible for environmental degradation. But local experience is that the areas of low or falling populations and decreasing fertility rates are where you find extreme and growing environmental degradation. The fact is that extremes of wealth and poverty and patterns of human settlement have a stronger demonstrable relationship to environmental degradation than the population size per se. Women's fertility rates decline when women's basic rights are respected, their livelihoods are respected, and they have access to adequate reproductive health care.

3. From

Population and Women

Karen Rindge

(*The Egg: An Eco-Justice Quarterly* 12 [4], Fall 1992)

In contrast to the strong statements of concern about population given at *Rio Centro* [where the official proceedings of the United Nations Conference on Environment and Development were going on], the voice coming from many NGOs [nongovernmental organizations] at the Global Forum had a different tone. Speeches made at the Planeta Femea—the women's conference—spoke harshly about the "population control" movement and insisted on a new direction for addressing population, one which does not focus on demographics, per se, as a problem.

None of the women speaking on population at Planeta Femea acknowledged a direct link between population and the environment, and they completely rejected the notion that population growth is the main problem affecting environment. Their emphasis was on the need to address the basic needs of people in poverty, and the paramount importance of putting women at the center of all development and reproductive health programs.

We need to maintain a dialogue on population, both within the U.S. and with women of the South. Politically, we cannot afford to be divided from the international women's movement on this critical issue.

While varied views on population exist, there is much common ground. We must be open to a broader concept of the issue and how to resolve it. Some women expressed to me personally the need to come to terms with the population problem, but they had very real fears about manifesting too much emphasis on it. Women believe that family planning should not be a means to an end—that is, an end often seen as oppression of the poor. They view women's health as an end in and of itself.

Women recognize that birth rates decline when women's social, economic, and health status improves and general living standards rise. Thus, all these areas must be addressed—along with family planning.

I was impressed with how comprehensively Southern NGOs look at global issues, and I think we can learn from them. This means considering additional actions we can take to improve, and increase funding for, maternal and child health, women-centered development projects, literacy, contraceptive research, and so on. We also need to consider additional measures for increasing public education on consumption patterns at home.

4. From

Linking Population and Development at Cairo

Bernadine Grant McRipley

(*Eco-Justice Quarterly,* 15 [1], Winter 1994–95)

Women of color were very evident in the official and unofficial circles in Cairo [at the United Nations International Conference on Population and Development (ICPD)]. Although the media played up the controversy over abortion created by male religious leaders from the Vatican and fundamentalist Muslims, this did not reflect the main concern of women of color. Leaders from delegations from developing nations were very explicit in stating, "Abortion is not our issue," but wanted the conference to address issues of development. Women of color were justice activists leading up to and during the ICPD and are continuing advocacy after Cairo.

By linking the concepts of population and development, the Cairo conference affirmed that it is not realistic to seek to curb female fertility or limit population growth in developing countries, without also making changes in development policies and in the production and consumption practices of privileged classes and nations. The ICPD produced a blueprint for a twenty-year global effort on population and development. The Program of Action adopted by consensus outlines principles for national population programs that support sustainable development.

A real concern about the Cairo conference, as with any UN conference, is moving from talk to action. A major theme that emerged out of the ICPD is for the empowerment of women. Although the issue could not be denied nor attention distracted from it, there is still concern that the agreed upon objectives will not be adequately funded.

Some advocates for improving the status of women fear that some developing countries may refuse to divert money from military to social expenditures. There is also concern that sustainable development will be equated with economic development and growth. In certain countries, the impact of economic development has worsened the status of women and increased their workloads without producing a corresponding increase in rewards.

Dr. Nafis Sadik, general secretary of the ICPD, spoke to this point: "There can be no sustainable development without the full involvement of women as equal partners. In many if not most societies, women are still considered less valuable than men. And despite their significant roles in the home, in the workplace and in the community, the social and economic contributions of women are often overlooked and undervalued."

Dr. Sadik continued, "Investing in women means widening their choice of strategies and reducing their dependence on children for status and support. . . . That means granting them access to land, to credit, to rewarding employment, establishing their effective personal and political rights—as well as access to reproductive health care and family planning information and services."

5. From

The Values Debate: A Native American View

Helen Locklear

(Eco-Justice Quarterly, 15 [1], Winter 1994–95;

written originally for the *Stewardship of Public Life* Program, Presbyterian Church [U.S.A.])

If the earth seems inhospitable toward humanity, it is primarily because we have lost our sense of the sacred character and delicate balance of the biological system. We have not protected the earth. We have dammed the rivers, and cut down the trees. The land, air and water are so toxic that the very conditions of life are being destroyed. Many forms of plant and animal life are extinct.

The crisis that threatens the destruction of the earth is more than social, political, economic or technological; it is at root spiritual. We have lost the sense that this earth is our true home and we fail to recognize our profound connection with all beings in the web of life.

Native Americans say "all my relatives," acknowledging their connection to everything that is alive—fire, water, wind, the earth and all the creatures that exist on and in the earth. They understand the delicate balance of the system; there is no separation between individuals, community and the land, between plant and animal life. All are viewed as relatives, with a place in the ordered universe: the earth and all its inhabitants are viewed as one.

The earth and sky, the animals and plants, the ground and all living things make up the whole. Yet we poison the rivers and seas and the ground on which we stand, so that we can have television and air conditioning. We engage in wars of conquest and exploit other people's labor in order to take the resources of their land. We forget that we are all connected in the web of life.

Section F

Economics, Good Work, and Sustainable Development

Editor's Notes

The subject matter of economics is simply the arrangements that a human society makes to meet its needs and wants. Material goods come necessarily from nature. Basically, an economy consists of the practices, regulations, and institutions for drawing sustenance from nature. These arrangements, of course, employ technologies. They entail cooperation always, competition sometimes. In any case, the structures and rules of the economy, which human actors have fashioned and can change, operate under the laws and systems of nature, which human actors can employ and perhaps enhance, which they can violate and disrupt, but which they cannot defy with impunity or repeal. Thus, economics is a subset of ecology. One of the tragedies of the modern world is that most economists do not know this. As social scientists, they have less excuse than the executives of corporations, whose commitment to the economy of endless growth is unqualified. But most justice advocates, labor unions, socialists, and "progressives" also fail to come to terms with the limits imposed by nature.

In Selection 17, "Sanctioning Resource Depletion," Charles A. S. Hall presents a severe critique of neoclassical—that is to say, mainstream—economics. Hall wrote this article in early 1990, originally for The Ecologist, *and supplies ample notes to back up his argument. At that time, as he says, the centrally planned economies of the Soviet Union and Eastern Europe were in ruins.*

Hall could still speak of two worlds, communist and noncommunist or capitalist. But he points at the outset to the assumption, already widespread, that "free market" economics provides the only viable path for any country to pursue. The communist countries, notably China and Russia, which had followed a centrally planned alternative to capitalism, were fast privatizing and pressing hard to learn and follow the neoclassical model.

One need not be expert in neoclassical theory to know that Hall's critique applies generally to market economies, privatized or fast privatizing, intent on attracting investment capital, oriented to growth and trade and a larger piece of the expanding global market, with the least possible government regulation or restriction.

Hall discusses five fundamental flaws in mainstream economic theory as a tool in economic decision making. The central criticism is the one indicated in the article's title: economic growth and development require and approve the depletion of finite, nonrenewable resources. Metal and mineral resources have remained cheap only because cheap fossil fuels make it possible to mine and refine low-grade ores. But fossil fuels too are finite and nonrenewable. Even if there were no greenhouse effect to take account of, to continue in the path of extreme fossil-fuel dependence in the industrialized world, with the rest of the world straining to go the same way, would be folly. Moreover, as developing countries take this route, the quality of the renewable resource base is degraded, so that when fossil fuel subsidies can no longer be applied, conditions will be worse than before they were introduced. Meanwhile, still larger numbers of people make ever greater demands, especially for food.

Hall prescribes as "most important" the reduction (and reversal?) of population growth for most of the world, and reduced reliance on depletable, polluting resources for the developed world. But such considerations do not enter into routine market decisions. When prices catch up with impending scarcities, Hall says, no economic adjustments will restore the depleted resource base.

After the trade expansion, far-flung industrialization, global integration, and capitalist triumphalism of the 1990s, while the global population passed the 6 billion mark, it should be clear that both of Hall's most important goals apply to both sectors of the world.

Selection 18 is a portion of an article by James Robertson on "A New Economics for the 21ˢᵗ Century." Robertson combines a citing of the outmoded and injurious tendencies of economics today—which keep it from being enabling for people and conserving for the earth—with a citing of the goals of a new economics.

One of the prominent features Robertson envisions is "self-reliant local communities." This decentralization will still belong to a "one-world economy." In his book, Future Wealth: A New Economics for the 21ˢᵗ Century *(Bootstrap Press, 1990), Robertson speaks of the world economy as a "multi-level system," with "autonomous but inter-dependent sub-economies." He says that "we must define the principal function of each larger, higher level unit as being to enable its component sub-economies to be more self-reliant and more conserving." (p. 17)*

Robertson sees the emergence of a worldwide community in search of eco-justice—organizations, movements, and groups seeking an order that will reflect the new needs and realities of the twenty-first century, which differ radically from those which capitalism assumes.

The Eco-Justice Project and Network identified and listed "good work" as a distinctive eco-justice issue, so important that we did not take for granted that it would get proper attention under "economics," even though a good economy has to be one in which all may participate as able an gifted in good work. Influenced by E. F. Schumacher, we meant work that meets a social need, provides a livelihood and fulfillment to the worker, fosters community, and enhances, or at least does not diminish, the quality of the environment.

In Selection 19, "Good Work, the Big Chill and the Sadness of Dinks," Ingrid Olsen-Tjensvold recalls the best dreams of the turbulent sixties, dreams chilled in the decades that followed. But "when a dream fails, we must dream it again, or dream another." She offers her "green dream" of the "perfect law office." It is a beautiful dream. It may make you weep.

In Selection 20, "The Development Debate: Coalition for a New Alternative?" J. Ronald Engel traces the intense global preoccupation with economic development and growth, in the second half of the twentieth century, to President Harry Truman's Inaugural Address in 1948. His famous "Point Four" proposed to make U.S. scientific and industrial progress "available for the improvement and growth of [the world's] underdeveloped areas." Truman gave impetus to a priority focus on economic development that made it descriptive and evaluative of the entire social process. Thereby, says Engel, "the all-encompassing purpose of the state was economic growth."

Engel traces the failures of the development fixation. Its negative consequences for economic liberation, for environmental protection, and for cultural and religious authenticity have mobilized three major global constituencies to expose these consequences and seek a concept of the social process that will be more liberating, more sustainable, more meaningful. He finds "promise for the future" in the molding of these heretofore disparate and sometimes antagonistic constituencies into "one united counterdevelopment movement in pursuit of a new paradigm to replace the Truman creed: a new paradigm that is authentically democratic, ecological, and spiritual."

Does a widespread growing consciousness of the absurdity and the peril—a consciousness to which our authors in this section point and contribute—provide the key to making the economy participatory, just, and sustainable? Certainly a keener perception and understanding are indispensable. Many of the elements of the new paradigm, suggested in the following articles, seem quite clear. But the will and the capacity of the people who are now aware, with their leaders, organizations, and movements, remain insufficient to press the world decisively toward eco-justice. Corporations and governments and international agencies for trade and finance remain far more focused on growth than on sustainability. The discussion of "sustainable development" has waned. To be sure, sustainable development, to meet real needs sustainably, happens in many local situations, but remains vulnerable to the industrial juggernaut. The movements have not gathered the hoped-for momentum. The U.S. economy has been too successful in conventional terms to generate receptivity to the penetrating critique that must be heard and absorbed. The movements, in which we do place hope, must struggle to find a more effective strategy. It has to address the power realities that stand in the way of a new paradigm, a new economics, an effective democracy, and the cooperative mechanisms to achieve a sustainable sufficiency for all.

17

Sanctioning Resource Depletion: Economic Development and Neoclassical Economics

Charles A. S. Hall

(*The Egg: An Eco-Justice Quarterly* 11 [1], Spring 1991;

reprinted by permission from *The Ecologist*
[www.theecologist.org], 20 [3], May/June 1990)

With centrally planned economies in ruins, it is assumed that "free market" economics provides the only viable path for economies to follow. However, the neoclassical economic model followed in the noncommunist world is based on many untested assumptions and fails to take adequate account of natural resource use and environmental costs. Neoclassical economics "works" only because it assumes the availability of massive quantities of nonrenewable fossil fuels. Development, by making societies more and more dependent on polluting, finite resources, is a two-edged sword that destroys economic systems that once supported people without making them overdependent on nonrenewable resources.

It is widely believed that the problem of feeding the world's growing population has been solved. Contemporary economics, and its handmaiden technology, are thought to have been applied successfully to development (especially that of agriculture) in both the western and the developing world. Although large pockets of extreme poverty, malnutrition and starvation still exist, the average person, it is argued, is better fed than two or three decades ago, despite a doubling of the human population. This trend is generally attributed to some basic economic-political concept or ideology, variously called "free enterprise," "centralized planning" or whatever, depending on one's political or economic leanings. Where there are failures, and there are many, the opposing ideology tends to get the blame.

Unfortunately this view is incomplete, misleading and a recipe for the ultimate failure of development. The words "development" and "economically successful" do not describe accurately the processes that have taken place. In virtually all cases, these terms should be replaced by "exploitation of resources" and "industrialization." Although wealth may appear to be produced through economic growth, wealth production occurs generally only through the increasing exploitation of natural resources, normally in an increasingly nonrenewable manner, and almost entirely through the increasing use of fossil fuels. Cheap oil and its derivatives continue to be used to alleviate the principal impacts of depletion and environmental degradation and mismanagement, giving too often the appearance of solutions, whereas in reality solutions are only being deferred.

In short, existing economies—whether centrally planned or free market—"work" only because we extract oil, coal and other resources out of the ground to make them work.[1] Meanwhile, populations grow relentlessly, oil reserves are drained, and our air and water are increasingly fouled, destroying those remaining nonpetroleum-intensive economic systems.

These problems are not taken into account in most economic analyses, because contemporary neoclassical economics fails to assess the total social costs and benefits of most projects. Nevertheless, neoclassical economic assumptions are used routinely in economic decision making as if there were no alternatives, and their use sanctions many projects unworthy by most other criteria.

Economics as Ideology

A natural scientist tends to view knowledge, especially models of that knowledge, as tentative, even ephemeral, as ideas that are examined, tested and subjected to rigorous assessment. Natural scientists tend to be suspicious of established knowledge because they have watched some of their most trusted principles crumble.

Economists, however, cannot easily apply the empirical criteria used in science. As the economist Milton Friedman has stated: ". . . a theory cannot be tested by comparing its 'assumptions' directly with 'reality.' "[2] In general, very few economic papers test hypotheses. This led Leontief to ask: "How long will researchers working in adjoining fields . . . abstain from expressing serious concern about the splendid isolation in which academic economics now finds itself?"[3] This attitude often confuses natural scientists, who expect theoretical models to be tested before being applied or developed further. But major decisions that affect millions of people are often based on economic models that, although elegant and widely accepted, are not validated.[4]

My criticisms are both fair and unfair: fair because they do apply to most contemporary neoclassical economics *as taught and practiced*, unfair because some economists (for example, Samuelson, Mishan, Hotteling, and Daly) have made extremely thoughtful contributions to a consideration of these problems, and because many social scientists use extremely rigorous procedures in difficult terrain. But the influence of such thought on routine economic analysis seems very small and is still inadequate.

An additional problem for many natural scientists is that economics pays almost no attention to the physical characteristics of economic systems.[5] Economists have no laws of thermodynamics to constrain economic activity. In the anthropocentric view of Barnett and Morse, authors of the 1963 *Scarcity and Growth: The Economics of Natural Resources Availability*, which presents the archetypal neoclassic economist's position on resources, it is incorrect even to consider the physical characteristics of resources if one is interested in future resource availability.[6] In their view, resources are supplied not by nature but by human ingenuity, and the only interesting index of scarcity is the *price* per unit resource. Barnett and Morse tested for the effects of scarcity by examining inflation-corrected prices for resources over the period 1870–1957. They found that, except for forest products, there was no clear pattern of price increases, and hence, in their view, no increasing scarcity of resources.

Most neoclassical economists have accepted this assessment and therefore totally neglect resources in their analysis. In 1974, Solow suggested that "the world can in effect, get along without natural resources," but more recent assessments, some by economists, show that natural resources have become scarcer even by Barnett and Morse's criteria.[7,8]

Some Critiques of Economics as a Discipline

It has been said that, "the purpose of studying economics is not to acquire a set of ready made answers to economic questions, but to learn how to avoid being deceived by economists."[9] The intellectual basis of economics as a discipline (more specifically the neoclassical model that dominates the economic analysis in the noncommunist world) is fundamentally flawed, and it is therefore unsuitable to use it to guide development in either the developing or developed world.

As Marxism, the only important viable intellectual alternative to the neoclassical model, has faded in appeal, the neoclassical model is often accepted as an appropriate model to follow by default. Recent events in eastern Europe have been interpreted as showing that the neoclassical, western approach to economics "works," but this success appears to be principally because this economic system helps nations to run through their resource stocks faster.

In West Germany, it may be noted, capitalism was aided enormously by the fact that the high-grade black coal there has twice the energy content of the brown coal underlying the communist block countries. Serious environmental pollution in the east results from the use of this highly polluting soft brown coal in a region with ten times the population density of North America.

A Flawed Paradigm

There are at least five fundamental flaws underlying the use of contemporary economics as the principal tool for making economic decisions.[10]

1. *Economics normally uses the gross national product as a proxy for human wellbeing*: Projects tend to be evaluated only on their projected contribution to a country's gross national product (GNP). But, as has been well documented, GNP is only a partial measure of those conditions that contribute to human happiness and wellbeing, the supposed goal of economic activity. GNP says nothing about the distribution of wealth, and it is an inaccurate measure of production, especially in areas where development is being introduced.[11] GNP does not measure nonmarket transactions, and therefore undervalues both environmental services and nonmarket sources of materials such as food. There is no provision made within the use of GNP for

including the economic benefits of properly functioning ecosystems, or their degradation, because such processes do not normally interact with markets.[12]

GNP does not measure the actual wealth citizens enjoy, but rather the flow of new wealth into the economy. Thus, GNP rises if people buy replacement goods more frequently because the original goods are poorly made, even though that process produces more pollution today and decreases the resource base available for the future. Development policies whose principal goal is to increase GNP, as opposed to meeting basic human needs, can encourage developing countries and their entrepreneurs to liquidate stocks, such as forests, as rapidly as possible to increase the flow of money through the economy.[13] When rivers flood and rains fail as a result of the removal of the forest, there is no system to account for the losses to GNP. In fact, GNP actually increases as villages destroyed by floods are rebuilt.

2. *Economic models have not been validated*: The most fundamental assumptions of neoclassical economics are virtually untested. In most economic text books, there is a complete lack of any hypothesis-forming and data-testing.

   Most noneconomists do not appreciate the degree to which contemporary economics depends upon arbitrary assumptions. Nominally objective operations, such as determining the least cost for a project, evaluating costs and benefits, or calculating the total cost of a project, normally use explicit and supposedly objective economic criteria. In theory, all economists might come up with the same conclusions to a given problem. In fact, such "objective" analyses, based on arbitrary and convenient assumptions, produce logically and mathematically coherent, but not necessarily correct, models. As one example, both classical and neoclassical theories were originally developed using concepts of markets as they existed in agrarian societies. These theories have been transferred more or less unchanged to applications in the modern industrial world. No changes have been made to the basic theory to take account of industrialization, the consequences of the development of the power of money itself, the development of large corporations and institutions or the development of advertising, each of which characterizes contemporary society and the "markets" where we buy and sell.

3. *Economic analysis leads to the destruction of nature and of the basis for real wealth*: Neoclassical economics argues implicitly for the destruction of the natural (as opposed to the developed) world, and as such assists in the destruction of many existing nonmarket economies, since the services of ecosystems (such as controlling hydrological cycles or moderating climates) are rarely reflected in market prices. Thus, neoclassical economics destroys real economic wealth while encouraging the generation of other, often less important, forms of wealth that happen to enter markets.

In the developing nations, investment policies based on neoclassical economic analyses encourage borrowing from developed countries and hence growing indebtedness. Pressure to serve the debt encourages the mining of natural resources to get a quick return on the investment so that the lending banks get their cash return, a process which is not taken account of in the original analyses. In the rare cases where natural resources are utilized, their value is heavily discounted. In one particularly good analysis, Repetto showed that many tropical countries sell their trees at a price far below their worth to either the buyer or, especially, the seller.[14] Canada does much the same, as does the U.S. in the Tongass and Flathead National Forests.[15]

Discounting the value of resources means that a gain of a thousand dollars today could weigh more heavily than tens of thousands of dollars gained slowly over a long period of time. Since many of the direct benefits of natural ecosystems are gained at low rates (as measured in dollars) but over very long, even indefinite time scales, their value tends to be heavily discounted. For example, natural areas which yielded limited financial gains in conventional terms, but did not require fossil fuel-derived inputs (in contrast to virtually all modern developments), are developed on the basis of an expected stream of economic revenues from that development. Hence the monetary benefits from filling in and developing a marsh, which might otherwise have continued to serve as a regional flood or hurricane buffer or a nursery for fish, might be expected to be much greater than both the initial and the continuing costs of development. But should the cost of the fuel or other inputs required to make the development work rise dramatically in the future, as it will, it might be found that the monetary value of the costs exceeds the gain.

Thus the practice of discounting leads to the destruction of natural systems. When the petroleum subsidies are gone or become too expensive, however, the benefits of development will be gone, and the natural systems may no longer provide their original solar-powered services. This has already happened in southern Louisiana where the economic boom brought by petroleum production has been replaced by economic depression in an area that now has neither petroleum nor the original natural environment that once supported local livelihoods.

Society cannot afford to discount the future. If forests are destroyed, the rainfall, and hence agricultural production, of a region may be diminished. This may be only a small amount for any given year, but the effect over many years would be large. If discounting is used in economic analysis, the value of the agricultural loss would appear negligible. Much of the Levant was forested and farmed in biblical times, but is now desert, probably due largely to human activities. The money gained from that original deforestation was almost certainly trivial, even if invested, compared to the loss of a thousand or more years' agricultural production.

4. *The market is the wrong yardstick for large scale analysis or decision making:* Neoclassical economics leaves the economic decision making of entire nations to the day-to-day commercial tastes of individual consumers. It is assumed that consumers will budget monetary resources in a way that is "best" for them. Consumers are assumed to be "rational"—meaning selfish and entirely materialistic. Since neoclassical economics is based on the assumption that people's wants and needs are best expressed by their behavior (purchases) in the marketplace, then no further discussion of the future investments made for a nation is needed. Those decisions will be determined only by entrepreneurs providing for anticipated routine consumer purchases. Those items that are not explicitly available in the market place, such as public health, clean air, or justice

before the law, will not be provided.[16] Thus neoclassical economics destroys the necessary discussion of economic means and ends, and replaces it with socially sterile and simplistic objectives based essentially on short-sighted and often manipulated human greed.[17]

5. *Price does not always reflect scarcity*: Price, the economist's usual measure of scarcity, reflects very poorly many important aspects of scarcity. Many scientists, especially environmental scientists but some economists as well, have argued vehemently against the perspective of Barnett and Morse that inflation-corrected price changes are the only relevant measure of scarcity. The original analysis of Barnett and Morse (which found no indication of increasing scarcity of raw materials as reflected by their price) was incomplete because the decreasing price of energy, and its increasing use, masked the consequences of resource depletion.[18]

For many resources large increases in energy use have been required to supply society with cheap raw materials as these materials were depleted and/or mismanaged.[19] Since energy was not scarce in the United States during the period analyzed by Barnett and Morse, and since cheap energy has allowed ever lower grade domestic reserves as well as foreign resources to be increasingly exploited, there is no reason for prices to increase even though the highest grades of virtually all major U.S. resources have become exhausted. Should energy become scarce in the future, as it did for a period in the 1970s, then probably all resources would become scarce by Barnett and Morse's criteria, as indeed occurred in the immediate aftermath of the oil crisis.[20] When international prices of energy declined again, so did the prices of raw materials.

It is possible that new technologies will be developed that will compensate for the lower availability of conventional fuels in the future. *That is an article of faith and the essence of the neoclassical economist's lack of concern about resources.* The evidence for technology overcoming any scarcity in the past without increased fuel use is ambiguous at best.[21] Thus, in a sense, the fundamental argument is philosophical, at least until such time as the world faces a major petroleum shortage again.

Despite these and other major problems with the essentials of contemporary economics, the basic concepts of the neoclassical approach have been recently adopted in principle by the International Monetary Fund (IMF) and the United States Agency for International Development (USAID) and are routinely used by other development agencies and government institutions around the world.

The Need to Refute Bogus Economics

It is not only ecologists who have serious reservations about economics as a discipline. The economist F. E. Banks has stated that:

> The difference between science and economics is that science aims at an understanding of the behaviour of nature, while economics is involved with an understanding of the behaviour of models— and many of these models have no relation to any state of nature that has ever existed on this planet, or any that is likely between now and doomsday. The word that comes to my mind when confronted by these fantasies is fraud. . . ."[22]

Banks concludes by suggesting that the most important thing that researchers in economics can do is not to continue in the same old way but to refute that previous work which is bogus.

Leontief, another economist, has noted that many economic models are unable "to advance, in any perceptible way, a systematic understanding of the structure and the operations of a real economic system."[23] Instead, they are based on "sets of more or less plausible but entirely arbitrary assumptions" leading to "precisely stated but irrelevant theoretical conclusions."[24]

The Example of Agricultural Development

Most increases in agricultural yields which have occurred around the world in the post-war years are attributable to the industrialization of farming.[25] When the fossil-fuel-derived inputs of fertilizers, pesticides and modern machinery, which make the dramatic increases in *yields possible, are removed, yields tend to fall to levels below their original value because the quality of the agricultural land has declined.* Although the intrinsic quality of most of our major agricultural soils has declined substantially, this is not reflected in yields because of increasing inputs.[26] For example, the

United States and Canada are losing considerable quantities of topsoil but crop yields are increasing because more fertilizers, and crop varieties bred to use the fertilizers, are used. Thus conventional economics may show an increase in the value of agricultural production while the resource base for agriculture is undergoing serious degradation that is not reflected in the market.

New Economic Goals

The world's human population, and thus its requirement for food, has been doubling every thirty years. The conventional "solution" to the problem of how to feed this increasing population *is not technology per se but rather the industrialization of agriculture.* Can this be sustained? Whether or not the world "runs out" of oil in thirty or more years is probably far less important than the fact that within a decade or two most of the oil left to be exploited will be in about four countries, which will be able to dictate the price.

If, and eventually when, energy resources are withdrawn, we will be faced with even lower yields on remaining farmlands and the destruction of economies that cannot function without fuel. Our present day economic paradigm will have failed catastrophically.

Of course, any form of development, no matter how well thought out, will eventually run up against the roadblock of increased population growth if present patterns continue. If people and their material requirements exceed the resources that a region can provide from the basic renewable biotic systems without supplementary fossil fuels or other external subsidies, the region simply cannot support these people. When this occurs, no economic analysis can produce solutions that will work, and both natural environments and human conditions will deteriorate. This is already occurring throughout the Third World.

It seems impossible not to conclude that, over the longer term, the most important economic goal of most of the world's nations should be to decrease the human population growth rate, so that each nation can retain the option of maintaining its own agricultural production without an increasing reliance on uncertain industrial resources. Likewise, it should be agreed that the most important economic goal for *developed* nations is to decrease their reliance on depletable and polluting nonrenewable resources. Unfortunately these considerations, like others discussed earlier, do not enter into market decisions for routine economic purchases. If fuel and its derivatives become too expensive, then no market economic system can readjust the depleted resource base to the increased human population. This is the most important economic question facing humanity; and it is exacerbated rather than resolved by contemporary neoclassical economics.

Notes

1. C. A. S. Hall, C. J. Cleveland, and R. K. Kaufmann, *Energy and Resource Quality: The Ecology of the Economic Process* (New York: Wiley-Interscience, 1986).

2. M. Friedman, *Essays in Positive Economics* (Chicago: University of Chicago Press, 1953), 41.

3. W. Leontief, "Academic Economics," *Science* 217 (1982), 104.

4. See R. U. Ayres and I. Nair, "Thermodynamics and Economics," *Physics Today*, November 1984, 62–71.

5. For example, see ibid.; C. Cleveland, R. Costanza, C. Hall, and R. Kaufmann, "Energy and the United States Economy: A Biophysical Perspective," *Science* 225 (1984), 890–97.

6. H. J. Barnet and C. Morse, *Scarcity and Growth: The Economics of Natural Resources Availability* (Baltimore, Md.: Johns Hopkins University Press, 1963); see also V. K. Smith, ed., *Scarcity and Growth Reconsidered* (Baltimore, Md.: Johns Hopkins University Press, 1979); A. Fisher, *Resources and Environmental Economics* (Cambridge, UK: Cambridge University Press, 1981).

7. R. M. Solow, "The Economics of Resources or the Resources of Economics," *American Economics Review* 64 (1974), 1–14.

8. M. E. Slade, "Trends in Natural Resource Commodity Prices: An Analysis of the Time Domain," *Journal of Environmental Economics and Management* 9 (1982), 122–37; Cleveland, et al, "Energy," supra 5; D. C. Hall and J. V. Hall, "Concepts and Measures of Natural Resource Scarcity with a Summary of Recent Trends," *Journal of Environmental Economics and Management* 11 (1984), 303–79.

9. Robinson, quoted in J. K. Galbraith, *Economics and the Public Purpose* (New York: Houghton-Miflin, 1973).

10. Based in part on N. S. Makgetla and R. B. Seidman, "The Applicability of Law and Economics to Policy Making in the Third World," *Journal of Economic Issues* 23 (1989), 35–78.

11. See A. A. Schnid, *Property, Power and Public Choice: An Inquiry into Law and Economics*, 2ᵈ Edition (New York: Praeger Publishers, 1987).

12. For the example of the public service functions see C.A.S. Hall, "The Biosphere, the Industrio-Sphere and Their Interactions," *Bulletin of Atomic Scientists* 31 (1975), 11–21; and Hall et al., "Energy and Resource," supra 1.

13. R. Repetto, *The Forest for the Trees? Government Policies and the Misuse of Forest Resources* (Washington, D.C.: World Resources Institute, 1988).

14. Ibid.

15. Canadian Broadcasting Corporation, *Cut and Run: The Assault on Canada's Forests,* CBC Transcripts, Box 440, Station A, Montreal, 1985.

16. M. Dohan, "Economic Values and Natural Ecosystems," in C. Hall and J. Day, eds., *Ecosystem Modeling in Theory and Practice* (New York: Wiley-Interscience, 1977), 134–71.

17. H. E. Daly, " Energy, Growth and the Political Economy of Scarcity," in V. K. Smith, ed., *Scarcity and Growth Reconsidered* (Baltimore, Md.: Johns Hopkins University Press, 1979), 67–94.

18. Hall et al., "Energy and Resource," supra 1.

19. Ibid.

20. Cleveland et al., "Energy," supra 5, figure 7.

21. See, ibid., 5; Hall et al., "Energy and Resource," supra 1.

22. F. E. Banks, "Truth and Economics," *International Association of Energy Economics Newsletter* 1 (1988), 9.

23. Leontief, "Academic Economics," supra 3, 104.

24. Ibid.

25. For example, L. Brown, "World Population Growth, Soil Erosion and Food Security," *Science* 214 (1981), 955–1002; Hall et al., "Energy and Resource," supra 1; E. P. Odum, "Input Management of Production Systems," *Science* 243 (1989), 177–82.

26. See "World Agriculture and Soil Erosion," *Bio-Science* 37 (1987), 277–83.

18

A New Economics for the Twenty-First Century

James Robertson

(*The Egg: A Journal of Eco-Justice* 9 [1], Spring 1989)

> *"I believe myself to be writing a book on economic theory which will largely revolutionize—not, I suppose, at once but in the course of the next ten years—the way the world thinks about economic problems."* —John Maynard Keynes

In his letter to George Bernard Shaw, written in 1935, a year before he published *The General Theory of Employment, Interest and Money*, John Maynard Keynes overestimated the long-term effect that his book would have. As the end of the century comes nearer, it grows more and more obvious that the need to revolutionize the way the world thinks about economics still exists, and indeed is greater than ever.

A crucial task for the 1990s will be to work toward a new economics, centered on creating well-being for people and the earth. The word "wealth" should recover its original meaning of well-being. Economy and ecology, now at odds with one another, should be brought into harmony as the management and the science of our earthly home—as the derivation of the words suggests.

213

We Are Now on the Road to Catastrophe

Our present way of economic life is leading the world to catastrophe. The 1980s have increased the amount of human poverty and misery in the world, and ecological disaster now threatens. Today's rates of tropical deforestation, the spread of acid rain and other forms of air and water pollution, soil erosion and the advance of deserts, climatic change from the greenhouse effect, depletion of the ozone layer, and mass extinction of species, are all causing growing alarm. By the early twenty-first century, if present trends continue, one-third of the world's productive land will have turned to dust, one million species will be extinct, and the world's climate will be irreparably changed. The recurring famines in Africa are just the most striking among many symptoms of the growing sickness of people and the earth.

This damage is being done by a world population that is now [1989] just over five billion. Of these five billion people, about a quarter live in the so-called "developed" countries and the other three-quarters in "developing" countries. Per capita, the quarter who live in developed countries consume far more than the three-quarters in the developing countries—fifteen times as much paper, ten times as much steel, and twelve times as much energy. The consumption of energy by the 750 million people in the richest countries—the industrial market economies of Western Europe, North America, and Japan—is actually seventeen times as high per capita as that of the 2,500 million people in the lowest income countries. So, even if world population were to remain stationary, bringing consumption in poor countries up to present rich-country levels would mean multiplying today's ecological impacts something like ten times over. But world population will not remain stationary. By the year 2000 it is projected to rise to 6.1 billion and by 2025 to 8.2 billion. Thereafter, it is not expected to stabilize below 10.2 billion on some projections and 14.2 billion on others—twice or three times what it is today.

Although awareness that the world is on this collision course has been spreading rapidly in recent years, conventional economic strategies offer no solution to the problem. Quite the reverse. Modern communications, especially television, are hooking the rising population of the world more and more firmly on the consumerist values propagated by rich-country businesses and governments. This is evident throughout the nonsocialist Third World. Even in socialist economies, most notably the Soviet Union and China, the reforms now taking place convey to the outside observer, not so much that a switch is taking place to a genuinely new direction of development, as that decisions have been taken to follow more closely the consumerist example of the market economies of the industrialized West. Meanwhile, as the richest countries gear themselves up to drive still further along the conventional path of economic growth—this being, for example, the stated purpose of the single European market in 1992 and the recent Free Trade Treaty between Canada and the USA—the wealth gap grows wider between rich countries and poor, and between rich people and poor people within each country.

We Need to Reject Today's Assumptions

A new economics for people and the earth must be enabling (for people) and conserving (for the earth). But those two principles— enabling and conserving—are directly opposed to two basic tendencies of conventional economic practice and thought today:

- the tendency to create and reinforce economic dependency for people, localities, and nations, and to widen the gap between the rich and the poor, the powerful and the weak;

- the tendency to be wasteful of natural resources and damaging to the natural environment.

We also have to reject other basic tendencies and assumptions of today's economic order. These include:

- the assumption that the wealth of nations is still what matters and that the paramount unit for economic policymaking must be the nation state;

- the assumption that all economic life must conform to a materialist model;

- the assumption that all economic activity must be governed by the impersonal mechanisms of the market and the state;

- a model of human beings as amoral maximizers of their own self-interest who, as economic agents, should not be expected to exercise moral or social choice;

- the notion that economics can be a science that is objective and value-free.

A Historical Watershed

These features of today's economic practice and thought originated in the seventeenth and eighteenth centuries. Modern economic development began with the deliberate creation of dependency, when the common people were pushed off the land, excluded from their subsistence way of life, and made dependent on paid labor. Modern economic thinking had its roots in the perceptions of the English philosophers Bacon and Hobbes—of nature as a limitless resource to be exploited for "the relief of the inconveniences of man's estate," of wealth as power over other people, and of human life as an incessant competitive struggle for power.

When Adam Smith came to articulate the workings of the modern economy—in place of the vanished medieval economic order that had been based on the rights and obligations of a divinely sanctioned, hierarchical, static society—he followed Bacon's and Hobbes' perceptions of "man" and nature and society, and Newton's value-free system-building in the sciences. That Smith emphasized the wealth of nations, rather than the wealth of people or cities or the world, and took material production and consumption as his model of economic life, reflected the most notable economic phenomena of his own time: the struggles between European nations to dominate overseas trade, and the unprecedented growth of industrial production and its accompanying division of labour.

The time has now come once again for the prevailing economic order to be transformed. The new economic order must reflect the very different realities and needs of the twenty-first century world—a world perhaps even further removed from Adam Smith's than his was from the middle ages.

A Common Cause

Active supporters of many specific causes are especially well aware that today's economic order stands in the way of what they are working for. For example, it makes it difficult to:

- eliminate poverty and famine;

- conserve natural resources and the environment;

- develop a personal capacity for cooperative self-reliance;

- develop self-reliant local communities;

- develop mutually supportive urban and rural economies;

- develop self-reliant Third World economies and humane postindustrial economies;

- manage the international economy as a one-world economy;

- achieve international peace, security, and disarmament;

- provide healthy conditions of life for all;

- provide adequate food for all, produced by humane and ecologically safe farming methods;

- provide all with opportunities for useful and rewarding work and leisure;

- enable all to have adequate housing;

- develop environmentally safe technologies that enhance, not diminish, people's capacity for self-reliance;

- value the capacities and rights of women as well as men, poor as well as rich, old as well as young, children as well as adults, ethnic minorities as well as majorities;

- live by spiritual and religious values;

- stabilize world population at a manageable level.

People who, like supporters of eco-justice, are working to change things for the better in one or another of these respects, belong to a worldwide community of organizations, movements, and groups. We share a common cause. For we all find that the practices, policies, assumptions, and imperatives of conventional economics place formidable obstacles in our way.

A Task for the 1990s

Those of us who founded The Other Economic Summit (TOES) in 1984 hoped increasing numbers of these organizations and movements and groups would come together in a sustained campaign to bring the new way of economic life and thought into being. This initiative has taken root. The challenge for the 1990s is to step up the pace, involving many more people and organizations in a loosely but purposefully linked worldwide program of advance through the decade. We cannot create utopia in a bare ten years, and we would be very foolish to try. But we can aim to make sure that, when the year 2000 arrives, enough thinking people all over the world recognize that the twenty-first century needs a new economic order, and know what they must do to bring it into existence.

19

Good Work, the Big Chill, and the Sadness of Dinks

Ingrid Olsen-Tjensvold

(*The Egg: A Journal of Eco-Justice* 8 [3], Fall 1988)

Once upon a time, say twenty years ago (though it was earlier in the west and later in the east), there was a generation of college-age young people markedly different from their parents and predecessors of "the silent generation." A surprising number of these young people did nothing more than grow hair, forsake bathing, and take up dope in a big way and were therefore perfect analogs of any slack-minded, fashion-conscious, group-following young people of any time at all.

But around the core event of this country's ill-fated involvement in the small and lovely country of Vietnam, a population of young people grew who *thought*. They thought very long and hard about what sort of a country would lure young men to war by promises of manhood and glory, or failing that, would drag them to war by threat of incarceration and disgrace. They thought about what sort of country would have such odd ideas about communist dominion that it would engage in such a war in the first place, and then go on and on with it when it became clear that the outcome would only be suffering and death over there and deep disenchantment over here.

Since everything is connected to everything else, the war in that tiny, lovely country led to thinking long and hard about the environment (note that Vietnam is one of the most beautiful subtropical areas on earth, and that we bombed it, burned it, and poisoned it from the air). And about men and women (how easily men were lured to war, how the mentality of military heroism requires a loathing of women and a ruthless suppression of men's feminine side). About blacks, hispanics, and the poor (who were dragged to war in grossly disproportionate numbers). And about work (how Dad could go off to Dow Chemical every day in his three-piece suit and great big car and make napalm).

The most thoughtful of this hard-thinking group dreamed a new future for themselves, their country, and the earth. It was a dream with a lot of green in it, and it meant living simply, gently, and close to the earth and the poor. Good work became an issue. Fritz Schumacher was much read and much admired, for he said we should turn our inventiveness towards things like egg cartons and bicycles, windmills and water pumps. We can do things better without doing them bigger, noisier, faster, and more violently. He sounded like the Gandhi of appropriate technology, and he was sometimes followed. Sometimes not.

Too often not, for the revolutionaries of that earlier day became the stock-brokers, corporate lawyers, plastic surgeons, and investment bankers of the late 1970s and early 1980s. They became indistinguishable from the later, younger yuppies, pursuing unenlightened self-interest with all the single-mindedness of the generation they had purported to surpass in morals and farsightedness. Thus *The Big Chill* became the movie to watch and to weep at. That was us; what has become of us?

Now, *Time* magazine tells us, there is a yuppie sub-group, the DINKS. Dual income, no kids couples, both with jobs in the fast lane, who work for their enormous salaries ten hours a day and communicate with one another through the medium of their home telephone answering machines [and now their cell phones]. They all seem to have dogs, but the dogs are left home alone, for everyone knows that children have needs but dogs have none. Which is why they have dogs rather than children. This is very sad.

More About the Failure of Dreams

I attended a panel discussion sponsored by the Women's Law Coalition. The panelists were a lawyer, a therapist, and a sociologist whose special field was women and work. All were women. All said this: Professional women get very tired. If they are married and have children, they work two full-time jobs, for the feminist dream of the sharing of household and parenting tasks equally with men has failed. If they are divorced and have children, child care is a constant, nagging worry, for industry has not provided in-house child care facilities and the government does not give a damn—and a single woman does not make enough money to buy the services of competent private caregivers.

What is more, the workplace is utterly unchanged from what it was in the 1950s. There is no paid maternal leave (or paternal leave for that matter) and no time off for care of sick children. Professional women are cautioned not to put photographs of their family in their offices, for it communicates divided loyalties and unseriousness. They are told that the bottom line is this: to make it in the professions, women must act as men always have, sharply divorcing their home and family lives from their role in the workplace, and always putting the latter above the former.

Oh, brave new world!

Good Work

Humans thrive on dreams. Failure of the imagination is a terrible thing; so when a dream fails, we must dream it again, or dream another.

Even lawyers have dreams, and mine is this. Because I believe that we have gone wrong in going back to work as a means of gaining the whole world while losing our souls, I dream of the perfect law office. It is a green dream.

It is green literally, for it seems to me that professional offices of all kinds are cold, ugly, and as unlike a home as the architects and designers can make them. They are intentionally unlike places where people feel safe, welcome, and at peace. The perfect law office will be full of window-light and plants. It will be decorated warmly and informally, with soft places to sit and good paintings to look at. It will smell like coffee.

It will have people in it, busy, purposeful grown-ups. It will also have dogs and cats and very small children, for lawyers *have* dogs and cats and very small children, and it is no use pretending (even going so far as not to put photographs on their desks) that this is not so. It is more efficient in the long run to have an office where those who must be there many hours of many days a week can be fully and roundly human—rather than half-beings who look at the clock and long for home.

The family comes first. A sick child, an injured wife, a recently widowed father comes before a client, so every lawyer in the firm will be thoroughly familiar with the cases of every other and can take over in these emergencies. We'll try flex-time, *any* alternative to caving in to industrial imperatives which take no account of what humans are really like.

There will be no isolates in this firm, and no bosses and no underlings. There will be lengthy once-a-week case conferences which all lawyers will attend and in which all will have an equal say. The right hand will always know what the left is doing. Knowledge will be shared. So will the crummy tasks, like running papers to the courthouse and checking the client trust accounts for errors and irregularities.

There will be sliding-scale fees. The poor pay costs when they can, nothing when they can't. The less poor, costs and a little something. The rich, plenty, for the laborer is worthy of his or her hire and it is amazingly expensive to practice law.

Every lawyer will have one community activity in which he or she participates. And every lawyer will faithfully attend the bar's continuing legal education programs and share what they have learned with others.

And we will *think* what we are doing. If this real estate development would harm the community, we will not grease its legal wheels. If this business wants to go worker-owned, we'll help with enthusiasm. If this client has money to invest, we'll aim her toward socially responsible investments. If that client's marriage is failing because of alcohol abuse, we'll suggest counselors and programs. If another client wants to shield his assets from his estranged wife by putting them in his girlfriend's name, we'll tell him we're off the case if he does.

It sounds like a modest dream. It isn't. It is unheard of, it isn't done, it will cause talk. And if it does work, it might be imitated. And if it's imitated, we will have built a small but sturdy footbridge to the future seen clearly once in a green dream.

20

The Development Debate:
Coalition for a New Alternative?

J. Ronald Engel

(*The Egg: An Eco-Justice Quarterly* 12 [1],
Winter 1991–92)

The term "sustainable development" is used with increasing frequency to describe the global ethic we need for the twenty-first century. Generally speaking, it is much more prevalent outside the United States than within. One document that recently crossed my desk proposes that "sustainable development" be made an amendment to the Constitution of Poland. Another indicates that Austria has proposed the following "Preamble" for the Earth Charter to be adopted at the United Nations Conference on Environment and Development meeting in Rio de Janeiro, June 1992: "Whereas all individuals, organizations and states share the duty to make sustainable development a reality for all people on earth. . . ." "Sustainable development" is also making an impact on the religious community. The spring 1991 Newsletter of the Evangelical Lutheran Church in America Hunger Program includes this passage:

> Development is the ultimate solution to poverty. . . . The road that leads to sustainable development is rough and tedious—but it is the road that Christ expects us to travel. . . .

> May we walk together on this road and challenge ourselves, and those who have power, to achieve sustainable development.

In its 1987 report, *Our Common Future*, the UN Commission on Environment and Development concludes that "human survival and well-being could depend on success in *elevating sustainable development to a global ethic*." Unfortunately, the report does not go very far toward defining "sustainable development," except to say that it means a kind of economic development that "meets the needs of the present without compromising the ability of future generations to meet their own needs," and that it must go hand in hand with environmental protection. Nonetheless, in spite of its vagueness, the term "sustainable development" signals something of significance: a growing unease in many quarters of the world community about the current trajectory of global development, and at least the beginning of a search for "another way." What we are talking about is basic change in our "way of life"—both personal lifestyle and objective social and economic structures. It involves what we do or do not choose to do together, as citizens.

January 20, 1949

In order to understand the idea of "sustainable development," we need first to understand the idea of "development" that preceded it. And to do that we must go back to the snowy afternoon of January 20, 1949, when Harry Truman, flushed with victory, rode down Pennsylvania Avenue to Capitol Hill to give his inaugural address before the American people. It is no exaggeration to say that Truman's speech anticipated both the greatest promise, and the greatest problem, of the second half of the twentieth century— although not quite in the way he intended.

Truman began his address by correctly noting the crucial nature of this moment in world history: "It may be our lot to experience, and in large measure to bring about, a major turning point in the long history of the human race." The American people, he said, desire to work for "a world in which all nations and all peoples are free to govern themselves and to achieve a decent and satisfying life . . . based on genuine agreement freely arrived at by equals." On this point Truman spoke with no ordinary authority. He inherited the mantle of Franklin D. Roosevelt and it was the personal crusade of Roosevelt's widow, Eleanor Roosevelt, that had made possible the signing of the Universal Declaration of Human Rights in San Francisco the year before.

But there was a major obstacle to the realization of the global promise of democracy, and Truman minced no words in identifying it: communism. In a long litany he set forth what he considered to be the radically opposing convictions of communism and democracy, beginning thus:

"*Communism* is based on the belief that man is so weak and inadequate that he is unable to govern himself, and therefore requires the rule of strong masters."

"*Democracy* is based on the conviction that man has the moral and intellectual capacity, as well as the inalienable right, to govern himself with reason and justice."

Up to this point it is difficult to fault Truman. The year 1949 *was* a crucial juncture in world history: the world *was* looking to the United States for wise leadership; a more universal embodiment of democracy and human rights was the great promise of the last half of the twentieth century; the ideology of communism under the Stalin regime was a great obstacle to freedom and self-government throughout the globe. But was it the greatest or only problem?

At this point in his speech Truman made a choice that was in many ways as fateful as the decision to drop the atomic bomb. He chose to fight communism with a weapon many persons four decades later would consider as deadly as the atomic bomb: western-style industrial and economic development. (As Shiv Visvanathan comments in a recent issue of *Alternatives* [16, 1991]: "Today, a hydroelectric dam or a hamburger can create more refugees than war.") Truman devoted the remainder of his inaugural address to describe his famous Point Four Program for international economic assistance:

- First, "unfaltering support to the United Nations."

- Second, reduction in the barriers to world trade, for "economic recovery and peace itself depend on increased world trade."

- Third, collective defense arrangements among free nations.

- Fourth (and most crucial for our purposes), a "bold new program for making the benefits of our scientific advances and industrial progress available for the improvement and growth of underdeveloped areas."

Note what is happening here. By introducing the term "underdeveloped" Truman in effect is refuting his earlier position—that the nations of the world need to work together "as equals." He is now assuming a quite different position, one in which the world is divided into two categories: the "developed" areas—industrialized nations of the north; and the "underdeveloped areas"—most of the southern hemisphere. By the simple act of naming half the world "developed" and half the world "underdeveloped," Truman in effect said that nations are to be classified by how far they have traveled the road of modern economic progress. Moreover, the direction of that lay clearly before his eyes: "Greater production is the key to prosperity and peace," he pointed out, "And the key to greater production is a wider and more vigorous application of modern scientific and technical knowledge." The "model" for what lay at the end of that road also lay clearly before his eyes: it was postwar American society: "The United States is preeminent among nations in the development of industrial and scientific techniques," he declared.

A considerable conflation of interests and concepts has occurred. What began as a transcendent vision of the peoples of the world working together "as equals" to establish a global democratic civilization narrows down to "development" of the world in the image of American industry and commerce. The struggle for democracy for all is assumed to be equivalent to the achievement of the American "standard of living" by all.

Democracy Equals Development?

By seeing western-style industrial and economic development as the principal *means* to the fulfillment of democracy, indeed, as virtually equivalent to democracy, Truman inadvertently created, rather than solved, the greatest problem of the second half of the twentieth century: the problem of modern development.

It is possible, of course, to argue that Truman was correct in his identification of the threat as communism, and in the means he chose to fight it: capitalist economic development. Indeed, with the fall of communism, and the apparent victory of what is euphemistically called the "free market economy," it seems to many observers that the American model of industrial and economic organization is, as Truman implied, the only alternative future for world history.

But this would be a premature conclusion. The fact that a state-centrist version of modern industrial development proved inadequate to feed, clothe and sustain a major portion of the world's peoples does not mean that a western capitalist-corporate version is adequate to feed, clothe, and sustain *all* the world's peoples, or that it is the basis for a democratic global civilization. In fact, if the controversy over sustainable development means anything, there are good reasons to think it is not.

Stop and think about it: in one consummate metaphorical stroke, Truman articulated a global teleological creed. All the peoples of the earth were henceforth to aspire to the same goal—"development." The word "development," a biological concept, laden with rich connotations of the creative process at the heart of life, became a metaphor for a particular form of economic and social organization—the American system of mass production and consumption as it emerged on the foundations of the World War II industrial machine. Henceforth, the diverse human societies of the world were no longer to be seen as a mosaic of the rich possibilities of being human, as any authentic notion of democracy would require, but were placed on a single progressive track, more or less advanced according to how closely they approximated the United States.

Truman took the metaphor of "economic development" and used it to describe the societal process as a whole. Never before had it been suggested as a matter of state policy that the degree of civilization of a country could be measured by the level of its material production, that the all-encompassing purpose of the state was economic growth. Even John Maynard Keynes, the father of neo-classical economics and the chief architect of the post World War II financial institutions created at Bretton Woods, once proposed a toast, "To economics, and to economists, who are not the trustees of civilization, but of the possibility of civilization." Thus did Keynes acknowledge the purely instrumental value of the economic sphere.

Apparently Truman was acting with the best of intentions, but with typical American hubris, to empower historical forces whose consequences he could not anticipate, and which he did not really understand. The real wonder of it all is that most of the world bought it! And that so few religious liberals or religious conservatives questioned it at the time!

Truman *totalized* the concept of development, so that industrial production became the end as well as the means of the democratic state: politics and culture were now subsidiary to economics. In spite of some battering and some disappointments, the Truman creed is still alive and well in 1992. In public policy arenas, development is still ideologically equated with democracy and operationally defined as maximum economic growth, i.e., ever higher quantitative levels of industrialization, consumption and population.

I don't think George Bush has any idea how much his "new world order" owes to the initiative of that crusty old Democrat of the 1940s.

The Development Debate

Development has made some positive contributions. According to the World Bank, each year ever larger numbers of people have more food, more comfortable lodgings, greater variety of clothing, access to medical services, and so on. On a global scale, human life expectancy has risen, as has adult literacy. Development has also brought to traditional societies some growth in freedom to associate, to organize, and to expand individual vocational possibilities. Peter Berger contended that with modern development people are more free to choose what they will believe, which values they will adopt, how they will live. To this extent, there are legitimate reasons to associate democracy and development.

But for three decades, beginning with pioneer analyst Louis Lebret, critics have warned about "anti-development," "maldevelopment," and more recently "unsustainable development." Negative consequences from development—social, environmental, and cultural—are now more evident, and each points to one of the failures of the Truman creed. On the whole, development resulting from the Truman initiative failed to achieve much social and political democracy, failed to preserve the environment, and failed to enhance cultural authenticity or religious faith.

In each case a major constituency has mobilized to protest these negative consequences, giving rise to movements for social and economic liberation, to the international environmental movement, and to various ecumenical and other religious movements concerned for the plight of the global community. *First*, consider the social consequences in the "developing countries." Poverty has appeared where it never existed before, and it has increased precisely in the shadow of wealth. In addition, both in absolute numbers and in percentage of population, unemployment has grown, not diminished. Women have been especially hard hit. They are left with double work: to raise family and raise food while men are lured to the cities to earn cash. In many parts of the world, both the food situation and the availability of basic material goods have deteriorated.

To make matters worse, repressive dictators have often emerged in the wake of development rather than democratic governments. Development reports out of South Korea and Kenya, for example, remain discreetly quiet about the political repression that has accompanied adoption of northern development strategies with the infusion of large amounts of western capital. To this must be added the growth in crippling external debt, as even relatively rich developing countries, such as Mexico, Brazil, or Nigeria, have seen their dependency increase due to their participation in the global lending and commodity system. This has meant a widening gap between rich and poor nations, with the few rich nations consuming an ever larger share of the world's resources.

In the developed countries themselves things have also gone awry. A synonym for "development" is "urbanization." All one has to do is to consider the concrete social (and environmental) effects of the massive urbanization of the United States in recent decades to grasp the reality we are dealing with. A permanent urban underclass has appeared. We have also seen an ever-widening gap between rich and poor as well as massive social displacement, not to mention the new diseases of "affluence." At the same time, the political life of most urban societies such as our own has deteriorated; many are burdened with citizen apathy and withdrawal from public responsibility. If there is any meaning to those words of Truman's—"We believe that all men have a right to equal justice under law and equal opportunity to share in the common good"— it is simply not possible to defend the proposition that development has brought more democracy to the world.

Second, the ecological consequences. We all know the bad news: topsoil is eroding and deserts are expanding, forests are dying and disappearing, air pollution is warming the earth and depleting its protective ozone shield, species are becoming extinct at the greatest rate in evolutionary history, industry and agriculture are putting toxic substances into the food chain and groundwater supplies. I do want to note one factor, however, that is often misunderstood.

There is growing evidence that the so-called "demographic transition theory" is fallacious, and that modern development creates unsustainable levels of population growth—not the stabilizing of population levels that was anticipated. In fact, as Virginia Abernathy at Vanderbilt University, editor of the journal *Population and Environment*, has recently concluded, rising expectations regarding the material standard of living lead to increase in family size, whereas a sense of limited resources promotes small family size. In her view, "motivation" is the major determination of reproduction.[1]

Finally, the cultural and religious consequences. Over the last two decades the "sleeping giants" of the world religions have begun to awake under the onslaught of development programs that impact traditional cultures and their core religious beliefs. Development has the undeniable effect of dissolving what Wolfgang Sachs calls "the whole texture of societies," in effect, making the rich diversity of the world's cultures into tourist attractions.[2] Thinkers such as Arnold Toynbee, Paul Tillich, Alfred North Whitehead, Albert Schweitzer, and Jacques Ellul among others warned long ago that the dominance of technical rationality would evacuate the meaning systems of the world's communities, from the family to the nation. But only recently have leaders of western religious communities discerned the degree to which modern development is antithetical to religious consciousness *as such*; it eradicates from the cultural memory those transcendental symbols that recall us to the gracefull character of our existence. The modern development paradigm simply treats questions about the ultimate purpose of life as insignificant or meaningless.

As a consequence, religious doctrines which have been tabled for seven hundred years are being reexamined. We begin to catch glimmers of why St. Francis talked about the redemptive meaning of "poverty" in the thirteenth century as capitalism began to gather steam in the Italian city states, and why the most spiritual or "otherworldly" ages of the world were also the most ecologically sustainable. Few of the teachings of the great traditions are compatible with modern development; none can really support the notion that the public good derives from personal greed, or that the spiritual aims of human life are furthered by the accumulation of technological power and wealth.

The Alternative Development Movement

As each of these three negative consequences has become visible, each of the three constituencies involved has become increasingly radicalized, and the possibility of a worldwide coalition of the three has become a real and present possibility. Each movement is becoming aware of how much its problems are intertwined with the problems of the other two; and how all these problems are traceable to a common source: the dominant pattern of western social and economic development, especially as that achieved global dominance after World War II.

It was possible for quite awhile to keep the three constituencies busy in warfare between themselves. At one time or another, each of the three has perceived each of the other two as its dire enemy. There has been distrust especially between the environmental movement and movements for social liberation ("jobs vs. environment"), and the environmental movement and the religious community (as evidenced by the Lynn White debate over the role of Christianity in precipitating the environmental crisis). Now all three are finding that they have far more in common than they do in opposition to one another. They are finding, for example, that persons deprived of their traditional means of livelihood bear the greatest brunt of ecological destruction; and conversely, ecological destruction deprives persons of livelihood. As I try to show in my introduction to *Ethics of Environment and Development* (University of Arizona Press, 1990), there is also growing awareness that social and environmental protests are ultimately grounded in ethical and religious values. The lesson of history is that religious motivations are necessary to keep the "desire for possessions" within bounds and subordinated to the common good. Most important, religious faith or reverence for life generates the idea that "justice" should take precedence over growth in material wealth, that the rest of life has value beyond its economic utilization.

We must not let our enthusiasm for these new understandings blind us to the fact that, in each case, we are still talking about a *minority* of individuals and organizations, and that in the world picture as a whole, we are still very much referring to a *minority movement*. Most persons and governments in the world are still enthralled by the modern development paradigm; most environmentalists (themselves a minority) have yet to grasp the connections between social justice, religion and the fate of the earth; most serious advocates for social justice (also very much a minority) have yet to take the environment seriously; most members of most synagogues, churches and temples still see religion as something separate from either of these worldly concerns. One has only to examine the premises of the largest and most heavily funded Christian missions to see how far a "new development paradigm" is from their perception of what the world needs. The Seventh Day

Adventists, for example, explicitly include a western-style economic development package as part of their missionary efforts.

In summary, I would say that the past thirty years have seen the *beginning* of an awakening from the spell of the "development dream," as each of these three constituencies has become mobilized. Criticism of development has moved from questions of equity and distribution of wealth, to issues of resource depletion and survival, to the question of the quality of our wants, to the deepest questions we can ask: On what terms are we to live on earth? How ought we to live and die?

I believe that the promise for the future lies in molding these three great constituencies, historically isolated from one another, into one unified counter-development movement, in pursuit of a new paradigm to replace the Truman creed: a new paradigm that is *authentically democratic, ecological, and spiritual.*

Practically speaking, this is no idle thought. In recent years, coalitions of nongovernmental organizations concerned with poverty, human rights, population, and environmental issues have begun to appear in different parts of the world, and this has been made possible by the recognition that their goals are ethically coherent and mutually reinforcing. Many religious groups are now cooperating with these coalitions, as the consultative process for the writing of an Earth Charter indicates. ·

Notes

1. Virginia Abernathy, "The True Face of Compassion," *Proceedings of the Earth Ethics Forum 1991* (Seminole, Florida, 1991).

2. Wolfgang Sachs, "On the Archaeology of the Development Idea," *Interculture* 23 (4) 1990, 1–32.

Section G

Lifestyle and Community

Editor's Notes

In an eco-just world people would live differently than people live or aspire to live in the United States today. In accordance with the norm of sustainability, the habits and patterns of their lives would treat the earth more gently, respectfully, and appreciatively. In accordance with the norm of sufficiency, they would find satisfaction in having enough and in careful, frugal enjoyment of nature's gifts. The norm of participation would sustain the consciousness that the Creator intends these gifts for the sustenance of all through good work, cooperative enterprise, and mutual sharing. And the norm of solidarity would keep strong the bonds of community and of a fulfilling engagement with human and nonhuman companions for the common good.

Lifestyle education constituted a large part of the program of the Eco-Justice Project and Network. Its centerpiece was our curriculum manual, A Covenant Group for Lifestyle Assessment *(1978 and 1981), which was used by church covenant groups all over the country. For several years a part-time staff member, Anita Jaehn, promoted and facilitated its use in our more immediate New York State region.*

In the manual and in various programs and workshops, we pointed participants toward enjoyment of community and satisfaction with sufficiency, with the covenant group itself designed to be a community of support for appropriate changes, responding as people of faith to the eco-justice crisis. We encouraged participants to consume less and to be more political. We showed that the individual and family changes for conserving and sharing, which they were beginning to make, needed to be accompanied by political action to make social policies and institutions more conducive to such changes.

The journal carried numerous articles on lifestyle, not only on our theory and philosophy of lifestyle assessment and change, but case stories of changes that members of the Network undertook.

Chris Burger, a member of the Eco-Justice Coordinating Council for many years, did real pioneering work on cutting household waste to an absolute minimum. Starting years before recycling became popular and "in," he and his wife, Cindy, and later their two daughters combined a routine home collection system with ingenuity to get metals, paper of all kinds, food scraps, old clothing, and eventually plastics to the places where they would still be useful. Eventually a year's residual trash that had to be discarded was such a small package that it became an exhibit at the Smithsonian Institution.

But Chris's concern to cut waste and pollution extended beyond the family project to public policy. He gave leadership on resource recovery and waste management to the Broome County (New York) Environmental Management Council and then to the county legislature, where he is still serving as an elected representative.

When Earl Arnold joined the Eco-Justice staff as Associate Coordinator, he took a risky leap of faith—giving up a position with a large corporation for one where the pay was far less and where tenure depended on precarious fundraising. "It's been a stimulating journey," he wrote in the March 1985 issue of The Egg. *"I've gotten much more in touch with the realities of living, much more sensitive to my real needs for food, shelter and community, and much less anxious about my bank balance or stock prices. The nonmonetary rewards of my work have become much more important, as I have felt myself playing a role in promoting significant changes in our society. My sense of myself and my relationship to the world is much less stereotyped, and I feel much more in control of the most important choices for my life."*

Selection 21 by James Nash did not appear in the journal but is new material written in 2001. Nash captures and advances the rationale for serious lifestyle change by comfortable Americans as an absolutely essential part of the eco-justice journey. The title declares the issue: "Prodigality and Frugality: Core Conflict of the Times."

Nash's concept of frugality makes it immediately clear that the eco-justice norm of sufficiency applies not only to people who need more but equally to those whose consumption is excessive, wasteful, and unfair. He does not regard frugality as world-denying asceticism. It is contrary to both overconsumption and underconsumption. It delights in the "enhanced lives for human communities and other creatures that only constrained consumption can make possible on a finite planet." But frugality is a "feared" and "subversive" virtue, alien and threatening to the "national ethos of abundance" with all its stimuli to excess.

Nash acknowledges that "present political prospects for the socialization of [frugality's] countervision are, of course, bleak." It still depends upon moral education to build "awareness of the values of frugality and the disvalues of alternatives."

The lifestyle work of the Eco-Justice Project, beginning in the mid-1970s provided an early model of this kind of moral education. The still greater need for it in the new century shows the persistent unawareness and denial in our churches and our schools.

This brings us to Selection 22 by John B. Cobb, Jr., on "Sustainability and Community." It makes a fitting final article for Part II on the eco-justice issues, because it shows their connections to each other. Cobb touches on most of them—economics and development, hunger, population, pollution, energy, and technology. He delivered this essay as the keynote address to the Eco-Justice Conference on "Eco-Communities: Toward Global Sustainability."

Cobb views the modern world as enthralled—in a quasi-religious way—by the great god Growth. This persists despite the mounting evidence that by any valid measurement (which the GNP is not) the costs of further quantitative growth exceed the benefits in many places, including the United States. Sustainable development understood as growth is an oxymoron, but development as community development can be sustainable. The two types of development are antithetical. The economy of growth, globalization, and "free trade" destroys communities and oppresses the poor and the earth throughout the world. Sustainable community development puts the economy in the service of the community and makes the values of the community govern development. To this end the United States must reinvent itself. It will happen from the bottom up, but support from "above" will be required.

Yes, he speaks of the eco-justice journey, and the road is rocky. The obstacles are huge.

21

Prodigality and Frugality: Core Conflict of the Times

James A. Nash

Prodigality, a Moral Problem

Let us focus our attention on what may be the central moral problem of our age: prodigality. Prodigality is a moral problem in the basic sense that it involves value judgments about what is good or bad, right or wrong, or what we ought to be and do, for the sake of the well-being of humans and other creatures in our relationships.

At issue are economic excess and its environmental harms:

- excess in the goods we extract from the earth, such as the fossil fuels we use to empower oversized vehicles and oversized houses;

- excess in the abundant products we make and consume, from wasteful packaging to ostentatious and quickly abandoned fashions;

- excess in the wastes we dump on the land and in the air and waters, such as the profligate emissions of synthetic chemicals and the trillions of tons of sewage produced annually by more than six billion people.

The moral problem is not mainly that we want and seek "bad things," though, of course, there are plenty of examples of people grasping for products they shouldn't have at all, not even in moderation, such as billiard balls made from elephant tusks. Instead, our main problem is wanting and seeking too much of the many good things in life. In the language of classical Western thought, the prosperous people of the planet are guilty of gluttony, one of the seven deadly, or primary, sins. Gluttony applies not only to the excessive consumption of food and drink, but also to excessive production and consumption in general. Gluttony and greed are often partners in producing excess.

Of course, there are degrees of excess, from elementary indulgences to obscene opulence. We may act better than our neighbors, but that fact does not exonerate us from prodigality. All of us who have tasted the enticements of affluence participate to some extent, more or less, in the ethos of excess. Thus we all are guilty though in different degrees.

The profligacy of the prosperous is a prime expression of one of the fundamental failures at the roots of the ecological crisis: the failure to recognize and respect the limiting conditions of the planet—in other words, the carrying, the absorptive, and the regenerative capacities of our earthly habitat.

Excess has always been a moral problem for our species. The difference now is the vast scale of excess, the sheer magnitude of the human impact on the planet, made possible by our vast numbers and our sophisticated technical tools.

We have taken too many steps too far. The result has been a host of serious environmental woes, including climate change, resource scarcities, collapsed fisheries, endangered species, and pollution in a multitude of forms. We need now to reverse directions, to pull back from the brink and beyond. We need also to discover and develop a new ecologically and socially sensitive code of conduct, one that restrains us from excess and enables us to recognize and respect the limits of life, to the benefit of all nations and all species, in this generation and all future generations. Frugality is the antidote to prodigality.

The Cornucopians and the Ethos of Abundance

One of the critical moral questions under debate for the past thirty or so years is: Do we live in an age of ecological abundance, in which the resources necessary to sustain prosperous economies are practically inexhaustible and even greatly extendable by technological innovations? Or do we live in an age of ecological scarcity in which there are pressing biophysical limits on using the rest of nature as the source of our materials and the sewer for our wastes?

The dominant U.S. answer to this question is, of course, an enthusiastic affirmation of abundance. The earth has bounteous resources and we have every right to use these resources without restrictions. If perchance we encounter a shortage in some resource, we can trust in technology to fix it. For example, we can increase fish and forestry yields through biotechnology, or substitute a common resource for a relatively scarce one, like fiber optics to replace copper. With vision and technological innovation, we can have both ecological security and unrestrained economic growth—reminiscent of the "guns and butter" theme from another era. This is the affirmation of those I shall call the *cornucopians*.

Economic abundance is the central paradigm that has shaped our national character and cultural institutions. Through most of the media of value transmission—obviously commercial advertising, but also our much-celebrated family values—our citizens have been socialized to seek the superfluous, in both quantity and quality of goods and services, on the assumption that the earth is a place of perpetual plenty. Our national ethos sanctions and even celebrates excess. The excesses are constantly present but reach their pinnacle, ironically, at the celebration of the birth of one who was a model of charitable restraint.

Political salutes to this "great" nation really mean this "rich" nation. The American Dream now means little more than fulfilling the fantasy of affluence. The "good life" or even "life abundant" has been redefined as material prosperity. The "pursuit of happiness" now implies the quest of acquisitions. "Success" is defined not as social service or creativity but as wealth—and gaining the property, prestige, and power that wealth provides. Indeed, excess is the main sign of success. And excess is the primary evidence of progress.

This ethos is inherently wasteful. In fact, the more we can afford to waste, the better off we are—and too many delight in showing off that fact, particularly in the size and style of our possessions. Remember that maxim from yesteryear, "Waste not, want not"? It's meaningless to many now, because they can waste wantonly without wanting.

A dominant moral assumption in this ethos of excess is that economic growth is good, with growth meaning ever-expanding material prosperity. In some current economic thought, even efficiency, the central moral norm of economics, is defined as maximum productivity; it is a virtual synonym for economic growth.

Growth is one of our nation's few bipartisan commitments, uniting Democrats and Republicans, conservatives and liberals. Moreover, internationally a commitment to "global growth" for "global prosperity" now unites capitalist, socialist, and mixed economic ideologies. The prevailing rationale is that economic growth is the prime cure for poverty. The goal is not a reduction of affluence for the affluent in a redistribution of wealth, but rather the inclusion of the poor as equal players in the system.

Allegedly, the perpetual expansion of production and consumption is necessary for progress and prosperity, to satisfy the basic needs and growing wants of national and international consumers, and to provide employment opportunities for rapidly expanding populations. We are counseled to consume liberally—even indiscriminately at times of economic slowdown—to keep the system going and growing. In this context, frugality is not only unfashionable; it is an unpatriotic vice.

Indisputably, the cornucopian paradigm in the United States has a positive side. It has nurtured some important values: jobs in the scores of millions; a multitude of goods and services, many of which we can applaud; capital for investments and improvements; tax revenues for government programs, including social services and environmental protections; technological innovations, many of which are socially and environmentally beneficial; pension systems, including social security; and philanthropic benefits that have strengthened nonprofit associations, including the religious and educational. We dare not forget that the abundance model has provided some significant and genuine benefits to most Americans, and we must ensure that any ecologically sensitive alternative to this system provides sufficient jobs, goods, revenues, and other benefits that will enable human communities to flourish.

Nevertheless, the ethos of abundance has significant liabilities. It is a Jekyll/Hyde phenomenon: the benefactor is also the destroyer. It is a major factor in destroying the planetary ecosystems on which all life depends, and on which the health of all social and economic systems also depends. Unconstrained production and consumption are key factors in the excessive exploitation and toxification of the renewable and nonrenewable gifts of nature.

The Frugalists and the Acceptance of Limits

In sharp contrast to the believers in abundance are those who argue that the planetary condition is ecological scarcity—prospectively at least, but also actually in many particulars. Let us call them *frugalists*.

The fundamental argument of the frugalists is that we face a severe economics-ecology dilemma, involving conflicts over the conservation of nature's systems and the consumption and destruction of its resources. This dilemma can be resolved only by abandoning the current growth model and replacing it with a new paradigm of economic goals—one characterized by the moral norms of equity, sustainability, and frugality. The global growth policy is a chimerical hope, grounded in an ecological myth of practical inexhaustibility. In reality, we live in age of ecological scarcity—and we need to adapt to that reality.

One of the elementary lessons of ecology is: We live on a finite planet. There are no infinite bounties, no inexhaustible resources, no limitless systems. There are biophysical boundaries beyond which we cannot go, not even with our awesome technological talents to extend limits. We face limits everywhere—limits on the number of humans the planet can support, limits on using the rest of nature as the source of our products (like food and fuel), limits on using the rest of nature as the dump for our wastes (from CO_2 emissions to plain garbage in its astonishing variety), and limits on the capacities of species and ecosystems to recuperate from human intrusions. Virtually everything material can become scarce—if it is not so inherently—as a consequence of overuse or abuse. If there is a fundamental "law of nature," it is that humans must stay within the bounds of nature—or face the effects of our folly. In large measure, the ecological crisis represents humanity's failure to learn this lesson of limits.

But even when we are not yet near a particular biophysical boundary, there are also moral limits beyond which we should not tread. The question about environmental limits on population or consumption is not simply a matter of empirical calculation, determined by examining the biological demands of a species in relation to the supply of its environment. Clearly, this empirical assessment is important. But the question is also an ethical matter, involving moral judgments about desirable ends or living conditions, just distribution, and benevolent sharing. Ethically, the essential questions are: What is a good quality of life for humans, and what material and demographic conditions are necessary to ensure that good quality for all on a finite planet? What are our moral responsibilities to the rest of humanity, other species, and future generations? What then are the moral limits to human production and consumption in order to fulfill these responsibilities? In fact, when limits are defined ethically, the tolerances are considerably tighter than when defined only biophysically. We reach the bounds of the ethically bearable long before we reach the edge of the biophysically possible, because of the concern for qualities of being and our responsibilities to others.

Let it be clear, moreover, that the rejection of current patterns of economic growth among the frugalists is not generally simplistic opposition to growth per se. Rather, it is opposition *to indiscriminate material growth* in both resources used and wastes produced. It is not only an appeal for *qualitative* growth—in social responsibilities, ecological sensitivities, and cultural aesthetics. It is also a call for discriminating judgments and "selective growth" (Ian Barbour, *Ethics in an Age of Technology,* 52, 189). For example, material economic growth is necessary and just in poor nations, though within ecological limits. In a context where almost 50 percent of the world's population, according to the World Bank, lives on the equivalent of less than $2 per day, and where the ratio of resources between the richest fifth and the poorest fifth of the world's peoples is at least 78:1 and growing, it would be callous and cruel to oppose economic development for them.

Yet, none of this seems possible without limits on production and consumption in the affluent nations to enable the material conditions for well-being globally, nor without magnanimous economic and technological assistance from the industrialized nations. On a finite planet, if we want floors on the consumption of environmental resources, so that "enough" can be available for all, humankind and otherkind, present and future, we also need ceilings, to prevent some from hogging more than their fair share. On a finite planet, the two are inseparable.

The frugalists are rightly alarmed: We the prosperous are living gluttonously, to the detriment of poor nations, other species, and future generations. We are approaching or surpassing both moral and biophysical limits in numerous areas through our excesses. We need to abandon the utopian illusions of the cornucopians, and to develop ethical standards that curtail our excesses and respect the lesson of limits.

Steps Toward Flourishing Frugality

How then shall we counter excess in the land? I wish I had an answer that I could offer with some confidence! The barriers to reform are abundant and formidable. The ethos of excess is so deeply engrained in our cultural institutions—including our colleges and religious institutions—that it seems at times impossible to change—at least not without tragedies that terrify us into transformation. But such tragedies are what we want to avoid. So we dare not succumb to fatalism or self-fulfilling prophecies about the prospects of change. We must avoid both the romantic illusion that cultural shifts are easy and simple, and the cynical illusion that cultural shifts are unrealistic.

The conversion from gluttony to moderate consumption certainly requires changes in our personal lifestyles. We are presently manipulated to want more, bigger, better, faster, or "state of the art" in everything from computers to can openers. We feel humiliated, inadequate, unfashionable, or deprived unless we have what we have been told we need. It takes courage of commitment to resist these pressures, especially when they come from family, friends, and peers. But that is not impossible, especially if institutions such as churches can provide supports or even support groups for courageous acts of constrained consumption.

Certainly this conversion to moderation will also require a lot of changes in public policy, because the voluntary acts of isolated individuals are never enough. We are social beings who can function effectively only with the collaborative supports of social institutions. We can't even recycle as individuals unless we have recyclable products and recycling centers, all made possible by governmental regulations. Among these necessary social changes are shifts in social incentive structures, which the Worldwatch Institute emphasizes. For example, in the use of water and electricity, consumers generally pay the same rates or even lower rates the more they use. Why not reverse that process, as many communities are now doing, so that the more one uses electricity or water, or the more waste one produces in, say, garbage, the higher the rate one pays? That would be a deterrent to waste and an incentive to conservation of resources, especially among corporate consumers. Or instead of a mineral depletion allowance as a tax benefit to the extractors of oil, minerals, or aquifer water for irrigation, why not impose a mineral depletion *tax*, to discourage waste?

We also will need what businessman and environmentalist Paul Hawken calls "restorative economics" (*The Ecology of Commerce*). This redesigned process of sustainable production and consumption mimics natural cycles and constraints (such as choosing crops that fit the climates of particular places), minimizes wastes, and operates on solar and hydrogen power.

We need not only to recycle and redesign but also to *reduce* production and consumption. This, however, is the very message that even some major environmental organizations seem reluctant to send, if in fact they believe it, perhaps for fear of alienating actual or potential members. But affluent societies must receive this discomforting message: We will not solve the problem of excess simply by enhanced efficiencies. Substantial reductions in everything from CO_2 emissions to forest products are essential. Our national focus should not be on increasing oil supplies by drilling, for example, in the Artic National Wildlife Refuge, but rather on decreasing oil demand, by a variety of practices, including taxes on gas gluttons and expanding public transportation. Ecological responsibilities entail some sacrifices.

A major moral mandate for an age of scarcity is: Ask not only what you can do for your country. Ask also what you can do *without* for the good of your country and the good of all the peoples and all the ecosystems of the planet.

Perhaps the most formidable challenge for the discipline of economics in the future will be to help societies develop economic systems that will produce enough goods, enough jobs with adequate incomes, sufficient profits and investments—but all without the stimuli of unconstrained production and consumption. That task would return economics to being truly the science of scarcity. Perhaps our motto for the future should be: Flourish frugally!

Subversive Virtue and Countervision

The main moral problem with excess is not that it hurts the prodigal actors. In fact, it often does not; it may even be beneficial to them economically and politically. Rather, the problem with excess is that it harms those whom it deprives, whether other humans or other life forms. Our excesses in goods are really excessive regard for ourselves at the expense of others, which is the essence of sin in Jewish and Christian thought. That in fact is why greed and gluttony as the roots of excess are central vices. Excess is wrong primarily because it is unfair to others. And it must be restrained in defense of fairness to others. These restraints I call frugality.

Frugality is one of the virtues or standards of moral excellence that we need to cultivate in our personal lives, our communities of faith and learning, and our social institutions to counteract the social and ecological vices of our age. It is indispensable as an instrument of social justice and ecological integrity. It is a standard for both character formation and social transformation.

Frugality is the most feared norm in modern morality. Indeed, it is considered a "vice" by some economists, because it is "inefficient," adversely affecting economic growth. It is the most subversive of the virtues, because it is a revolt against the most sacred values of prodigal societies. Yet, solutions to every social and environmental crisis in this age depend on the revival of this classical virtue, and its reformation from a strictly personal trait into a norm for social practices. Frugality is an antidote to the gluttony that is corrupting the planet.

Frugality means moderation, thrift, material sufficiency, even temperance (so long as that word is not understood in a Prohibition sense). It incorporates careful conservation, comprehensive recycling, material efficiency, restrained consumption, and product durability and repairability. Frugality is morally disciplined production and consumption. It is a middle way that struggles against both profligacy and poverty. It opposes both overconsumption by the affluent and underconsumption by the poor.

Contrary to the modern and demeaning stereotypes, frugality is not a world-denying asceticism that makes us feel deprived and envious. Not at all. In fact, its Latin root, frux, connotes fruitfulness and joyfulness. Frugality is an earth-affirming and enriching norm that delights in the nonconsumptive and less-consumptive joys of the mind and flesh, especially the enhanced lives for human communities and other creatures that only constrained consumption can make possible on a finite planet. Frugality minimizes harm to humans and otherkind, enabling thereby a greater thriving of all life together.

In the great religious traditions, frugality is an expression of love—that is, seeking the good of others in response to their needs. Frugality is also a necessary condition of justice and sustainability in situations of relative scarcity, where "enough" can be available for all—humankind and otherkind—only if essential resources are shared and not "hogged" by some.

Prodigal societies need to learn what the world's religious traditions have long understood: The fullness and richness of life will not be found in the abundance and luxuriousness of our possessions. Rather, genuine joy is found in justice and generosity, to ensure that all have enough to thrive together.

Frugality is more than an alternative lifestyle; it is rather a countervision of being a purposeful and responsible human being in a purposeful and responsible society. The present political prospects for the socialization of this countervision are, of course, bleak. But we are not fated. Political possibilities can be transformed, particularly when serious initiatives are undertaken to create a widespread awareness of the values of frugality and the disvalues of alternatives. That is a major challenge to moral education in these times.

22

Sustainability and Community

John B. Cobb, Jr.

(*The Egg: An Eco-Justice Quarterly* 12 [3], Summer 1992)

For more than a century the world has been taught that the great choice is between capitalism and socialism. Now capitalism has won the struggle in terms both of public power and of human loyalties. But over the last quarter of a century, many of us came increasingly to realize that capitalism and socialism have not really been so very different. They are two sects in a larger quasi-religious movement. This movement has been based on commitment to economic growth as the organizing principle of personal and social life and as the way of dealing with all the important problems of humanity.

Capitalism has sought growth through the reduction of social restrictions on individual initiative. It has accepted enormous disparities in wealth and power as contributory to increasing the total amount of goods and services. It has taught that impersonal market forces lead to the greatest efficiency in allocating resources and thus to rapid growth.

Socialism has held that it is the task of government to encourage, manage, and direct growth for the sake of the people as a whole. It has undertaken to distribute the products of labor so that all will benefit to a more equal degree. All this is to be attained by planning on the part of those best able to understand and shape the entire process.

Socialist ideas, translated into practice, mean bureaucratic management. But it is now clear that the impersonal mechanisms of the market deal with the complex problems of allocation far more effectively than could the most conscientious, diligent bureaucrat. Also, removal of the profit motive reduces the incentive to work hard and implement efficient procedures. So capitalism wins hands down in the contest to see who can grow fastest.

Growth as Salvation

Why does the great god growth control the hearts as well as the practice of so many thoughtful people? Some people adopt a religious position out of self-interest, and devotion to growth lends itself especially well to this use. But I am focusing on those whose conviction is sincere. Let us review the history of salvation that shapes their perception of the past, present, and future.

According to this history, most human beings throughout recorded history have lived near the threshold of survival. When the weather has been unfavorable, or when the soil has become impoverished, or when social discord has disrupted normal patterns, hundreds of thousands have perished. Even when matters have gone well, the great majority have barely subsisted. The total production of goods has made a few wealthy, but it has not sufficed to provide the amenities of life to the many.

The industrial revolution changed this. It was in part a new organization of labor that enabled the same number of people, working the same amount of time, to produce far more goods. It was in part a technological advance that harnessed fossil fuels to increase the productivity of human labor. By these means, the economy grew.

Economic growth outstripped population growth, wages rose beyond mere subsistence, and prosperity led to less desire for large families. Family size dropped in industrialized nations, population growth slowed, and economic growth translated into a higher standard of living for the great majority. For the first time in human history, even the poor came to enjoy what had previously been considered the luxuries of the rich, as well as many luxuries of which even the rich had not earlier dreamed.

After World War II the religion of growth became global. Seeing the success of this religion in the developed countries, those that were not yet industrialized looked to it as their salvation as well. Global economic growth became the goal of international organizations as well as of national governments. The question was only to which sect to subscribe in pursuit of this growth. The World Council of Churches did not oppose growth when it committed itself to justice and participation. It only argued that these values should not be obscured or subordinated in the process of seeking growth.

Uncounted Costs

No one can question that a great deal of suffering accompanied industrialization, especially in England, which pioneered it. No one can question that since World War II enormous suffering has been endured in many Third World countries for the sake of the economic growth generated by industry. In most instances the sufferers could be controlled only by military governments.

In addition, industrialization, with its accompanying urbanization, intensifies social problems. Families are less stable. There is more loneliness and loss of meaning, accompanied by increased use of alcohol and other drugs. Crime increases. Employment becomes less regular and secure.

Believers in growth acknowledge these social costs, but they are not deeply troubled by them. Some of them are outgrown as industrialization progresses. Wages rise, working conditions improve, and the unrest of labor declines. Democratic institutions guaranteeing civil rights replace authoritarian regimes.

Although urbanization increases some social problems, it also offers many advantages when compared with rural life. Further, affluence allows cities to respond to these social problems with social services. Indeed, the presence of these problems only accents the need for the growth that allows societies to pay for the institutions required to deal with them.

At present this orthodox doctrine governs the affairs of the world, with little regard for the costs of growth. Some economists recognize that these costs should be internalized—that all social and environmental costs should be included in the market price. This, they rightly argue, would steer growth in more benign directions.

This brings us to the problem of the costs of disposing of wastes. Here the orthodox commitment to growth confronts its greatest difficulties. It is hard to see how advances in technology can add to the capacity of the earth to cope with the greenhouse gases, for example. Of course, some reduction in these gases can be effected by technological advances in industry and transportation. But the most traditional economists advocate that we cope with the problems caused by global warming as they arise. When one properly discounts costs to be incurred twenty or thirty years from now, some argue, it is more economical to relocate people from flooded coastal areas then, or to build dikes to protect them, than to make the drastic changes needed to slow global warming.

The Counter Argument

Even if it were possible to continue indefinitely to increase production in each country, i.e., to enlarge GNP, much of this production would be "defensive." That is, GNP includes costs entailed by its increase, such as the costs of urbanization and protection from criminal activity. Increasingly, there are costs for environmental protection as well. If all the growth of GNP were in these defensive costs, or if these defensive costs grew more rapidly than GNP as a whole, then continued devotion to growth as measured by GNP would have to be acknowledged as absurd. If a nation spent hundreds of billions of dollars relocating its people away from coastal lands and building dikes to protect those who remained, this would all be counted as increasing the GNP. In this sense, continued growth of GNP might be sustained. But since this would not enable people to obtain more of the goods they desired, it makes no sense to claim that this kind of growth is beneficial.

In my opinion we are already at the point in the United States where the costs of growth, even in strictly economic terms, exceed its benefits. Together with Cliff Cobb, I have tried to show this in an Index of Sustainable Economic Welfare. According to our figures, during the last ten years covered by our study, 1979 to 1988, while the per capita GNP grew by 20 percent, per capita sustainable economic welfare fell by 10 percent.

Now that we see that the growth to which the world has committed itself does not directly improve the human lot, we can raise other questions about the standard history of salvation. Was the life of the English yeomanry, before they were dispossessed by the enclosure movement, really as miserable and precarious as depicted? Was life in the cities of the Renaissance, with their guild economies, so terrible? Indeed, was the poverty of those days worse than the poverty of the present? Has economic growth benefited the poor?

We can also ask to what extent the prosperity of Europe and North America was generated through exploitation of Latin America,

Africa, and Asia, rather than by the efficiency of the manufacturing system. Certainly it was closely accompanied by the colonialism that destroyed indigenous cultures and that devoured both natural and human resources. Could it have occurred without this? Does it occur now apart from neocolonial exploitation of the tropical world?

If great claims are to be made for past achievements of the industrial system and its accompanying ideology of growth, they should be justified by comparisons of the total global situation before and after industrialization. The claim that industrialization has improved the human condition, even in strictly economic terms, is difficult to sustain. The issue today is whether, when unfettered from government regulations and social constraints, it can do so. The global campaign for free trade expresses the faith that it can. But the amount of free trade we now have is doing appalling harm. The further extensions in the Uruguay Round of the GATT and the NAFTA will be an unmitigated disaster.

The growth establishment, finally realizing the importance of sustainability, has called for "sustainable development." By this it means "sustainable growth," as is made very clear in the report of the World Commission on Environment and Development, the channel through which this phrase has passed into wide use. It fosters the orthodox view that the Third World can grow only through trading with the First World. And from this it follows that the First World must also increase its production and consumption sixfold. On a planet in which economic activity is already causing severe stresses in the natural environment, the call for a sixfold increase in this activity, whatever the rhetoric about sustainability, is absurd. "Sustainable growth" is an oxymoron.

Sustainable Community Development

But what if the phrase "sustainable development" were taken away from those who are devoted to growth and employed by those who are committed to sustainability? Could we fill it with meaning? If not, are we not turning our backs on the teaming populations of Latin America, Africa, and southern Asia, condemning them to misery and worse?

The answer depends on what we can make of the other word in my title, "community." Alongside the dominant meaning of development as growth of per capita production and consumption, there is another meaning to be found in the term. *I believe there can be "sustainable community development."*

Note that these two types of development are not simply different. They are emphatically not complementary. They are antithetical. The dominant model of development as growth requires a systematic assault on existing communities together with the values they nourish and live by. Third World development requires the "rational" embracing of First World values, which means persuading individuals to subordinate their concern for their communities to their efforts to gain more goods for themselves. People who are content with meeting their basic needs must be taught to have infinite wants. Those who have prized spiritual values above material ones must be persuaded to put material goods first. When persuasion and indoctrination do not suffice, economic and political force must be used.

We do not need to go to the Third World to see how the economic order devoted to growth assaults community. In this country, it has been applied in systematic ways to agriculture. The results has been a great success in economic terms. Fossil fuels have been substituted for animal and human labor in such a way as greatly to increase productivity, defined as product per hour of human work. The result, of course, is that most of the people who once lived on the land have lost their farms. Those who lived in the towns that were based on the economy of small family farms have lost their jobs. Thousands of rural communities have been destroyed.

In the past two decades a different feature of the growth economy has destroyed hundreds of urban communities. The quest for productivity not only involves substituting fossil fuels for animal and human labor. It also requires that capital should be invested where it is most profitable. In places where workers were organized and demanded high pay and good working conditions, or where the public demanded that industry avoid pollution of its environment, costs went up. Capital was, accordingly, less profitably invested in these places than in others where labor was cheaper and more docile, and where there were fewer restrictions on the use of the air, land, and water. Being "rational," the owners of capital have closed long-established factories in large numbers and reinvested their capital, sometimes in other sections of the United States, but now more often in Mexico and other Third World countries. "Free trade" means that products manufactured by badly-paid workers, and with few costs associated with environmental protection, re-enter the U.S. market to undercut goods made here, where manufacturers must meet higher standards.

Sustainable community development returns to the traditional view that the economy should be in the service of the community. This means that the values of the community govern what is considered to be development. It means that the process of development strengthens the community.

In much of the Third World, a large part of the population still lives in rural villages. Much of the practical outcome of adopting the principles of community development would be development in and for these villages. This was the form of development advocated by Gandhi. The symbol of community development for him was the sewing machine. Technology of this sort would enable village women to become more productive. An improved plough might help in the farming. This is the kind of equipment that E. F. Schumacher taught us to call "appropriate technology." It is appropriate because it enables people to accomplish their tasks more successfully without changing the basic structure of their lives or their communal values. It is equipment that can be maintained and repaired by village people.

Of course, the desires of people in many villages will not be for sewing machines and better ploughs. In many places the most urgent problem is the lack of fuel for cooking. The greatest help may be to introduce solar cookers or stoves that can produce more heat with less wood or dung. Reforestation of local hillsides may be called for. In other places the major problems arise from the fact that development of the standard variety has made people dependent on fossil fuels and tractors that have become unaffordable and cannot be maintained. The need may be to return to a system based on the water buffalo.

In many places the problems of the villagers are caused by external economic and political forces. For example, they may be displaced to give the best land to agribusiness for production of export crops. Their need is political organization against their oppressors and a shift of public thinking from the present growth-oriented, export-driven enterprise to sustainable community development.

Community development enables villages to become more self-reliant instead of making them more dependent on decisions made about them by others. This requires that in essential matters they be able to survive on their own resources. This does not preclude trade. The village produces a surplus that it can exchange for goods it does not produce. But the less its survival depends on this exchange, the freer it is to seek fair terms of exchange and thus to escape the economic exploitation to which so many villages have been so long subjected. Community development moves toward self-sufficiency in essentials.

Development of this kind *can* be sustainable. It sometimes increases the use of scarce materials, but more often it is a matter of developing more sustainable practices and more efficient use of renewable resources. If Third World development since World War II had followed this Gandhian model, hundreds of millions of poor people would be better off, even though their standard of living measured by per capita GNP would still be very low.

Urban Implications

A new approach to urban development is also required. Community development in urban areas must become neighborhood development. Some neighborhoods already have some of the same cohesion as rural villages. It is then possible to work with existing neighborhoods, discovering felt needs, and responding to them. It is possible to strengthen neighborhoods politically and to help some of them to become more nearly self-sufficient economically—even in the production of food!

In considering communities thus far, I have emphasized small ones—rural villages and urban neighborhoods. Larger groupings of people should be thought of as communities of communities. It is of great importance that cities become communities of neighborhoods.

Cities as they are now built are inherently unsustainable. They require enormous input of energy for their very survival. They grow like cancers, often over the most fertile parts of the land. They claim resources from distant places.

The most positive alternative proposal of which I am aware is that of Paolo Soleri. His "archologies" would meet their energy requirements chiefly from passive solar power. They would eliminate the need for motor transportation within the city. They would occupy far less land. And together with the surrounding countryside, they could become largely autonomous economic units. Further, they would encourage the kind of participation by their citizens that makes for true community.

Eco-Communities Here and Now

Perhaps the most difficult country in which to implement the vision of eco-communities is the United States. We have worshipped the great god growth so long in theory and in practice that stable communities, rural or urban, have become rare. Even those of us who recognize the need for community prize our mobility. We may find it exciting to experiment with community living, but we have internalized the values of individualism too deeply to set them aside.

Precisely for this reason, this is the country in which experimentation in eco-communities is most widespread, most important, and most fruitful. We have so embodied the values and ideologies of the modern world that traditional communities are too broken to inhibit us or to restrict our vision. We are truly free to experiment. It is imperative that our own nation re-invent itself. That will have to be from the bottom up, though it also requires support from "above" through better economic policies and sensitive courts. Re-invention must be in terms of communities, not individuals, and these communities must become sustainable. For this we can hope and work.

Part III

The Journey Continues

The eco-justice journey is far from finished. In the early years of the new century it continues on its rocky course, despite the distressing evidence—especially in the U.S. political arena—of denial more deeply entrenched. This denial of the need for a radical turn actually generates around the nation the conditions and energies for accepting and pressing its imperative.

Part III consists entirely of material written after the *Journal of Eco-Justice* was no longer published. It demonstrates and exemplifies the continuing journey. Indeed, it suggests a new stage of the journey, which may come from a more solid grasp of the eco-justice crisis and a more courageous acceptance of the radicality of the turn that is required.

Dieter Hessel in Selection 23 picks up on the story of "The Church's Eco-Justice Journey." In this essay church means the scholars, institutions, agencies, and church leaders and members who understand themselves as part of the one ecumenical church and have worked within the context of the ecumenical movement, international and national. It is a story that needs telling, for it has been neglected by the secular media and even by most of the church press.

It begins with the basic and central insight of eco-justice, "that there will be little environmental health without social justice, and vice-versa." Over time a "fulsome ethic of eco-justice" emerges, incorporating the norms that have been cited repeatedly in this volume: solidarity, sustainability, sufficiency, and participation.

Hessel sees ecumenical environmentalism as part of "a historic movement toward the alternative paradigm of mutually enhancing human-earth relations." Christian and secular travelers have mutually benefited each other and made it a movement not just for the environment or for social and economic justice but for both together. This larger, maturing movement contributed to the development of the Earth Charter, clearly an eco-justice document.

Hessel sees nothing less than the beginning phase of a comprehensive ecological reformation of Christianity. This will encompass profound and far-reaching new understandings of scriptural interpretation, theology, ethics, liturgy, church practice, and Christian faithfulness. The reformation has clearly come onto the ecumenical agenda. The unanswered question is "how alertly and energetically" will Christians participate in the unfinished journey.

Selection 24 is "The Earth Charter" itself. After wide and varied input and much work over a number of years by the Earth Charter Commission, this document received considerable favorable attention among delegations to the World Summit on Sustainable Development in Johannesburg, South Africa in 2002. The Charter is expected to gain increasing currency in UN circles. It constitutes a major expression of, and impetus to, the continuing journey.

In Selection 25, "The Earth Charter, Globalization and Sustainable Community," Larry Rasmussen provides an extended explanation and commentary on the Charter and its implications.

"Respect Earth and life in all its diversity" is the fundamental principle of the Earth Charter. This parallels the fundamental principle of the Universal Declaration of Human Rights, which is human dignity, requiring respect for every human life. "But the parallel," says Rasmussen, "hides a moral revolution." If respect for the whole community of life has become the fundamental ethical principle, this de-centers the human self and necessarily places that self within the basic context of Earth community. The moral revolution—opening up a new moral world—implies and indeed finally requires a social revolution—in Rasmussen's words, "redoing the world created by that [now de-centered human] self." The Charter deeply affirms the dignity of every person, but it does not accept the aspect of the rights tradition that asserts "a practical and deeply institutionalized morality of the sovereign human subject as legislator over all else."

In the light of respect for the whole community of life, Rasmussen goes on to discuss global capitalism, the huge concentrations of corporate power, and the assault by such power upon community and democracy. The concept of sustainable development has been reduced to a "greening" of capitalism, which leaves the power reality and its inevitable perpetration of injustice unbroken. As Rasmussen says, the language of the Charter is "mild and careful and never truly confrontational." Perhaps the revolutions to which it would surely lead are too hidden either to alarm or to inspire.

But community and democracy will not be empowered and deadly excesses of power disassembled without confrontation and fierce resistance. The ethics of eco-justice must prepare itself for the coming stage of the journey in which the life-or-death issues will become both more obvious and more controversial.

In Selection 26 I offer my own "Concluding Considerations" about the "Continuing Journey." Both the ecological reformation in the church and the drive for a global ethic, as represented by the Earth Charter, must address and debate more explicitly and creatively the revolutionary nature of their eco-justice vision and the force that opposes it all along the way. The obsolete paradigm, which they seek to replace, still serves the prevailing powers, which work constantly to keep it embedded and unquestioned in people's assumptions, habits, and defenses. In the coming stage of the long journey it will be necessary to get serious and specific about the hard questions, the challenge and the task, of preparing for and actually effecting the radical turn, all the while drawing upon the resources of a faith that is radical both in its realism and in its hope.

23

The Church's Eco-Justice Journey

Dieter T. Hessel

As planet Earth becomes hotter, stormier, less biodiverse, more crowded, unequal and violent, a growing number of theologians and ethicists, seminaries and colleges, church agencies, intentional communities, and discerning church members on six continents are joining the eco-justice movement. They are fostering ecologically responsive Christianity that challenges prevailing patterns of church and society. This essay will review recent ecumenical Christian involvement in this environmental and social responsibility journey, and then draw out some implications from that story for us.[1]

I. International Ecumenical Awakening
to the Environmental Crisis

Cultural historians looking back at the last third of the twentieth century with renewed appreciation for religion's ambiguous power may see that religious leaders, scholars, and organizations had to relearn from the ecologists that, in addition to the human species and culture, *nature* in all its biodiversity is real and valuable. But historians should also see that twentieth century environmentalism often lacked passion for, or adequate principles of, social justice. So, it was left to working groups of ecumenical theologians and ethicists—informed by the insights of environmental activists and social ecologists, as well as by the Hebrew Bible's Sabbath

261

sensibility and Covenant ethics—to emphasize that *there will be little environmental health without social justice, and vice-versa.* Once the ecumenical movement came to this realization, its gatherings and leaders began to express an inclusive vision of *eco-justice* that seeks what is ecologically fitting and socially fair through democratic decision making for the common good.

The global ecumenical movement and its member churches began to address the environmental challenge in the mid-1970s, following the Stockholm Conference on Environment and Development (1972). In response, the Nairobi Assembly of the World Council of Churches (WCC) (1975) emphasized the need to establish a "just, sustainable, and participatory society." In his address to that Assembly, Australian biologist Charles Birch explained:

> A prior requirement of any global society is that it be so organized that human life and other living creatures on which human life depends can be sustained indefinitely within the limits of the earth. A second requirement is that it be sustained at a quality that makes possible fulfillment of human life for all people. A society so organized to achieve both these ends we can call a sustainable global society in contrast to the present unsustainable global society. If the life of the world is to be sustained and renewed . . . it will have to be with a new sort of science and technology governed by a new sort of economics and politics.

After Nairobi, a 1979 WCC Conference at Massachusetts Institute of Technology on "Faith, Science and the Future" pursued the subject in more detail. To sample some mature Christian ethical reflection from that era, read Roger Shinn, *Forced Options* (Harper & Row, 1982), and the reports of the WCC's Vancouver Assembly (1983) around the theme of Justice, Peace and the Integrity of Creation.

Even with these prominent initiatives, it took at least another decade to gain wide ecumenical acceptance of a fulsome ethic of eco-justice that features basic moral norms of *solidarity* with other people and creatures; ecological *sustainability* in development, technology and production; *sufficiency* as a standard of organized sharing, requiring floors and ceilings for equitable consumption; and socially just *participation* in decisions about how to obtain sustenance and to manage community life for the good of all.

And not until the late 1980s, in a consultation at Annecy, France, did the WCC begin to address a theology and ethic for the liberation of life that demands respect for animals and preservation of species for their own sake, not just for their benefit to humankind.[2] That report informed the WCC's Canberra Assembly theme, "Come Holy Spirit, Renew the Whole Creation." Through the 1990s, the WCC mission in society unit developed an action/reflection emphasis on Theology of Life that has focused the critical ecumenical reflection, and several WCC publications, on environmentally and humanly destructive effects of *economic globalization.*

Similarly, in 1998, the World Alliance of Reformed Churches (WARC) issued a study paper to guide a "Committed Process of Recognition, Education, Confession and Action regarding Economic Injustice and Ecological Destruction." (*Processus Confessionis*) A paragraph in that WARC report said:

> It is not enough for our communities to denounce injustice and point to the seemingly irreparable damage done to the earth [by economic globalization]. We need to travel further towards the embodiment of a just society living in tender relationship with the earth. We need to celebrate the "mustard seed" signs of the realm of God. We can give thanks for the ferment of the Holy Spirit in and through people who resist threats to life.

Meanwhile, the WCC launched a climate change program led by David Hallman of the United Church of Canada. And in the late 1990s the Orthodox ecumenical Patriarch Bartholomew received considerable publicity for declaring pollution to be a sin against God. Nevertheless, concerns about violence, racism, and economic injustice have continued to elicit much more international ecumenical attention than has the ecological crisis.

The Roman Catholic story unfolded more slowly, beginning with the Pope's 1979 trip to the Americas (first Puebla and then Des Moines), where John Paul II emphasized land stewardship. It took another decade for the Vatican to issue a 1990 message on *The Ecological Crisis: A Common Responsibility.* Then, on Pentecost 1992, in Brazil, parallel to the Earth Summit (the 1992 UN Conference on Environment and Development), an inclusive gathering of Protestant, Orthodox, Roman Catholic, and Anglican leaders facilitated by the WCC issued a *Letter to the Churches*, which concluded its confession of complicity and expression of commitment with these words: "The Spirit teaches us to go first to those places where community and creation are most obviously languishing, those melancholy places where the cry of the people and the cry of the earth are intermingled. [There] we meet Jesus, who goes before, in solidarity and healing."[3]

II. Phases of Ecumenical Environmental Response in the U.S.

(Here I am pointing to the most noticeable aspects, and will not go into some parts of the story, such as individual denominational activity, earth-honoring practices by intentional Christian communities, interfaith efforts to preserve endangered species, progress in "greening" institutional practices to serve sustainability, ecumenical relief for environmental refugees from human-induced disasters, and support of indigenous people struggling for human rights.)

1. Cultivating Quality Ecotheology and Ethics

This started with essays by forerunner theologian Joseph Sittler, and developed through a National Council of Churches (NCC) Work Group on "Faith-Man-Nature" formed in 1963-64 by biologist Philip Joranson. Daniel Day Williams, H. Paul Santmire, John B. Cobb, Jr., and Rosemary Radford Ruether soon added contributions. This early period is well-summarized in Roderick Nash, *The Rights of Nature: A History of Environmental Ethics* (University of Wisconsin Press, 1989). But Nash does not discern the beginnings of a theological bent toward eco-justice ethics, for example, in a 1971 Friendship Press anthology entitled, *A New Ethic For a New Earth*. He also overlooks what the churches actually said and did in proximity to the first Earth Day, and shows no awareness of extensive church engagement with hunger and energy policies in the 1970s.

Ecotheology and ethics languished in the 1980s, and then developed with vigor again in the 1990s. Now diverse voices representing both genders and people of color as well as whites across the Christian spectrum are contributing, as can be seen in *Ecology, Justice and Christian Faith: A Critical Guide to the Literature* (Peter Bakken and Joan and J. Ronald Engel, eds., Greenwood Press, 1995), and in *Christianity and Ecology* (Hessel and Ruether, eds., Harvard University Center for the Study of World Religions, 2000). Although few theological schools actually *feature* this important advance in theology and ethics, most seminary and religious studies programs offer electives on this subject. Still, neither the churches nor the National Religious Partnership for the Environment have been all that interested in the intellectual task. So TEMEC, Theological Education to Meet the Environmental Challenge, was launched in 1992 to foster the in-depth theological reflection and cross-disciplinary study needed for sustained environmental response by scholars, pastors, and laity.

2. Fostering Sustainable Food Systems and Lifestyles

During the 1970s progressive churches were prominently involved in protecting the rights of farm workers. National boycotts of grapes and lettuce, spearheaded by the United Church of Christ, lent strong support to the United Farm Workers. Boycotts (selective buying) of other commodity producers, because they violate labor rights, have also occurred with less fanfare in recent years.

Meanwhile, the churches working together in the NCC became quite knowledgeable about U.S. government food and farm programs, as well as problems of international aid and trade. The churches invested considerable energy in leadership development for hunger education/action through new denominational initiatives and the ecumenical effort named WHEAT—World Hunger Education/Action Together (of which I was the founding chair). The hunger programs institutionalized by the churches in the late 1970s gave some attention and project funding to the environmental dimensions of sustainable food systems, for example, how to decrease monoculture, pesticide use, export cropping, and grain-fed meat consumption, while using appropriate technology for food production in poor countries. Today we face deepening problems of inappropriate technology in export crops, controlled by corporations that patent and produce genetically modified organisms (GMOs) such as pesticide resistant plants or "killer" seeds. So far, ecumenical critique of these developments seems muted.

As the crisis of family farmers deepened in the 1980s and 1990s, church groups, influenced by Wendell Berry, Wes Jackson, and Dean Freudenberger, began to focus on the need for sustainable agriculture, church- and community-based agriculture, and local food security. In the United States much of the solid analysis, education and advocacy has been led by creative clergy—often Lutherans—working with centers for land stewardship and rural life, especially in the upper plains.

Roman Catholics have approached these concerns in a different style, featuring regional pastoral letters (drafted in both of the following cases by John Hart of Carroll College, Montana). In 1984, Catholic bishops of twelve midwestern states issued *Strangers and Guests: Toward Community in the Heartland*. In February 2001, twelve northwestern Catholic bishops issued a pastoral letter on the *Columbia River Watershed: Caring For Creation and the Common Good.* That international watershed is threatened not only by inappropriate dams and logging, but by water diversion for irrigated agriculture, and a regional population explosion of high consumers.

Speaking of consumption, the pioneering work of campus minister William E. Gibson and the Eco-Justice Project based at Cornell University fostered quality education for lifestyle change as an emphasis of the church's hunger programs. It focused on reduced consumption, voluntary conservation, appropriate private diet and recreation, plus public engagement. In the 1990s, education for lifestyle integrity has returned to prominence again, thanks to the initiative of another regional ecumenical project called Earth Ministry, in Seattle.

(Lester Brown, of the Worldwatch Institute, has said, "We need an environmental revolution of an order of magnitude that matches the agricultural and industrial revolutions, and at the same time transforms them. Numbers 2 and 3 of these ecumenical environmental responses illustrate his point.)

3. Advocating Responsible Energy and Climate Change Policies

Before the first oil shock from OPEC, U.S. churches were not involved in energy policy debates, viewing them as too technical or merely political. But in 1974 the Division of Church and Society of the NCC formed a committee of inquiry, chaired by Margaret Mead and Rene Dubos, on the use of plutonium as a commercial nuclear fuel. When, in October 1975, the committee proposed a policy statement condemning such use of plutonium, the nuclear industry and utility executives attacked the NCC for being irresponsible. A resolution calling for a moratorium was substituted for the policy statement, and in the same action the Council mandated a broad study on the Ethical Implications of Responsible Energy Production and Use, led by the late Chris Cowap, NCC Director of Economic Justice. She wrote a concise, instructive overview of that highly conflicted study for a book entitled *Energy Ethics* (Friendship Press, 1979). Her description of the outcome of the three-year process, involving a panel of 120 knowledgeable persons, shows how intellectually demanding and politically sophisticated was this timely ecumenical endeavor.

The energy study shows that the church can be powerfully present among competing interests with contradictory answers to the environmental challenge. This policy study coincided with the grassroots movement to delegitimize nuclear power and take a "soft energy path" (Amory Lovins). It was followed by inter-church programs to foster local energy responsibility, by substantive denominational energy policy statements, and by interfaith efforts to demand corporate accountability to communities on the part of utilities building power plants. Local congregations, however, tended to limit their participation to retrofitting their buildings for energy efficiency.

Now, three decades later, we have come back full circle to the same aspects of energy policy that the 1970s NCC study explored, including: fossil fuel dependence, reliance on dangerous nuclear and carbon dioxide emitting coal-fired generators, as well as lack of public accountability by power companies, and federal indifference to renewable energy technologies, conservation incentives, mass transit subsidies and carbon taxes that would reduce consumption.

Moreover, the world faces an urgent need to halt global warming, regarding which the United States—with 4 percent of the world's population, but responsible for 25 percent of the world's heat-trapping gasses—is dragging its feet. Ecumenical work on climate change emerged through workshops in different parts of the world organized by Canadian David Hallman as a way to focus on the links between economic injustice and environmental destruction. WCC workshops and its 1988 study paper on "Climate Change and the Quest For Sustainable Societies," plus reinforcing reports and statements by denominations, presented scientific facts about climate change, and theological-ethical reflections on social and ecological justice. This was followed by a worldwide petition campaign involving the churches and other faith communities, which got the attention of government officials and positioned an ecumenical team of church representatives to become active advocates at climate change negotiations from Kyoto forward. Ecumenical advocacy on this issue emphasizes that the most industrialized countries must demonstrate global responsibility and show fairness to poor countries by making real cuts in greenhouse gas emissions, rather than relying on "trading" emission credits.

Churches in the industrialized countries are also engaged in advocacy work with their public officials. Currently in the United States, this is done through Interfaith Climate Change Campaigns—occurring in eighteen states coordinated by the NCC Eco-Justice Working Group, working with State Councils of Churches. *The Christian Century* (April 18–25, 2001) printed an editorial on U.S.

responsibility for global warming, but made no mention of ecumenical studies or public policy advocacy work by churches.

4. Community Organizing for Environmental Justice.

The U.S. churches' most distinctive involvement with the environmental movement has been to foster "environmental justice." The UCC Commission on Racial Justice first prepared, published and circulated the documentation of severe inequity in locating toxic dumps and incinerators. [See Selection 7.] The churches also took the initiative to contact community organizations fighting toxic facilities, to bring some of their leaders together, and to find funding that enabled community organizations to challenge unjust waste management. Though the Citizens' Clearing House on Hazardous Wastes (now the Center for Health, Environment and Justice) deserves more credit for starting this kind of organizing, the ecumenical churches helped to make environmental justice more possible for communities of color, rural areas, and Indian nations.

By 1987, these initiatives were being coordinated through the Eco-Justice Working Group (EJWG) formed in 1985 by the NCC, with Chris Cowap as staff director, and myself as founding co-chair. Support of community organizing for environmental justice led the EJWG to subsidize participation by leaders of community groups in the National People of Color Environmental Leadership Summit (Washington, D.C., 1991), where they pushed the leaders of established environmental organizations to support basic principles of environmental justice, and to help "build a movement of all peoples of color to fight the destruction and taking of our lands and communities . . . and to secure our political, economic, and cultural liberation." Lutheran layman Jim Schwab, *Deeper Shades of Green* (Sierra Club Books, 1994) points out that this unique summit "drew more than 600 activists, combining the colors of the rainbow in one giant sharing and strategizing meeting that has literally and permanently changed the complexion of the U.S. environmental movement." The environmental justice emphasis also strengthened collaboration between para-church groups and non-governmental organizations (NGOs) at UN forums such as the Rio Earth Summit (1992), the Cairo Conference on Population and Development (1994) and the Beijing Conference on Women (1995).

The environmental justice focus also carried over into the work of the National Religious Partnership for the Environment, which provided funding for the NCC to hold special meetings with leaders of the Black churches and the Orthodox communions. But preoccupation with community organizing to combat toxics tended to preempt other styles of engagement and, for a time, to narrow eco-justice work to become a subset of economic justice advocacy.

5. Developing Leadership for Earth Community Ministry

At this point, the churches remembered that it is not enough to support grassroots groups of activists siding with the powerless. The environmental agenda is also concerned with preserving biodiversity and special places. To grapple with a broad agenda the churches must continuously develop leaders and nurture members, gain a voice in the media and a hearing with public officials, and challenge indifferent or hostile institutions to care about the web of creation and human relations with other kind. In other words, for there to be significant implementation of a preferential option for the oppressed, there must be more pedagogy of the privileged and careful structuring of environmental ministry.

Since the mid-1990s, the NCC EJWG and the U.S. Catholic Conference, with generous funding from the National Religious Partnership for the Environment, have concentrated on leadership development to mobilize congregations and to integrate creation-care into parish life—always with a strong social justice component. The NCC group now gathers its grassroots network annually to share the latest educational resources and to give focus to public policy advocacy.

Before drawing out some insights from this review, I must frankly acknowledge that the story also has a negative side. Most churches and members remain indifferent to the eco-justice movement or ethic, and are not yet involved in significant environmental ministry. In comparison to widespread church involvement in programs of social service and peace education/action, Christian communions have not institutionalized much care for creation. Church bodies and congregations continue to affirm and practice social "stewardship" apart from ecological responsibility. They have yet to grasp the depth of the eco-justice crisis, nor do they see mission in terms of communing and suffering with creation, or building sustainable community in healing and liberating ways. Rare is the church that celebrates and ministers to earth community in worship, education, institutional practices, and public witness. Except perhaps for recycling some waste, talking about reducing unnecessary consumption, and planning to retrofit church buildings for energy efficiency, congregations typically conduct religion business as usual with little time for the most basic human vocation—earth keeping (see Gen. 2:15).

Many clergy and lay leaders of local, denominational and ecumenical communities of faith still leave creation's well-being to others called "environmentalists." And even where Christians do see ecological problems, church leaders display ambivalence about working with the environmental community. For example, the Statement on Global Warming issued by Oregon Religious Leaders in October 2000, when launching their interfaith campaign declared, "We speak not as members of an 'environmental movement,' but as people of faith giving thanks to God for the blessings of creation by working to preserve them for present and future generations." As if faith, but no influence from environmental science and activism, had led the Oregon religious leaders to begin a global warming campaign.

III. Learning from the Church's Eco-Justice Journey

First, the U.S. ecumenical environmental responses that I have just reviewed are aspects of a historic movement toward the alternative paradigm of mutually enhancing human-earth relations. Churches that think and act in terms of God's commonwealth ("kingdom") can appreciate and respond positively to these concrete signs of a better future. In other words, ecumenical examples of eco-justice journeying offer wisdom for ongoing efforts to embody the more appropriate paradigm. With that perspective and commitment, we can recycle theology and ethics, foster sustainable food systems and lifestyles, advocate responsible energy and climate change policies, help to organize communities for economic and environmental justice, protect species, restore ecosystems, and develop leadership for earth community ministry.

Second, church leaders and environmental community leaders have positively influenced each other in a reciprocal relation that needs to continue. On the one hand, environmentalists pushed the ecumenical churches to rethink theology, ethics, and mission in light of the ideal of a sustainable society, to which the churches came slowly. While the ecumenical movement affirmed its social calling, in light of Jesus' public ministry, to care for and seek distributive justice to other humans, the environmental movement was focusing world attention on the plight and rights of the rest of nature, challenging the narrowly human-centered preoccupation of modern culture. Environmentalists, in addition to clarifying global ecological problems, contributed important concepts such as carrying capacity and interconnectedness. They defined the norm of sustainability in terms of ecological integrity, which forbids human activities that diminish earth's biodiversity or life-carrying capacity. The environmental movement also insisted that humans are called to feel respect and show care for all forms of life, not just other humans—an emphasis that broadens the meaning of "solidarity."

Instructed by these ecological insights, as well as critical social analysis, ecumenical ethicists came to a holistic understanding of what eco-justice requires to meet the world's dual crisis: degradation of the natural environment and oppression of poor people. Therefore, on the other hand, ecumenical eco-justice sensibility about human-earth relations began to spread throughout the environmental movement. This pushes environmental organizations to explore beliefs about what is sacred, and (moving beyond the insights of environmental philosophy and ecological science) to broaden their thinking about ecological sustainability to encompass principles of socio-economic justice. That advance was demonstrated vividly in two events that bookend the 1990's: the October 1991 People of Color Environmental Leadership Summit that I discussed above, and the Earth Council's release in March 2000 of a finished Earth Charter text (Selection 24; also available on the internet at earthcharterusa.org). The Earth Charter actually illumines basic eco-justice values, without using the term, as the Charter's four parts discuss principles associated with solidarity, sustainability, sufficiency, and participation—in that order. The result is to foster an ecology of ethical values for earth community.

A perspective that first emerged to reconcile post-Earth-Day competition between social justice and environmental action groups has turned out to offer much more than "tradeoffs." Eco-justice provides a dynamic framework for philosophical and theological study, and environmental ethical reflection to meet the real needs of earth community. Ironically, environmental organizations have gotten the eco-justice message faster than the faith communities!

Third, the vision, values and virtues expressed in eco-justice praxis give shape to a contextual ethic for church and society that applies at every level of moral agency—individual, institutional and governmental. A contextual, non-absolutist ethic informs immediate choices at any given time and place, but does not tell us exactly what to do. In light of social experience and human reason, as well as scripture and tradition, the ethical task is to discern among real options the good to be achieved or the path of right relations, while expecting pluralistic solutions respectful of cultural and biotic diversity.

Solidarity with Earth and people, ecological sustainability, basic sufficiency, and fair participation all matter as mutually reinforcing and correcting norms that inform and qualify each other. Full-orbed efforts to achieve just and sustainable community, therefore, encompass these deep, practical values as essential, interactive components of a healthy future—that is, what earth community requires. Also notice that the eco-justice norms are both ends-oriented and means-clarifying, illumining both where we want to go and how to get there.

Fourth, Christians who journey with creation-awareness and eco-justice intention are contributing to the ecological reformation that promises to: a) shift the axis of Christian theology, ethics, and liturgy, and transform our human vocation, b) reshape and reconstruct the churches' theology, worship, mission and witness to meet the twenty-first century, and c) within our new historical context of real biophysical limits and a threatened earth, seek human rights and otherkind's well-being together. That is a comprehensive, long-term agenda—much bigger than dealing with an environmental issue or changing some lifestyle habits.

Ecological reformation impels leaders in theology and ministry, and alert church bodies to: a) *abandon the bad theological habits* that have separated history and humanity from nature, and separated human redemption from creation. Recognizing that the web of life embraces distant galaxies and that humans are an ecologically integrated, morally responsible species, b) we can *utilize the relationality paradigm within current cosmology, ecology, process thought, and ecofeminism*; c) we also learn to *read scripture in trifocal perspective*—combining the view from outdoors with the view from below and the view from abroad; and d) this reformation underscores the need to *represent theology in ecologically alert terms*, and accordingly to *recycle traditional affirmations* about God, Christ, Spirit, world, church, soul/body, sin and evil, redemption, and new earth. Other steps toward ecological reformation are to: e) *redefine faithfulness in common life* in ways that *embody eco-justice ethics*; f) *reshape liturgical life* so as to highlight God's loving and just relationship with habitat earth, not only human beings; and g) *model sustainability in individual and institutional practices* that are earth-honoring. The needed transformation encompasses our consumer lifestyles, what and how we learn, the work we do, the way our organizations operate, and the networks we join for public engagement—all to strengthen sustainable community for creation's sake on and around this planet.

Though many churches and members still don't "get it," the ecological reformation has emerged prominently on the ecumenical agenda (as suggested in the Introduction to *Christianity and Ecology*), and we know what it involves.[4] The question before us is, how alertly and energetically will we participate in the continuing eco-justice journey? Or as the prophet Ezekial put the question: Can these bones live?[5]

Notes

1. This essay updates my earlier article, "Where Are the Churches in the Environmental Movement?" in *Theology and Public Policy*, VII (I) (1995) 20–31.

2. The Annecy Consultation Report is reprinted in an Appendix to *Liberating Life*, ed. Charles Birch, William Eakin, and Jay McDaniel (Maryknoll, N.Y.: Orbis, 1991).

3. See Wesley Granberg-Michaelson, *Redeeming the Creation* (Geneva, Switzerland: WCC Publications, 1992), 70–73.

4. See my concluding chapter, "The Church Ecologically Reformed," in Dieter Hessel and Larry Rasmussen, eds., *Earth Habitat: Eco-Injustice and the Church's Response* (Minneapolis, Minn.: Fortress Press, 2001).

5. The prophet's vision of God breathing life into the dry bones is found in Ezekial 37. Note the role of human prophecy and nature's four winds in enlivening the church.

24

The Earth Charter

Preamble

We stand at a critical moment in Earth's history, a time when humanity must choose its future. As the world becomes increasingly interdependent and fragile, the future at once holds great peril and great promise. To move forward we must recognize that in the midst of a magnificent diversity of cultures and life forms we are one human family and one Earth community with a common destiny. We must join together to bring forth a sustainable global society founded on respect for nature, universal human rights, economic justice, and a culture of peace. Towards this end, it is imperative that we, the peoples of Earth, declare our responsibility to one another, to the greater community of life, and to future generations.

Earth, Our Home

Humanity is part of a vast evolving universe. Earth, our home, is alive with a unique community of life. The forces of nature make existence a demanding and uncertain adventure, but Earth has provided the conditions essential to life's evolution. The resilience of the community of life and the well-being of humanity depend upon preserving a healthy biosphere with all its ecological systems, a rich variety of plants and animals, fertile soils, pure waters, and clean air. The global environment with its finite resources is a common concern of all peoples. The protection of Earth's vitality, diversity, and beauty is a sacred trust.

The Global Situation

The dominant patterns of production and consumption are causing environmental devastation, the depletion of resources, and a massive extinction of species. Communities are being undermined. The benefits of development are not shared equitably and the gap between rich and poor is widening. Injustice, poverty, ignorance, and violent conflict are widespread and the cause of great suffering. An unprecedented rise in human population has overburdened ecological and social systems. The foundations of global security are threatened. These trends are perilous—but not inevitable.

The Challenges Ahead

The choice is ours: form a global partnership to care for Earth and one another or risk the destruction of ourselves and the diversity of life. Fundamental changes are needed in our values, institutions, and ways of living. We must realize that when basic needs have been met, human development is primarily about being more, not having more. We have the knowledge and technology to provide for all and to reduce our impacts on the environment. The emergence of a global civil society is creating new opportunities to build a democratic and humane world. Our environmental, economic, political, social, and spiritual challenges are interconnected, and together we can forge inclusive solutions.

Universal Responsibility

To realize these aspirations, we must decide to live with a sense of universal responsibility, identifying ourselves with the whole Earth community as well as our local communities. We are at once citizens of different nations and of one world in which the local and global are linked. Everyone shares responsibility for the present and future well-being of the human family and the larger living world. The spirit of human solidarity and kinship with all life is strengthened when we live with reverence for the mystery of being, gratitude for the gift of life, and humility regarding the human place in nature.

We urgently need a shared vision of basic values to provide an ethical foundation for the emerging world community. Therefore, together in hope we affirm the following interdependent principles for a sustainable way of life as a common standard by which the conduct of all individuals, organizations, businesses, governments, and transnational institutions is to be guided and assessed.

Principles

I. Respect and Care for the Community of Life

1. RESPECT EARTH AND LIFE IN ALL ITS DIVERSITY.
   a. Recognize that all beings are interdependent and every form of life has value regardless of its worth to human beings.
   b. Affirm faith in the inherent dignity of all human beings and in the intellectual, artistic, ethical, and spiritual potential of humanity.

2. CARE FOR THE COMMUNITY OF LIFE WITH UNDER-STANDING, COMPASSION, AND LOVE.
   a. Accept that with the right to own, manage, and use natural resources comes the duty to prevent environmental harm and to protect the rights of people.
   b. Affirm that with increased freedom, knowledge and power comes increased responsibility to promote the common good.

3. BUILD DEMOCRATIC SOCIETIES THAT ARE JUST, PARTICIPATORY, SUSTAINABLE, AND PEACEFUL.
   a. Ensure that communities at all levels guarantee human rights and fundamental freedoms and provide everyone an opportunity to realize his or her full potential.
   b. Promote social and economic justice, enabling all to achieve a secure and meaningful livelihood that is ecologically responsible.

4. SECURE EARTH'S BOUNTY AND BEAUTY FOR PRESENT AND FUTURE GENERATIONS.
   a. Recognize that the freedom of action of each generation is qualified by the needs of future generations.
   b. Transmit to future generations values, traditions, and institutions that support the long-term flourishing of Earth's human and ecological communities.

In order to fulfill these four broad commitments, it is necessary to:

II. Ecological Integrity

5. PROTECT AND RESTORE THE INTEGRITY OF EARTH'S ECOLOGICAL SYSTEMS, WITH SPECIAL CONCERN FOR BIOLOGICAL DIVERSITY AND THE NATURAL PROCESSES THAT SUSTAIN LIFE.
    a. Adopt at all levels sustainable development plans and regulations that make environmental conservation and rehabilitation integral to all development initiatives.
    b. Establish and safeguard viable nature and biosphere reserves, including wild lands and marine areas, to protect Earth's life support systems, maintain biodiversity, and preserve our natural heritage.
    c. Promote the recovery of endangered species and ecosystems.
    d. Control and eradicate non-native or genetically modified organisms harmful to native species and the environment, and prevent introduction of such harmful organisms.
    e. Manage the use of renewable resources such as water, soil, forest products, and marine life in ways that do not exceed rates of regeneration and that protect the health of ecosystems.
    f. Manage the extraction and use of non-renewable resources such as minerals and fossil fuels in ways that minimize depletion and cause no serious environmental damage.

6. PREVENT HARM AS THE BEST METHOD OF ENVIRONMENTAL PROTECTION AND, WHEN KNOWLEDGE IS LIMITED, APPLY A PRECAUTIONARY APPROACH.
    a. Take action to avoid the possibility of serious or irreversible environmental harm even when scientific knowledge is incomplete or inconclusive.
    b. Place the burden of proof on those who argue that a proposed activity will not cause significant harm, and make the responsible parties liable for environmental harm.
    c. Ensure that decision making addresses the cumulative, long-term, indirect, long distance, and global consequences of human activities.
    d. Prevent pollution of any part of the environment and allow no build-up of radioactive, toxic, or other hazardous substances.
    e. Avoid military activities damaging to the environment.

7. ADOPT PATTERNS OF PRODUCTION, CONSUMPTION,
AND REPRODUCTION THAT SAFEGUARD EARTH'S
REGENERATIVE CAPACITIES, HUMAN RIGHTS, AND
COMMUNITY WELL-BEING.
  a. Reduce, reuse, and recycle the materials used in production and consumption systems, and ensure that residual waste can be assimilated by ecological systems.
  b. Act with restraint and efficiency when using energy, and rely increasingly on renewable energy sources such as solar and wind.
  c. Promote the development, adoption, and equitable transfer of environmentally sound technologies.
  d. Internalize the full environmental and social costs of goods and services in the selling price, and enable consumers to identify products that meet the highest social and environmental standards.
  e. Ensure universal access to health care that fosters reproductive health and responsible reproduction.
  f. Adopt lifestyles that emphasize the quality of life and material sufficiency in a finite world.

8. ADVANCE THE STUDY OF ECOLOGICAL SUSTAINABILITY
AND PROMOTE THE OPEN EXCHANGE AND WIDE
APPLICATION OF THE KNOWLEDGE ACQUIRED.
  a. Support international scientific and technical cooperation on sustainability, with special attention to the needs of developing nations.
  b. Recognize and preserve the traditional knowledge and spiritual wisdom in all cultures that contribute to environmental protection and human well-being.
  c. Ensure that information of vital importance to human health and environmental protection, including genetic information, remains available in the public domain.

III. Social and Economic Justice

9. ERADICATE POVERTY AS AN ETHICAL, SOCIAL, AND
ENVIRONMENTAL IMPERATIVE.
  a. Guarantee the right to potable water, clean air, food security, uncontaminated soil, shelter, and safe sanitation, allocating the national and international resources required.

    b. Empower every human being with the education and resources to secure a sustainable livelihood, and provide social security and safety nets for those who are unable to support themselves.

    c. Recognize the ignored, protect the vulnerable, serve those who suffer, and enable them to develop their capacities and to pursue their aspirations.

10. ENSURE THAT ECONOMIC ACTIVITIES AND INSTITUTIONS AT ALL LEVELS PROMOTE HUMAN DEVELOPMENT IN AN EQUITABLE AND SUSTAINABLE MANNER.

    a. Promote the equitable distribution of wealth within nations and among nations.

    b. Enhance the intellectual, financial, technical, and social resources of developing nations, and relieve them of onerous international debt.

    c. Ensure that all trade supports sustainable resource use, environmental protection, and progressive labor standards.

    d. Require multinational corporations and international financial organizations to act transparently in the public good, and hold them accountable for the consequences of their activities.

11. AFFIRM GENDER EQUALITY AND EQUITY AS PREREQUISITES TO SUSTAINABLE DEVELOPMENT AND ENSURE UNIVERSAL ACCESS TO EDUCATION, HEALTH CARE, AND ECONOMIC OPPORTUNITY.

    a. Secure the human rights of women and girls and end all violence against them.

    b. Promote the active participation of women in all aspects of economic, political, civil, social, and cultural life as full and equal partners, decision makers, leaders, and beneficiaries.

    c. Strengthen families and ensure the safety and loving nurture of all family members.

12. UPHOLD THE RIGHT OF ALL, WITHOUT DISCRIMINATION, TO A NATURAL AND SOCIAL ENVIRONMENT SUPPORTIVE OF HUMAN DIGNITY, BODILY HEALTH, AND SPIRITUAL WELL-BEING, WITH SPECIAL ATTENTION TO THE RIGHTS OF INDIGENOUS PEOPLES AND MINORITIES.

    a. Eliminate discrimination in all its forms, such as that based on race, color, sex, sexual orientation, religion, language, and national, ethnic or social origin.

b. Affirm the right of indigenous peoples to their spirituality, knowledge, lands and resources and to their related practice of sustainable livelihoods.

c. Honor and support the young people of our communities, enabling them to fulfill their essential role in creating sustainable societies.

d. Protect and restore outstanding places of cultural and spiritual significance.

IV. Democracy, Nonviolence, and Peace

13. STRENGTHEN DEMOCRATIC INSTITUTIONS AT ALL LEVELS AND PROVIDE TRANSPARENCY AND ACCOUNTABILITY IN GOVERNANCE, INCLUSIVE PARTICIPATION IN DECISION MAKING, AND ACCESS TO JUSTICE.

a. Uphold the right of everyone to receive clear and timely information on environmental matters and all development plans and activities which are likely to affect them or in which they have an interest.

b. Support local, regional and global civil society, and promote the meaningful participation of all interested individuals and organizations in decision making.

c. Protect the rights to freedom of opinion, expression, peaceful assembly, association, and dissent.

d. Institute effective and efficient access to administrative and independent judicial procedures, including remedies and redress for environmental harm and the threat of such harm.

e. Eliminate corruption in all public and private institutions.

b. Strengthen local communities, enabling them to care for their environments, and assign environmental responsibilities to the levels of government where they can be carried out most effectively.

14. INTEGRATE INTO FORMAL EDUCATION AND LIFE-LONG LEARNING THE KNOWLEDGE, VALUES, AND SKILLS NEEDED FOR A SUSTAINABLE WAY OF LIFE.

a. Provide all, especially children and youth, with educational opportunities that empower them to contribute actively to sustainable development.

   b. Promote the contribution of the arts and humanities as well as the sciences in sustainability education.

   c. Enhance the role of the mass media in raising awareness of ecological and social challenges.

   d. Recognize the importance of moral and spiritual education for sustainable living.

15. TREAT ALL LIVING BEINGS WITH RESPECT AND CONSIDERATION.

   a. Prevent cruelty to animals kept in human societies and protect them from suffering.

   b. Protect wild animals from methods of hunting, trapping, and fishing that cause extreme, prolonged, or avoidable suffering.

   c. Avoid or eliminate to the full extent possible the taking or destruction of non-targeted species.

16. PROMOTE A CULTURE OF TOLERANCE, NON-VIOLENCE, AND PEACE.

   a. Encourage and support mutual understanding, solidarity, and cooperation among all peoples and within and among nations.

   b. Implement comprehensive strategies to prevent violent conflict and use collaborative problem solving to manage and resolve environmental conflicts and other disputes.

   c. Demilitarize national security systems to the level of a non-provocative defense posture, and convert military resources to peaceful purposes, including ecological restoration.

   d. Eliminate nuclear, biological and toxic weapons and other weapons of mass destruction.

   e. Ensure that the use of orbital and outer space supports environmental protection and peace.

   f. Recognize that peace is the wholeness created by right relationships with oneself, other persons, other cultures, other life, Earth, and the larger whole of which all are a part.

The Way Forward

As never before in history, common destiny beckons us to seek a new beginning. Such renewal is the promise of these Earth Charter principles. To fulfill this promise, we must commit ourselves to adopt and promote the values and objectives of the Charter.

This requires a change of mind and heart. It requires a new sense of global interdependence and universal responsibility. We must imaginatively develop and apply the vision of a sustainable way of life locally, nationally, regionally, and globally. Our cultural diversity is a precious heritage and different cultures will find their own distinctive ways to realize the vision. We must deepen and expand the global dialogue that generated the Earth Charter, for we have much to learn from the ongoing collaborative search for truth and wisdom.

Life often involves tensions between important values. This can mean difficult choices. However, we must find ways to harmonize diversity with unity, the exercise of freedom with the common good, short-term objectives with long-term goals. Every individual, family, organization, and community has a vital role to play. The arts, sciences, religions, educational institutions, media, businesses, nongovernmental organizations, and governments are all called to offer creative leadership. The partnership of government, civil society, and business is essential for effective governance.

In order to build a sustainable global community, the nations of the world must renew their commitment to the United Nations, fulfill their obligations under existing international agreements, and support the implementation of Earth Charter principles with an international legally binding instrument on environment and development.

Let ours be a time remembered for the awakening of a new reverence for life, the firm resolve to achieve sustainability, the quickening of the struggle for justice and peace, and the joyful celebration of life.

25

The Earth Charter, Globalization, and Sustainable Community

Larry L. Rasmussen

The dream of a common earth ethic and the unity of humankind is a hoary one, at least as old as the Hebrew prophets, Confucius, the Buddha, Plato, and Jesus. That should surprise no one since religions themselves, together with ancient philosophies and the primordial visions of first peoples, all have consistently staked out a highly audacious claim for "community." It is community sufficiently generous to include not only the neighbors (at least those we like!) but Earth as a whole, indeed the cosmos in toto. Creation as a community has not only been the aged and enduring dream; it has been a basic religious, moral, even metaphysical, claim.

Humans dream these dreams because community that surpasses our wee lives answers to restive stirrings deep within our humble creaturely souls. Indeed, religion and ethics may well arise from a yearning to align our lives with an order that outstrips them, an order attuned to the same powers that flung the stars and planets into their orbits, an order in which we are truly home to the universe itself.

In our time the old dream has found realization in the Universal Declaration of Human Rights, posited as it is on the notion of universal human dignity and endorsed as a common moral standard and instrument for all peoples everywhere. By all counts, it has been a powerful means for effecting and institutionalizing universal moral claims.

285

The Whole Community of Life: De-Centering the Human Self

The Earth Charter Movement and the Charter itself belong to the deep tradition of this irrepressible dream of earth as a comprehensive community guided by a shared ethic. There are a couple of new twists, however. The most remarkable one, at least for the children of modernity, is to render the ethics of homo sapiens derivative of Earth's requirements and to consider the whole community of life the bearer of compelling moral claims. "Respect Earth and life in all its diversity" is the fundamental principle of the Earth Charter. It is in fact the parallel of human dignity, or respect for every human life, as the baseline of the Universal Declaration of Human Rights.

But the parallel hides a moral revolution. The fabled "turn to the human subject" of modern Western ethics—a turn underlying modern psychology, philosophy, economics, politics, and the omnipotent science and technology of the industrial paradigm itself, as well as the turn that issued in the notion of human rights itself—this is the turn rejected by the Earth Charter and its moral world. The language is mild and careful and never truly confrontational, but the Earth Charter is an assault on the institutionalized anthropocentrism of reigning practices and their morality, especially patterns of production and consumption. To say "humanity is part of a vast evolving universe" and to view Earth as a remarkable niche in that universe, and as alive, because it is the bearer and sustainer of a unique community of life, is already to dislodge the morally transcendent human subject and invert the orientation of prevailing ethics. In fact, the very moral universe that gave us universal human rights does not accord with the Earth Charter ethic. The Earth Charter wants to de-center the sovereign human self (historically, an andocentric and white Western self) who is the moral legislator and whose very notion of freedom rests in giving ourselves the laws we live by. It wants to locate the ecology of all human action within the economy of Earth itself and temper the sovereign swagger of idolatrous human powers parading mastery on a grand scale. But the universal rights tradition *combines* the rightful assertion of human dignity as the norming norm *with* a practical and deeply institutionalized morality of the sovereign human subject as legislator over all else. This the Charter does not accept, even though it deeply affirms the dignity of all human beings and the ascription of freedom, equality and respect to every person as a condition of human fulfillment.

There is another theme that puts the Earth ethic of the Charter far from the reigning moral universe of present institutions and daily habits. Cosmologies now emerging in science, namely ones in which the web of life spreads to embrace distant galaxies and all 13–15 billion years of the epic of evolution, have little place in our moral sensibilities and conventions. Most all present worlds, at least dominant ones, still regard us morally as an ecologically segregated species. So we moved more rocks and soil and water in the twentieth century than did volcanoes and glaciers and tectonic plates, and we altered the thin envelope of the atmosphere more in that time than all humans together in previous and far longer stretches of time, yet none of this registered as a profoundly moral matter, much less a moral crisis.

In sum, the Earth Charter is trying to line out what Earth *as Earth community* means for ethics and moral agency. In moral theory it means de-centering the sovereign human self and in practice it means re-doing the world created by that self, what the words of an earlier draft dubbed as no less than "reinvent[ing] industrial-technological civilization." This primacy of Earth community for ethics—or a communitarian understanding of nature and society together, with the economy of Earth basic to all—is the new twist, at least for the modern ear.

A Uniquely Representative Process

Still another remarkable quality of the Earth Charter is its genesis and generation, the drafting process itself. The Charter initially failed. It was to be the international product of nation-state negotiations climaxed at the Earth Summit in Rio, 1992. That did not happen. The Earth Charter Commission, gifted with remarkable leadership, then decided to re-launch the effort as a global civil society initiative. This grassroots participation by communities and associations of all kinds resulted in what has been termed "a people's treaty." It is not a true "treaty," negotiated by appointed sovereigns and signed by their national bodies, but there is a call for the Charter's endorsement by the UN General Assembly in 2002 as a "soft law" document. [This did not occur.] Furthermore, its drafting has been coordinated with a genuine "hard law treaty" underway as "The International Covenant on Environment and Development."

This renders the Charter more than an inspirational document for a developing global consciousness and an educational tool and guide for action in many quarters, important as these are. It has the substance of a genuine charter seeking universal recognition and backed by international law.

The specific point about genesis and process, however, is the Charter's rarity among time-worn efforts at a global ethic. Few have been generated from the bottom up—or more precisely, from high levels of participation cutting across virtually all sectors of society, with a determined effort to include historically under-represented voices. Past efforts at an earth ethic were far less representative, and to my knowledge none were carried out by way of a democratic consultative process this open with this much revision over time. It is a remarkable instance, made possible by electronic globalization, of what in fact may be an emerging global society tuned to local communities and bioregions as well as myriad forms of expertise from every quarter—government, business, academe. Against the homogenizing forces of economic globalization, the Charter process has seen new local coalitions and cross-cultural alliances emerge. Dimensions of local and regional belonging have been strengthened and given voice in the face of economic invasions that have tended to weaken them and render them dependent—usually in the name of interdependence itself!

These two qualities, then, should get the attention of Christian ethics—the Earth Charter Movement's high levels of representation and agency in the effort to realize the ancient dream of an Earth ethic, and the Charter's assumed and proposed moral universe, with respect for the full community of life as foundational.

What brought this on? Changes in moral practice and habits of mind are usually compelled by altered material conditions, whatever our deep and lasting yearnings. And conflict and moral contestation is invariably present, together with a few moral conundrums. So what is compelling here? And where will the rubs be, if in fact the Earth Charter is significant in the ways just mentioned?

The Human Venture Within the Universe

What brought on such as the Earth Charter Movement has been laid out in different ways. Theodore Roszak says that ecological problems cannot "be fully solved, if at all, by the nation-state, the free-trade zone, the military alliance, or the multinational corporation."[1] These "awkwardly improvised human structures"[2] are powerful, but they aren't up to the task of addressing their own macroconsequences spread across a humanly dominated biosphere. Some kind of reinvention of inner and outer worlds together is necessary.

Lester Brown's "take" is that we are looking at the need for an environmental revolution on an order of magnitude that matches the agricultural and industrial revolutions—and necessarily transforms them at the same time. Like the agricultural revolution, the environmental revolution will also dramatically alter population trends. But whereas the agricultural "set the stage for enormous increases in human numbers," the environmental "will succeed only if it stabilizes population size" in ways that establish "a balance between people and nature." And in contrast to the industrial revolution, "which was based on a shift to fossil fuels," the environmental will have to shift away from them, on some other base.[3] (We might add that human beings, in order to arrange their own habitat by way of these and other revolutions, have always transformed ecosystems by simplifying them. That simplification is at the heart of both agriculture and urbanization and will no doubt continue, since the rest of nature is immensely more complex and dynamic than we can reckon. The most complex human system, to remember a comment attributed to Peter Raven, is to the rainforest as the squeak of a mouse is to the history of music! Yet now our simplifications must of needs be done with a view to preserving, indeed enhancing, biodiversity itself.)

Thomas Berry is the most dramatic of these witnesses. History is governed, he says, by overarching movements "that give shape and meaning to life by relating the human venture to the larger destinies of the universe."[4] Such a movement can be called "the Great Work" of a people and age. And the great work before us is effecting the transition "from a period of human devastation of the Earth to a period when humans [are] present to the planet in a mutually beneficial manner."[5] Berry does not shrink from describing this as nothing less than a shift of geological ages: from the Cenozoic, with its "irrational exuberance"[6] of life forms, to either the Technozoic, which essentially places the human as subject vis a vis all else as object, and extends present arrangements, or the Ecozoic, that age of mutually enhancing relationships struck between humans and the rest of the community of life.

Among Christian ethicists, Douglas Sturm approaches Berry's scale. The key point in Sturm's formidable essay on the Earth

Charter, titled "Identity and Otherness: Summons to a New Axial Age (Perspectives on the Earth Charter Movement),"[7] is that the recent turn to human subjectivity in ethics and society, as expressed in the varied modalities of modernity, was a subjectivity that saw all else—the supposedly external world—as fair game for manipulation, whether nonhuman or human. Thus an Enlightenment movement that both sought and proclaimed human liberation led by emancipated reason ended up organizing patterns of widespread domination of nature and of peoples considered "close to nature."[8] The need, Sturm argues, is for intersubjectivity, a subjectivity that understands relations to be profoundly internal, because interdependency is our lot at every level and the fiery core of ancient stars our origin. The Earth Charter is, as noted above, premised on such intersubjectivity as this.[9] (Steven Rockefeller's own summary of the Charter echoes this: "Interconnectedness and responsibility are the two main themes of the Earth Charter.")[10]

Sustainable Development or Sustainable Community

If "what brought this on" is essentially what is happening to the planet and the inadequacy of modern ways in addressing the jeopardy they have created, where are the rubs? What does the Earth Charter assume, cherish and pursue that will be difficult because of present ways? We elaborate only one here, albeit a far-reaching one—the conflict between the Charter's kind of democracy and global capitalism's. The way of doing so will use the rubrics of "sustainable development" and "sustainable community." First we introduce these key terms, then register the point about democracy.

The going lingo for the ways of global capitalism is "globalization," meaning the process of an increasingly porous movement of information, money, goods, images, ideas, and people across countries and cultures, driven above all by the progressive integration of all these elements into a single geopolitical economy. The players are many but most prominent are what Thomas Friedman tags "corporations on steroids."[11]

Most discussions of "sustainable development" assume the globalizing economy of corporate capitalism and seek to "green" that. That is, sustainable development is the necessary effort to wrap the global environment around the global economy in such a way that both economy and environment are sustained.

The Earth Charter, too, uses the language of "sustainable development." Yet most of its spirit and direction accord with what might better be called "sustainable community." Sustainable community works on the principle of subsidiarity and asks how you wrap both economy and environment around local communities and bioregions. In contrast to the ways of globalization as current corporate capitalism, even "greened," sustainable community tries to preserve or create the following: greater economic self-sufficiency locally and regionally, with a view to the bioregions themselves as basic to human organization; agriculture appropriate to regions and in the hands of local owners and workers using local knowledge and crop varieties, with ability to save their own seeds and treat their own plants and soils with their own products; the preservation of local and regional traditions, languages, and cultures and a resistance to global homogenization of culture and values; a revival of religious life and a sense of the sacred, vis à vis a present way of life that leeches the sacred from the everyday and has no sense of mystery because it reduces life to the utilitarian; the repair of the moral fiber of society on some terms other than sovereign consumerism; resistance to the commodification of all things, including knowledge; the internalization of costs to the local, regional, and global environment in the price of goods; and the protection of ecosystems and the cultivation of Earth, in the language of the Charter, as "a sacred trust held in common."

All this is global democratic community, not nativist localism. That is, it is not asking *whether* to "globalize," but *how*. And its answer—democratic community democratically arrived at—is *global* community by virtue of both its planetary consciousness and the impressive networking of citizens around the world made possible by electronic globalization. But adherents of sustainable community have this, rather than "development" in mind, because they are not trying to wrap the global environment around the integrating global economy pumped by corporations on steroids. They are asking, "What makes for healthy community on successive levels— local, regional, sometimes national, and global—and how do we wrap both economy and environment around that, aware that Earth's requirements are fundamental?" They are attentive to questions that global capitalism, even as sustainable development, rarely asks: namely, what are the essential bonds of human community and culture, as well as the bonds of the human with the more-than-human world; and what is the meaning of such primal bonds for the rendering of a healthy concrete way of life? What is cultural wealth and biological wealth and how are they sustained in the places people live with the rest of the community of life?

Enabling Democracy/Disassembling Power

But let us be more specific about democracy, globalization, and the Earth Charter.

A place to begin is with a reminder about U.S. antitrust laws. Antitrust laws were initially motivated by two concerns. One was to prevent large monopolies from overwhelming consumers and in effect dictating "choices." The other was to prevent big business from overwhelming democratic government and essentially laying down the terms of public policy. ("The best government money can buy" was H. L. Mencken's quip about it.) This happened when businesses grew, in the last part of the nineteenth century, beyond the control of local institutions and the states. They thus needed federal power to rein them in. Now businesses are growing to global dimensions but governments are still national, so governments struggle to keep pace and, in fact, to keep or lure the corporations. Michael Sandel's comment is this: "In a world without walls, we are going to have to come up with new ways for government to rein in the power of global corporations, and prevent them from buying up democracy. Instead of just being dazzled by these mega-mergers, there should be a nagging voice in us all asking: is democracy going to be bought up too?"[12]

What is at stake here is the loss of political control over fundamental economic decisions; or, more precisely, the failure to extend democracy from the political to the economic. What is at stake is a severe reduction of the three classic values of democracy: equality and community are largely sacrificed to the workings of liberty (and liberty is largely market liberty plus the vote). What is at stake is, in fact, the specific vision of democratic society itself. Is it, to draw from Robert Dahl, the vision of a society with virtually unrestricted liberty to acquire and enjoy wealth? Or is it a society in which citizen agency and effective self-government create the common good through the process of democratizing social, political, and economic power?[13] The kind of democracy mirrored in the Earth Charter process tilts clearly toward the latter. Here democracy resides in people's self-organizing, self-provisioning, and self-directing capacities. This is democratic agency of a multivalent kind, and it contrasts with that of regnant global capitalism. There public power is increasingly in private hands. There it comprises— strongly stated—a kind of corporate neo-feudalism that militates against citizen self-agency and effective self-government (unless you believe that citizenship is defined by the roles of consumer, client, stockholder, and service-provider, and that the essence of freedom is the room to maximally acquire and enjoy wealth).

In a word, the enabling of democracy and moral agency as citizen self-direction for an inclusive common good, which is the heart of community, is what is assumed and fostered by the Earth Charter, provided "inclusive common good" is inclusive of the full community of life. But just this is undercut by economic globalization processes.

This worry about disabled democracy and a shrunken common good is underscored by knowledge of how injustice happens. The reason is why the World Council of Churches and the American Catholic Bishops and a whole stream of Christian social thought running from the Social Gospel through Christian Realism into Black, feminist, womanist, and other liberation theologies have not given up on the social project of disassembling concentrations of economic power. It is that injustice flows from imbalances of power. As we learned by Reinhold Niebuhr and, before him, Frederick Douglass, the pyramiding of great concentrations of power by economic behemoths who then shape much of public policy itself is a prescription for disabling democracy and creating power arrangements that make for injustice. Requiring global capitalism to be greener does not of itself change these power arrangements, nor does it waylay the disempowerment they generate.

Differently said, conceding defeat on the democratizing of economic power means to lose on virtually every other front, political and cultural, as well. And given the transformation of Earth—land and peoples together—that capitalism has effected over several centuries, the relationship of economy, ecosystem and biosphere favors arrangements that disperse rather than concentrate power, in accord with subsidiarity.

The point of all this is that the Earth Charter seems both to express and to believe in the development of our powers as self-regulating community moral agents, with concomitant responsibility. Of course, such democracy must, for the Earth Charter to take account of the moral claims of otherkind, adopt patterns of production, consumption, and reproduction that safeguard Earth's regenerative capacities, human rights, and community well-being. And while this kind of community democracy is yet another way of naming sustainable community, it is also the case that we have far too little experience in community of this kind, in working versions of "bio-democracy." Sustainable community is, in any event, no panacea. Panaceas don't exist. Nonetheless, the direction of the Earth

Charter itself is correct; namely, a communitarian understanding of nature, society, even cosmos. It is far more promising than sustainable development as the green vision of global capitalism.

Notes

1. Theodore Roszak, "'Where Psyche Meets Gaia," *Ecopsychology: Restoring the Earth, Healing the Mind*, Theodore Roszak, Mary E. Gomes, and Alan D. Kanner, eds. (San Francisco: Sierra Club Books, 1995), 1.

2. Roszak, "Where Psyche Meets Gaia," *Ecopsychology*, 2.

3. Lester Brown, Foreward to Roszak, *Ecopsychology*, xv.

4. Thomas Berry, *The Great Work: Our Way into the Future* (New York: Bell Tower, 1999), 1.

5. Berry, *Great Work*, 3.

6. With apologies to Alan Greenspan for using his phrase (about stock market behavior) completely out of context.

7. Douglas Sturm, "Identity and Otherness: Summons to a New Axial Age (Perspective on the Earth Charter Movement)," an essay published by the Forum on Religion and Ecology, Department of Religion, Bucknell University, Lewisburg, Pa.

8. It might be noted that Dietrich Bonhoeffer surmised much of the same in the 1940s. What he calls "Euro-American" civilization and its neo-European extensions around the globe used the "emancipated" reason of the Enlightenment to trumpet its own autonomy in an expansionist journey of idolatrous confidence in progress and conquest, elaborated as an ethic of civilization. The Western aim, writes Bonhoeffer, is to be independent of nature. And it issues in what he calls "a new spirit," "the spirit of the forcible subjugation of nature beneath the role of the thinking and experimenting man." The outcome is technology as "an end in itself" with "a soul of its own." Its symbol "is the machine, the embodiment of the violation and exploitation of nature." See his *Ethics* (New York: MacMillan, 1965), 98.

9. Sturm, "Identity and Otherness," 8–9.

10. Steven Rockefeller, as quoted in "Earth Charter Launched at the Hague," *Boston Research Center for the 21st Century Newsletter* 16 (12) 2001.

11. Thomas L. Friedman, "Corporations on Steroids," *New York Times*, February 4, 2000, A29.

12. Cited by Friedman, ibid.

13. Robert Dahl, *A Preface to Economic Democracy* (Berkeley: University of California Press, 1985), 163.

26

Concluding Considerations, Continuing Journey

William E. Gibson

I. Eco-Justice Is the Journey

Originally I intended to title this book "Journey to Eco-Justice." We move and struggle toward an eco-just future. As a destination, the world of ecological wholeness and social justice remains far off. Nevertheless, we experience and celebrate its reality along the way.

Eco-justice is the journey. Eco-justice happens. It is the emerging, demanding, promising reality with which human moral agents must come to terms if there is to be a good and viable future for people and the planet. To journey toward eco-justice is to know and enjoy this reality—as only partial to be sure, but actual nonetheless.

Eco-justice happens when people of color and labor unions and their allies organize to stop the poisoning of air and water and people, as in the Great Louisiana Toxics March (Editor's Notes, Section A). It happens even though victory is incomplete. Even an apparent defeat sometimes contributes to an eventual achievement.

It happens when technology serves people, eliminates pollution, and enhances human work without displacing it (Section B). It happens when places are appreciated and defended, habitats are preserved, and wild creatures remain free (Section C). It happens as women not only play their nurturing role but become partners in development geared to need and the care of earth (Section E).

It happens as families and eco-communities cut unnecessary consumption, share equipment, space, and skills, grow much of their own food, and advocate for eco-just policy changes, insisting that the values of the community govern development (Section G).

Nowhere more than in community-based development does the eco-justice perspective get translated into practice. In 1993 as a member of the Presbyterian Task Force on Sustainable Development, Reformed Faith, and U.S. International Economic Policy, I traveled with that group to Honduras. Among the many Hondurans with whom we visited were representatives of the Union of Campesino Workers. These people told us that the main point of their struggle was access to land. "We have to work the land to live," they said. "This land is ours. We are trying to recover our land." They reported the concentration of the best land in the hands of some 460 large landowners, including some transnational corporations; and they feared that the new Modernization of Agriculture Act, aiming at increasing exports, would lead to a still greater concentration.

A few days earlier we had visited the Santa Rosita Cooperative. In 1986 a group of landless peasants had moved onto a piece of unused mountain land. They managed to stay despite repeated attempts to evict them. They received assistance, in partnership style, from the Christian Commission for Development. They finally obtained from the National Agrarian Institute the right to work this land. They wanted more land, both to rest periodically the fields used for subsistence grains and to expand their coffee and cattle projects. By 1993 they had greatly improved their lot and were determined to keep on. Proud of their community's achievements, they nevertheless worried that they did not have title to the land, and government policy was pushing exports even at the expense of community subsistence.[1]

Donella Meadows, in her *Global Citizen* newspaper column, tells the story of Gaviotas, a solar village in Colombia. Its locale is "the huge, wild, wet savanna called the llanos." The soil there was so toxic that nothing except a tough grass could grow.

When the founder of the village, Paolo Lugari, first saw the region in 1965, he told himself that if people could live in this desolate place, they could live anywhere. At that time there were only a few scattered ranchers in addition to some Guahito Indians fishing in the rivers and hunting in forest strips along the streams.

Lugari enlisted the inventiveness of professors and graduate students at Bogata universities, and then, increasingly, the ingenuity of llanos people. Meadows cites various ingredients of a remarkable community development. Fourteen parts of the terrible soil mixed with one part of cement produced a stony substance for constructing buildings and piping water. Ultra-light windmills suited the mild but steady llanos winds. The solar water heaters, invented for Gaviotas, were so cheap and efficient that the Gaviotans sold them all over Bogata. They built a hospital in Gaviotas cooled, heated, and powered by solar technologies. They met their need for fresh vegetables by growing them in containers of rice hulls watered with manure tea. They planted thousands of acres of a Caribbean pine from Venezuela; they had at last a plant that would thrive in the llanos soil once the seedling roots were dipped in a certain fungus. And they tapped the oozing gum from the pines and distilled it into turpentine and a resin valuable for paints, glues, cosmetics, and medicines. They found a big market for this resin.

The technologies from Gaviotas for windmills, solar collectors, and pumps are spreading around the world. They are all "simple, affordable, and purposely unpatented." "Gaviotans," says Meadows, "live in peace surrounded by narcotics dealers and guerrillas. They live without guns, without pesticides, willing to serve and teach all comers. They count their wealth in sun, water, and community."[2]

Much more might be said about where and how eco-justice happens. The final decades of the twentieth century were the time of a great awakening around the world, a spreading consciousness of the eco-justice crisis. Despite all the denials, this crisis has radically altered the global situation. As the new millennium begins, the course of history becomes in large part the drama of human societies in critical interaction with natural forces. Innumerable happenings reflect and increase the emerging reality: from Eco-Justice conferences to the 1992 United Nations Conference on Environment and Development; from the Eco-Justice journal to the whole body of eco-justice literature[3]; from local activism and municipal recycling to legislative measures, conservation agencies, worldwide wildlife protection, and international treaties.

In the face of the massive denial and the formidable systemic obstacles, I have often found it easy to underestimate and overlook the magnitude of the efforts and the movements since 1970 to address the eco-justice crisis. A little reflection, however, reminds me of the global scope, the host of travelers, and the many positive achievements of the eco-justice journey.

II. Heralding the Journey

The eco-justice perspective has always included a strong moral sensitivity and commitment. The normative values of eco-justice follow from ethical reflection about what *ought* to guide personal behavior, community action, public policy, and systemic transformation.

For many, probably most, of the travelers with whom I have walked on the eco-justice journey, the moral dimension of eco-justice is rooted in religious faith, a religious conception of existence. My assent to the moral authority of the eco-justice norms is a response to the inescapable claims of my fellow creatures, human and nonhuman, to be respected and valued. It is a matter not only of rationality and prudence but of loyalty to the ultimate source of those claims, the One who is the creative, ordering, purposeful, just, and compassionate force underlying and upholding all that is.

As a Christian, I have long had a major interest in the role of the church in addressing the eco-justice crisis. The church, I believe, should be a major player, a center of both proclamation and nurture, whereby all of its members may come to understand what is happening in the world, the salient facts about ecology and justice, in the light of the biblical/Christian themes of creation and liberation. The church should equip them, theologically, spiritually, and practically, for the eco-justice journey. (See Selection 5.)

A number of Christian communions have made statements of policy indicative of the role suggested above. By way of illustration, I want to call attention to three of these statements among those made by the denominations with which I have traveled in the Eco-Justice Working Group of the National Council of Churches (NCC).

The American Baptist Churches, U.S.A.

The General Board of the American Baptist Churches, U.S.A., unanimously approved a Policy Statement on Ecology in June 1989. The statement stresses human stewardship of creation as required by God's "everlasting covenant" with humankind. The creation belongs to God. We humans "are each related to God as one appointed to take care of someone else's possessions entrusted to us." The image of God in humankind makes it possible for us to be "responsive to God's self-revelation in the creation." We express that image by caring for the creation, and this is "our distinctive human vocation."

We can, of course, choose to be irresponsible and to use nature's resources only for what we perceive as our immediate self-interest. This is sin and is corporate as well as individual. But our model is Jesus, who proclaimed liberation of the oppressed and announced the Jubilee Year of Leviticus 25. This was a year for rectifying destructive and unjust social conditions, including the treatment of the land.

After affirming the interdependence of ecology and justice, the American Baptists declare: "God continues to create as well as to redeem. God asks us not only to call persons to redemption but also to teach them to be wise stewards." In this time of "unprecedented challenge" and "extraordinary peril and promise," "[the] Creator-Redeemer seeks the renewal of creation and calls the people of God to participate. . . . Our task is nothing less than to join God in preserving, renewing and fulfilling the creation."

This task "will be guided by the norms of solidarity, as we stand with the vulnerable creation and work with its defenders; sustainability, as we devise social systems that maintain the balance of nature; and sufficiency, as we give priority to basic sustenance for all life."

The statement ends with a call to American Baptists for acknowledgments, learnings, practices, and actions geared to the care of creation. These include influencing public policy and "insisting that industries, businesses, farmers and consumers relate to the environment in ways that are sensible, healthy and protective of its integrity."[4,5]

Presbyterian Church (U.S.A.)

The 202[d] General Assembly of the Presbyterian Church (U.S.A.) adopted a policy statement entitled *Restoring Creation for Ecology and Justice* in June 1990. (See my Notes introducing Selection 5.) This is a considerably longer document than that of the American Baptists. It begins, however, with a "Call to Restore Creation," which anticipates and indeed encapsulates much of the content that follows.

"Creation cries out," the Call begins, "in this time of ecological crisis." "Creation's Cry" is spelled out in some detail in Part I of the main document.

The Call cites the church's "powerful reasons for engagement in restoring God's creation":

- God's works in creation are too wonderful, too ancient, too beautiful, too good to be desecrated.

- Restoring creation is God's own work in our time, in which God comes both to judge and to restore.

- The Creator-Redeemer calls faithful people to become engaged with God in keeping and healing the creation, human and nonhuman.

- Human life and well-being depend upon the flourishing of other life, and the integrity of the life-supporting processes that God has ordained.

- The love of neighbor, particularly the "least" of Christ's brothers and sisters, requires action to stop the poisoning, the erosion, the wastefulness that are causing suffering and death.

- The future of our children and their children and all who come after is at stake.

- In this critical time of transition to a new era, God's new doing may be discerned as a call to earth-keeping, to justice, and to community.

The second of the "powerful reasons" exemplifies the theocentric emphasis of the whole document. It is about "God's own work in our time." Part II of the statement, "Response to an Endangered Planet," focuses in Section A on "God's New Doing: to Judge and to Restore."

We receive as judgment the evidence that the human creature, placed in "the garden . . . to till it and keep it (Genesis 2:15)— to draw sustenance from it and protect it—has tilled without keeping and failed to share equitably the fruits of tilling." The statement probes to the basic character of modern civilization.

> Surely we have been too uncritical, too unbiblical, too self-serving in going along with our culture's abuse of nature and its pursuit of affluence. . . . But God comes to judge our world—our civilization, our nation, our "tilling," our way of life—with righteousness and truth. By God's grace in the eco-justice crisis, we may receive and accept judgment and forgiveness and make a new beginning.

God comes not only to judge but to restore.

The biblical basis for restoring creation is very simple: the Creator is always also the Redeemer, and the Redeemer is always also the Creator. The God "who made heaven and earth, the sea and all that is in them" is the One "who executes justice for the oppressed" (Psalm 146:6f.). Because God the Creator loves the whole creation, God the Redeemer acts to save the creation when it is bowed down and cries out.

Section B of Part II takes up the "Norms for Keeping and Healing." These are instrumental to "a new faithfulness." They provide guidance because they "illuminate the contemporary meaning of God's steadfast love for the world." They are the eco-justice norms of sustainability, participation, sufficiency, and solidarity.

On the basis of the statement's findings and affirmations, the General Assembly: "recognizes and accepts restoring creation as a central concern of the church, to be incorporated into its life and mission at every level."

The Presbyterians move in Part III to some specific "Social Policies to Protect the Environment" in five areas of concern: sustainable agriculture, water quality, protecting wildlife and wildlands, reducing and managing our wastes, and overcoming atmospheric instability. Then Part IV gives directives and recommendations to the church's agencies, governing bodies, and congregations for new mission initiatives and the infusion of eco-justice concerns into existing programs.[6]

The Evangelical Lutheran Church in America

The Churchwide Assembly of the Evangelical Lutheran Church in America (ELCA) adopted a Social Statement on *Caring for Creation: Vision, Hope, and Justice* in August 1993. The three words of the subtitle provide structure for the statement. Part I discusses "The Church's Vision of Creation." "God blesses the world and sees it as 'good,' even before humankind comes on the scene. . . . By faith we understand God to be deeply, mysteriously, and unceasingly involved in what happens in all creation."

Humans, in kinship with fellow creatures, have a special responsibility to care for the earth. "Human dominion (Genesis 1:28; Psalm 8) . . . should reflect God's way of ruling as a shepherd king who takes the form of a servant (Philippians 2:7) wearing a crown of thorns." This responsibility is to be discharged within the covenant God makes with all creation and in accordance with God's wisdom in creation.

According to Part II on "The Urgency," the roots of the current crisis are human sin and captivity to "demonic powers and unjust institutions." The statement speaks of unprecedented environmental threats. It points to "excessive consumption by industrialized nations and relentless growth of human population worldwide." "Action to counter degradation, especially within this decade, is essential to the future of our children and our children's children."

Part III is a short but trenchant section on "The Hope." Sin and captivity are not the last word. Hope stems from the forgiveness of sins, the new life in Christ, the promise of new creation and of the ultimate consummation wherein "the creation—now in captivity to disruption and death—will know the freedom it awaits." As "captives of hope" we can act in the present crisis and "be a herald here and now to the new creation yet to come. . . ."

Part IV, "The Call to Justice" makes justice the summary word for what the care of creation intends and accomplishes— "justice in political, economic, social, and environmental relationships," which "means honoring the integrity of creation, and striving for fairness within the human family." Instrumental to justice are the same norms set forth in the Presbyterian statement. Here they are called principles.

Part V, "Commitments of This Church," lays out the commitments, by individual Christians and by the church as a faith community, that now follow. "We of the Evangelical Lutheran Church in America answer the call to justice and commit ourselves to its principles. . . ." The commitments pertain to individual and institutional lifestyles, worship and learning, moral deliberation, and public policy advocacy.

These commitments have to be made without any idea of a "quick fix—whether technological, economic, or spiritual." They require sustained effort. "The prospect of doing too little too late leads many people to despair. But as people of faith, captives of hope, and vehicles of God's promise, we face the crisis."[7]

Church Statements as Prophetic Heralds

These are strong statements. They show an accurate and sophisticated understanding of the many, interacting components of environmental degradation. They consistently link the plight of nature to the plight of people. In their repeated emphasis on this linkage they are ahead of secular environmental organizations and secular campaigns for justice to workers and the poor. They are eco-justice documents.

As such, they contribute to the development of a contextual theology responsive to creation's peril, and to an eco-justice ethic.

This ethic advances norms that translate abiding religious meanings and values into language that fits the contemporary context and makes ties with secular movements. The documents speak at times with an eloquence and a prophetic passion rooted in both covenantal loyalty and spiritual sensitivity. For those who hear their message, a motivating, undergirding empowerment transcends enlightened self-interest and prudential, strictly humanistic morality.

The Protestant denominational work constitutes part of a much larger ecumenical development, which moves also now into inter-faith dialogue. The World Council of Churches (WCC) has played a major leadership role in this development. The WCC has moved from its work on the "just, participatory, and sustainable society" of the 1960s and 1970s, to the conciliar process preceding and following the 1990 World Convocation on Justice, Peace and the Integrity of Creation, to work on "Economy as a Matter of Faith," to current work on theology of life. (See Selection 23.)

In 1992 in Rio de Janeiro at the time of the Earth Summit, a WCC-convened group sent a Letter to the Churches, noting that it was twenty years after the Stockholm Conference on the Environment, "and not one single major trend of environmental degradation has been reversed." The letter expresses the "conclusion that the prevailing system is exploiting nature and peoples on a worldwide scale and promises to continue at an intensified rate." It is therefore "extremely urgent that we as churches make strong and permanent spiritual, moral and material commitments to the emergence of new models of society, based in deepest gratitude to God for the gift of life and in respect for the whole of God's creation."[8]

One should not overestimate the impact of what the denominational bodies and ecumenical gatherings have said about ecology and justice. Although addressed primarily to their own members, these statements have provided an important policy base for the churches' public witness and advocacy. Through the NCC EJ Working Group and the WCC, the churches have had a consistent presence at United Nations conferences and the related preparatory and follow-up meetings. The WCC has provided notable leadership on global warning and climate change, urging Northern governments to lead in reducing greenhouse gas emissions, and providing church representation at all the meetings of the "Conference of the Parties," which implement and extend the 1992 Framework Convention on Climate Change. But if the membership of the churches on a significant scale had heard the message of their national bodies and taken the urgent call seriously as a matter of covenant loyalty and lively spirituality, the witness of the churches to the world would have multiplied many times. Some of the disastrous trends might have begun to turn around.

The hard fact is that social policy statements generally do not make much impact on Christians at the congregational level. Nor are they taken with great seriousness by most pastors, denominational leaders, and governing body staff. The eco-justice statements are accepted in an "of course" kind of way; they have not generated much controversy yet. They deserve study in every congregation, but most church members do not see them. The mindset of the churches has not changed in accordance with the word about the magnitude of the crisis and its religious significance. The environment is still departmentalized as one concern among many others, and its connections to those others—the far-reaching implications of the sustainability factor—are not often recognized. Some worthwhile new initiatives have been undertaken by the designated departments. Several denominations now have Eco-Justice Advocates or Restoring Creation Enablers at work in many of their judicatories or districts around the country. These volunteers have received training and resources, not only denominationally but ecumenically through the NCC EJ Working Group. By 1999, in a related development, some 460 Presbyterians were members of Presbyterians for Restoring Creation. But ongoing denominational and ecumenical initiatives, plus many additional possibilities, do not have the priority, the funding, and the staffing that would properly follow from the affirmations in the statements.

Nevertheless, I see these statements as heralding the eco-justice journey. The bodies that approve and issue them do so because they find them convincing—ringing true and timely—even if they do not grasp their full import or rise fully to the commitments they declare. The message heralded is indeed far ahead of the thinking of the church as a whole. But the church here is speaking a prophetic word to the church, alerting the community of faith to the crisis, discerning God in it, lifting up the vision of restored creation, challenging hesitant people to undertake the journey, and offering hope and encouragement for adventurous faithfulness.

Some hearers respond, and others will. The message heralds a journey that has a long way to go. It still will speak and call as the ripening times and the Holy Spirit increase the openness to hearing and responding.

III. The Opposing Force

Lessons Learned Along the Way

Massive evidence lay behind the warnings of the 1970s. Subsequent years substantiated and increased it. Without being refuted, the evidence has been widely disliked, ignored, and denied. In the 1970s there were national conferences on "alternatives to growth." The Society of Christian Ethics discussed the "global problematique." Bibliographies for eco-justice lengthened rapidly. But the momentum of those years, the early attempt to grapple with the evidence of limits, was itself not sustainable. Despite all the improvements that followed from legislation and regulation, the most destructive trends have not been turned around, the peril to the planet has not diminished. With all the endorsements of sustainability, prevailing economic theory and policy have not changed accordingly. One important lesson learned along the way is that the journey will be much longer than we thought.

Another lesson is that our leaders do not lead us where we need to go. Those with great influence and power have not embarked upon the journey. For the most part they stand in the way. Politically, to be "soft on growth" would be even more self-destructive than to be "soft on crime" or "soft on defense." The academic world has not moved out front to address the crisis. In departments of economics a steady-state or radical economist, in the unlikely event there is one, becomes increasingly lonely and isolated. The universities, overall, serve and buttress the existing order, with little response to its inherent destructiveness, despite their possession of knowledge that demands a different role. In the churches the limited influence of prophetic statements is due in no small measure to the paucity of prophetic preaching. And a business executive, even when trying to be environmentally responsible, must still maximize growth and profit. In all of our major institutions the voices I hoped to hear have been either too timid or too few.

A third lesson is that most church people, including most clergy, do not tend as a matter of course to think theologically about what is happening in the world. They do not have a lively sense that God is active today either in nature or in history. They do not endeavor to discern the presence and the will of God in the eco-justice crisis. The danger to creation and the world is not a compelling *religious* concern. And because as people of faith they do not see God in the crisis, they do not draw upon the equipment of faith to follow God's leading in it.

A fourth lesson is that the eco-justice crisis is a crisis of democracy. It is testing whether people can mobilize democratically to resist and overcome the enormous power of the institutions, the class, and the individuals that have a strong perceived self-interest in perpetuating the systems, assumptions, values, and practices that now propel the world on its socially and ecologically destructive course.

All of these lessons point toward the most important lesson. All our efforts on the journey, successful and unsuccessful, to make eco-justice happen and to hasten the eco-just future are pressing against the tide. They contend with an opposing force, a fierce and dominant political will that would maintain the consumer society, the growth economy, the global expansion of capitalism, the rule of the corporations, and the military/economic/cultural dominance of the advanced technological/industrial nations, the United States above all. This opposing force has been insufficiently named, scrutinized, exposed, and opposed.

The Most Critical Objectives

The destructive impact of humankind depends directly upon the size of the human population, the kinds of technologies people use, and the magnitude of their production and consumption. (See Editor's Notes, Section E.) These factors, inextricably connected to societal systems and power realities, point to two objectives as most critical in moving toward eco-justice.

One is the reduction of human numbers. The measures required for that include poverty reduction and the enhancement of women's status as well as effective contraception. (See Section E.) But the global population reached six billion in 1999. The demographic realities make additional billions certain. The realistic question is whether the population can be kept from another doubling—kept, say, at nine billion or less before declining. But even current numbers are far too many for sustainability and quality of life, even if we could achieve equitable distribution.

Turning to the other components of the human impact—production and consumption and the technologies they entail—we take a hard look at the economy of the modern world. The other most critical objective is to stop the destruction inflicted by industrial civilization and capitalist economics on the natural environment and the human community.

By focusing on the economy we need not underestimate the many simpler ways of working for eco-justice or the essential importance of the motivational and spiritual factors that empower people for the eco-justice journey. For over a quarter of a century the simple living movement has fostered the discovery that the good life does not consist in material accumulation—that enough is good, and big consumption is a phony substitute for true community. I applaud the ongoing work on this by Alternatives in Sioux City, Iowa, Seeds of Simplicity in the Los Angeles area, and Earth Ministry in Seattle.[9] But the economy of overconsumption, fueled constantly by seductive advertising, remains intact, unthreatened, and still destructive.

At the same time, the secular and religious programs—educational and experiential—to engender a deeper appreciation of nature, to teach the unity and diversity, the intricacy, the wonder, and the sacredness of all of life, and to inspire awe before the cosmic immensities of the universe story, all these are to be welcomed. They enrich and reinforce the biblical, continuing story of creation and liberation. ***But what then?*** How do we pursue the most critical objectives? An essential part of the answer is to name and face the economic realities in a way that most people have been unwilling, hesitant, or helpless to do. It is not enough to advocate reforms. We have to face the full extent to which the economy in its most essential features causes the destruction that it will not and cannot stop.

The Capitalist Economy

For many years the Worldwatch Institute under the leadership of Lester R. Brown has stressed the need for an economy that can accommodate sustainability. The opening chapter of *State of the World 1998* gave a particularly cogent factual analysis of the connection between economic activity and ecological deterioration.[10]

The expansion of the global economy in the twentieth century, especially the second half, was truly spectacular. In dollar terms the total world output of goods and services grew from not quite $5 trillion in 1950 to over $29 trillion in 1997. Forest cover has disappeared by half since 1900. Lumber use has tripled since midcentury. Paper use is up six times. The consumption of fossil fuels, the main culprit in the greenhouse effect, has soared since 1980 while the warnings about climate change have grown more urgent. The consumption of grains and other agricultural products has tripled since mid-century. Water tables are falling on every continent due to overpumping, most of which is to irrigate farmland. In much of the world, including India and China, people depend upon irrigation for most of their food. Water scarcity portends food scarcity. And then there are the facts about soil erosion, desertification, declining fisheries, species extinction, and air and water pollution.[11] Pressures for rising standards of living (desperately needed by the poor but not by the already comfortable) and the ever-increasing human population guarantee that the strains on the environment will continue to mount.

All of this is about economics—how people meet their needs and wants drawing on what nature provides within the operation of nature's laws. "The unfortunate reality," says Lester Brown, "is that the economy continues to expand, but the ecosystem on which it depends does not, creating an increasingly stressed relationship." The global economy, says Brown, *cannot* continue much longer to expand: "The challenge facing the entire world is to design an economy that can satisfy the basic needs of people everywhere without self-destructing." [12]

Brown speaks of "the unfettered optimism" of economists assessing the economic prospect.[13] In September 1997 the World Bank released an "upbeat" economic report forecasting new economic superpowers by 2020. The economy of China was expected to expand to more than five times its current size. India's economy would multiply four times, Indonesia's five, and Brazil's three. But Brown asks, "If the global economy is already overrunning its natural capacities, what happens as . . . fast-developing countries strive to emulate the American lifestyles?"[14] He concludes that the western model of development is not viable for the developing countries or even for the western industrial countries themselves over the long term.[15]

The Western model is capitalism, and expansion is of its essence. Expansion entails: capital accumulation; technological advances in productivity; labor understood as a cost of production, so that wage-earners are kept as few in number and low in pay as possible; the kind of competition that leads to larger and fewer firms and on toward monopoly or at least oligopoly control of the major sectors of industry by gigantic transnational corporations; and the continuous drive for new markets, more sales, greater profits, further expansion (with "free trade"), and the concentration of wealth and power in the dominant class.

Three Counts of Failure

I believe that such an assessment of the fundamental tendencies of the capitalist economy should be taken very seriously on the basis of empirical evidence and with an honest effort to avoid ideological bias. The evidence leads to three counts of unacceptable failure. (See Section F.) In the first place, the economy destroys the ecological basis of its own continuation. It is cancerously self-destructive. The evidence cited in *State of the World* and elsewhere compels this indictment. The present system is literally unsustainable over the "long term," which cannot yet be pinpointed, no matter how strong, dynamic, and successful its beneficiaries claim it to be.

In the second place, this system fails to discharge the function that is to be demanded of any economic order, the life-maintaining function that makes an economic order necessary. It fails to meet basic needs. Large minorities in the United States and other "developed" countries and the majority in "developing" countries live in unacceptable poverty, hundreds of millions without basic requirements for nutrition, sanitation, and security. This failure is neither ecologically nor technically necessary; but instead of giving priority to sufficiency for all, the capitalist economy generates monstrous inequalities.

In the third place, this system is destructive of community cohesion, cultural integrity and diversity, and religious and spiritual integrity and vitality. (See Selections 20, 22, and 25.) The system attempts to put a price on intellectual, aesthetic, cultural, and spiritual relationships and experiences—as though these could be weighed in the marketplace. This demeans their role in human fulfillment. Development projects have severely disrupted neighborhoods; the demands of the factory or the firm have pulled families apart. Both the colonial imperialism of the recent past and the economic expansion, modernization, and domination that succeeded it (continuing the long story of Western, capitalist imperialism) have failed at being respectful and careful toward the places into which they have thrust themselves. A 1996 Presbyterian policy statement, dealing with worldwide economic and human development, said this:

> [The General Assembly] acknowledges with deep regret that economic expansion and modernization in the less developed countries of the south, furthered by northern governments and

corporations, have often proceeded in ways that have demeaned local cultures, disrupted community support systems and community cohesion, displaced small-scale and subsistence agriculture, ignored traditional knowledge and wisdom, and disregarded the natural resource base.[16]

Justice (in terms of participation and sufficiency), ecological sustainability, and community vitality are not the aims of economic theory and practice. By its own standards, our growing economy, as perceived by its leading actors, has by no means failed. But the human and religious values and goals of justice, sustainability, and community require an economy that serves them.

Obstacles to Transformation

The existing system presents enormous obstacles to all our efforts to make it serve those values and goals. Our efforts strain against the force of a system that strenuously resists and blocks its own transformation. Here are three reasons why this is so.

First, the capitalist system generates inordinate concentrations of corporate power, firmly resistant to public accountability. This power is not limited to the marketplace; it extends beyond economic activity per se. It dominates politics and government, severely undercutting or eliminating the role of government in restraining the economy's violations of sustainability, justice, and community. It dominates and effectively restricts communications, entertainment, and the people's understanding of their plight, as huge corporations own the major media. It exerts profound influence and limitations upon education, culture, and religion. As David Korten has laid out in detail, "corporations rule the world."[17]

Second, the system depends upon unnecessary, wasteful, and injurious overconsumption. Without such overconsumption the economy cannot grow and would indeed under this system fall into depression. Millions of jobs depend upon producing goods and services that are unnecessary for sufficiency and detrimental to sustainability. People want these things. The culture, conditioned and perpetuated by advertising and the major media, does not embrace mere sufficiency. The highly consumptive lifestyle is seductively attractive and enjoyable in many ways. The sustainability factor will not permit it to be extended to all or even to most of those who do not have it. Those who do have it are reluctant, if not adamantly unwilling, to let any significant portion of it go. We face the absurdity of a self-destructive economy which most people in the developed world—including many who do care about the future—have a large, if short-sighted, stake in perpetuating. Without growth, or with negative growth, they might become nonparticipants in the economy, nonparticipants in affluence or even in sufficiency.

Finally, our economy institutionalizes selfishness and greed. Self-interest is the expected motivation in the marketplace. Ruthless, corner-cutting, cruelly impersonal tactics are expected or even required as corporations strive to survive or to increase market share or to drive out weak competitors. This is not to deny that many people in business want to provide a good product or a useful service. With the economy structured and understood as it is, however, as corporations gain size and financial and political clout, the overriding driving force is the self-interest of the firm and the further buttressing of the existing order, not the meeting of the most pressing human needs or long-term environmental protection or the honoring of community values.

The traditional, now fatally flawed, rationale for capitalism is that self-interest serves the common good even when the actors in the economy do not specifically so intend. But the common good is not served by the nonparticipation of the many who have no place in the economy as it actually operates, such as displaced peasant farmers or rootless youth in the abandoned sectors of inner-cities. It is not served by the exploitation of workers, at home and in developing zones of corporate expansion, who have neither job security nor a living wage. And it is not served by the extreme inequalities whereby those with great wealth undermine and dominate the processes of "democratic" government and make vastly disproportionate demands on nature's bounty.

The point is not that self-interest can ever be eliminated from economic life, but that for a viable future it must be put into a longer-term context and significantly restrained, qualified, and transcended by considerations of justice, sustainability, and community. These goals of eco-justice will not emerge as by-products of self-interest and greed. Capitalism does not lend itself to its own correction. The outcome would not be capitalism.

The Most Basic Task

In the early days of the eco-justice journey we knew that a first step was consciousness-raising—making people keenly aware of environmental degradation and the peril to life-support systems and human well-being and survival. A great deal of such consciousness-raising has occurred. But many people thought and still want to believe that environmental problems can be fixed without basic changes in lifestyles or economics or the size of families. They fancy, despite the evidence, that capitalism can be "greened." (See Selection 25.) The consciousness-raising to precede basic change still remains to be done. Lifestyles of responsible frugality will not be widespread enough to make much difference under the existing system. The "Two-Thirds World" voices say clearly that population will not decline until overconsumption is turned back in rich countries and poverty reduction gets first priority in poor countries. (See Section E.) Among the many things to be done, the most basic task—basic in really getting to the effective causes of environmental degradation and human misery—is to scrutinize, reconceive, and radically redesign the economic system.

The task could not be more formidable. Much in this volume has pointed to the system's entrenched power. See especially Sections D and F and Selections 3 and 22. Here I shall add the following two paragraphs, which come from a previous essay, slightly edited.

. . . Sustainability and justice *require*: an economy of universal participation without destructive growth; an economy oriented to need and the enhancement of community and the quality of life; an economy carefully protective of the natural life-support systems. . . . Universal participation means that all the members of a community engage, as able and gifted, in need-fulfilling, life-enhancing tasks and enjoy a sufficient livelihood. There will be ample good work needing to be done even with much less material consumption and accumulation by those whose impact on natural systems is now excessive and destructive.

Growth and profit cannot be the predominant driving forces. They will have their place, along with markets, to the extent that they serve the goal of a sustainable sufficiency for all. The new economy will not be ruled by huge corporations unaccountable to the public. The test of political democracy is whether it can finally fulfill its potential of protecting societies from dangerous concentrations of power. This now entails breaking up those concentrations and effecting a redistribution of economic power and access to resources. This does not mean an all-powerful state and a "command economy" but a major decentralization. Economic activity and development will be predominantly community-based and community-strengthening. Localities, regions, and nations will find appropriate ways to build self-reliance, with less dependence on imports for necessities, especially food. Governments at every level and international institutions will facilitate the initiatives of their respective subdivisions and will direct resources to enlarge the capabilities of deprived and damaged places. The right balance will be sought between decentralized responsibility and national or international planning and coordinating and protecting against localized inequities and abuses.[18]

The new field of "ecological economics" seeks better ways than the size of gross product to measure economic well-being. It distinguishes between beneficial economic activity and that which is actually injurious—or remedial in the sense of dealing with pollution and other injury resulting from production, consumption, trade, and growth. Ecological economics argues for "getting the price right"—by internalizing, that is, including in the price of a product the costs that have been externalized by being passed to the public. Valid measurements and "right prices" will reflect the "natural capital" upon which economics depends and the quantitative value of the services that ecosystems render to economic activity.[19] These considerations make a relevant contribution to reconceptualizing economics. Their application to the brutal arena of economic reality will encounter the opposing force.

Nothing is more important at this juncture in the journey than the realization that it cannot consist simply in pushing harder here and there against that dominating force. We need strategies and scenarios for getting from where we are to where we must go, strategies that include the politics of a sweeping realignment and democratization of the existing configurations of power.

Today most of those who call themselves "progressives" seem bent only on fixing the existing system. Their redoubled and partially successful efforts will not remove its inherent and fatal flaws. As we take on specific causes—against sweatshops or gas-guzzling cars—we need to remember and say that something far more fundamental is required, which will profoundly alter our way of living and our economic arrangements. Fuel-efficient cars (obviously needed now) will not get us where we need to go. Among many measures now resisted or scarcely contemplated, we shall have to phase out our dependence on the private automobile. In the just, sustainable, community-enhancing economy, the "good life" will mean *less* in quantitative terms. It can mean *more* in terms of convivial community, affinity with nature, democratic governance, and genuine fulfillment. That economy will not be capitalism. It will not be socialism or communism as we saw them in the Soviet Union or Eastern Europe. It does not yet have a name.

We do indeed face a test of democratic institutions, of bold, enlightened, inspired leadership, and of the capacity of people to mobilize against destructive powers and systems. The United States today, some say, has only the forms and appearance of democracy. A democracy requires a degree of relative equality that has long since been lost. The nation state is too large and powerful and too beholden to economic interests to be trustworthy, just, and respectful of freedom. More than ever, politicians depend upon big money to get elected; and big capital dominates the government and the media, and mightily influences the universities and the churches, which ought to be informing and equipping people to address the eco-justice crisis with a mobilization of democratic power.

These charges are valid. I do not believe, nevertheless, that democratic ideals and possibilities are dead. If democracy has perished from the earth, it has to be created anew. Against the odds, in response to great shock, suffering, and mind-changing realizations, people do rally, organize, mobilize, and struggle to right wrongs, actualize participatory governance, and secure a sufficient, sustainable livelihood. Here and there are signs that this does happen. In many places there is an emerging, still unpredictable potential for courageous and determined action. A deeper analysis of the opposing force is urgently needed, with a firm focus on the radicality of necessary changes. The changes that must come will not be granted by the established powers. The struggle to make them happen belongs to the eco-justice journey, a long, hard, enormously challenging adventure.

IV. Thinking Theologically, Acting Faithfully

About God, With God

The biblical authors witness consistently to the God who is in creation and in history. Using the biblical clues to who God is, we may look for God in the historical drama now unfolding. Among the clues too often overlooked by theologians is the biblical testimony to God's authorship of, and abiding concern for, the whole creation. It is somewhat harder to miss the testimony to God's concern for justice to human beings. But both of these clues require us to see and ponder the salient facts about the created order and the human story in which we ourselves are now enmeshed. And then we find the eco-justice crisis.

The biblicism of fundamentalist Christians blinds them to the necessarily contextual character of God's contemporary word. I am less concerned about this, however, than about the noncontextual thinking of "mainstream" church people. Their sense of where God touches their lives seems usually not to extend beyond personal and family concerns. But the Creator-Deliverer calls people of faith to a more exciting and meaningful engagement with God.

Theologians, preachers, and educators have the task of proclaiming, illuminating, and teaching what this means, so that it makes sense and resonates throughout the church. We need new theological work on the doctrines of God, Incarnation, and Holy Spirit, work that sees and seeks God in the crisis that is the megafact of our time.

Larry Rasmussen, drawing upon a 1991–92 review from the Canadian National Roundtable on the Environment and the Economy, speaks of three great social revolutions that have taken place in human history—agricultural, industrial, and informational—which now for the sake of survival are being superseded by a fourth great revolution. "All these [three] revolutions shared one crucial characteristic, which has determined the basic contours of our present world. They all reorganized society so as to produce more effectively." The fourth revolution "is the ecological revolution and its social-economic characteristic is qualitatively different—to reorganize society to produce without destructiveness." Rasmussen says society must also "reproduce without destructiveness."[20] I believe it is also clear that both production and reproduction must be *less* in order to cease their destructiveness. But they can be less and still be enough.

Thinking theologically about the fourth revolution, I venture to suggest and hope that God as Creator-Deliverer wants humankind to survive and the human enterprise to continue—despite all the destructiveness that incurs God's judgment. God wants otherkind to flourish along with people. Human communities must find a way (an economy) to meet their needs without destructiveness. A revolution indeed! And God is in it. But *how* is God in it? Certainly not by dictating what shall happen. Rather, in myriad, mysterious ways, by calling and commanding, chastening and restraining, inspiring and persuading, empowering and leading free human agents to live, work, witness, and struggle in the various ways of accomplishing harmony with nature and justice and fulfillment in community.

Larry Rasmussen's reference to the great social revolutions comes as part of the Introduction to a volume of theological/ethical essays. These come out of a program on Theological Education to Meet the Environmental Challenge, sponsored jointly by Dieter Hessel's Program on Ecology, Justice and Faith and Richard Clugston's Center for the Respect of Life and Environment. The contributors to this volume "expect schools of theology and departments of religion . . . to explore comprehensive implications of the environmental challenge for course work, community life, and institutional practice."[21] Perhaps this program will help to raise up a new generation of preachers and teachers who will equip and enlist committed participants in the eco-justice journey.

As people of faith think theologically *about* God, they will be energized for adventurous faithfulness by a lively sense of engagement *with* God in God's work in our time. This affirmation is packed with implications for the theological-ethical agenda.

About Sin, With Humility

I said recently to a group of clergy, "We need some new work on the doctrine of sin." They replied, "It is counter-productive to make people feel guilty. Guilt is disempowering." But the answer to the disempowerment from guilt is grace, forgiveness, and new beginning, not the soft-pedaling of truth and the offer of cheap grace.

The distinctive eco-justice norms for our time gain their power and relevance as responses to the distinctive contemporary character of social as well as personal sin. As the church learned or should have learned long since from Walter Rauschenbusch and Reinhold Niebuhr, sin indeed is institutional as well as individual.

> The economic forces which move [modern industry] are hardly qualified at a single point by really ethical considerations. If, while it is in the flush of its early triumphs, it may seem impossible to bring it under the restraint of moral law, it may strengthen faith to know that life without law destroys itself.[22]

Since Niebuhr wrote these words in 1928, the flush of early triumphs has swollen to a full-blown triumphalism that is truly self-destructive, and in a manner and degree that Niebuhr could not know, destructive to the planet as well as people.

Individual and institutional forms of selfishness and cruelty are of course inextricably entangled. While it is rarely possible to

speak of an institution or a nation as repenting (though certainly
the Hebrew prophets called the nation to repentance), personal
repentance and conversion can be instrumental to systemic change.

Theological, ethical reflection on distinctively contemporary
faithlessness and wrongdoing would probe and confess: the supreme
arrogance associated with the immense corporate, national, military, rich-world concentrations of power; the lust of power-wielders
to bring small competitors, client states, and all-world development
into a spreading and consolidating orbit of containment and control; the willful blindness of the elite class and the many beneficiaries
of economic expansion, technological brilliance, and material excess to the massive suffering of the human and nonhuman victims
of that expansion, brilliance, and excess; and the prostitution of
truth, as vested interests determine the selection and the slanting
of the facts and the news, and baldly disseminate disinformation.

The desecration of the planet was neither necessary nor inno-
cent. We can cite many instances of the unintended consequences
of good intentions, such as atmospheric destabilization from burning oil and coal. But when the warnings came, they were not heeded.
The campaign of the petroleum industry to spread doubt about
global warming and block the measures that could stem it provides
a flagrant example of the way self-defense causes deception, including self-deception, and persistent error. The planet's desecration,
moreover, could not have occurred but for the devaluation of everything not human and often the devaluation of the human as well
for the sake of unjust gain.

The institutional and systemic nature of our plight does not
absolve those in executive offices and board rooms who knowingly
make decisions with cruel consequences, like relocating operations
in order to hire labor for a pittance and to discharge toxics into
open sewers. It does not excuse their shameless discounting of the
future. And it does not relieve from responsibility the policymakers
whose insistence on "structural adjustment" for nations straining
to develop has pushed millions of children and their parents into
destitution or death. But there is also in American society a very
general acquiescence in, or at least a toleration of, these violations
of earth and people, and a timid, faithless unwillingness to accept
the very real risks of doing otherwise.

We need theological work on the complexities and subleties
and distinctive dimensions of sin manifest in the eco-justice crisis.
Our culture tends either to explain sin away or to reduce it to the
relatively trivial. A diminished moral sensitivity to the most

dangerous and damaging assumptions and attitudes, policies and practices, lies and deceptions, results in a diminished accountability. But there are conditions and atrocities toward which outrage is in order. Great evils are to be resisted, destructive forces to be turned back, idolatries to be renounced. The eco-justice journey includes "[withstanding] the evil day," for which, as Paul put it, we may put on "the whole armor of God" (Ephesians 6:10–17).

The appropriate outcome of theological work on sin, however, is not the division of the world into the righteous and the unrighteous. Any such division belongs to God, and Jesus passionately denounced self-righteousness. The appropriate outcome will be a new humility for the continuing journey. This means acknowledging complicity in arrogant stewardship, the proud overreaching, the shameful exploitation of the vulnerable; acknowledging how hard it is not to participate in the excessive demands on nature, and (for most of us) acknowledging unwillingness to break wasteful habits or let go of privilege. Humility entails starting over, accepting limits, exercising restraint that nature may heal itself, and admitting the sham and the hollowness of much that passes for "progress" and feeds the craving for unnecessary things that do not satisfy. It means remembering our own fallibility, guarding against defensiveness, and remaining open to new evidence and insights. We have to begin again, many times.

This new humility can generate a new boldness to face and speak the truth. With clearer sight and renewed integrity we can name, resist, and oppose the powers and systems that violate earth and people. In humility that frees and emboldens, we are better equipped to act with steadfastness and courage against the long evil day—and *for* the eco-just future, even though we know it will not be fully realized in a sinful world.

Hope and Grace

In this volume I have emphasized the obstacles that stand in the way of the changes that eco-justice requires. It is impossible to say how delayed or wrenching the necessary changes will be; but they pose an unsettling and frightening prospect, especially for all who want to hold on to the comforts and luxuries and jobs associated with the existing order. And many who do see the need for change feel that they are stuck, not knowing what to do.

So—we have to name the obstacles. We have to lift up and refine the vision of the eco-just future. We have to call for personal transformations in thinking, commitments, and courage to act. We have to identify and make plain the next steps that can be taken, both to hasten that future by anticipating it in the way we live, and to oppose the opposing force and finally turn it back. And all this will require religious, spiritual, educational, informational, political, and other kinds of leadership far beyond what we have now, together with popular outcries, protests, and persistent, widespread, multi-faceted assertions of organized democratic power.

I cannot be optimistic about the next few decades. But I live with hope.

I live with hope because eco-justice is not only the goal but the journey. Eco-justice happens.

I live with hope because the time is getting "full." The old order is truly unsustainable. Something new has to emerge. The challenge is to make it something better, and to minimize the destruction, disruption, and suffering along the way. We can expect surprises as history unfolds, astonishing events for the better which seem sudden but for which there has been long preparation. We have seen these in our own time, the fall of the Wall, the collapse of apartheid. The challenge is to speed the preparation.

I live with hope because I do believe God is in nature and in history and therefore in this momentous time of turning, this crisis of ecological wholeness and social-economic justice. I believe that God as both Creator and Redeemer moves, in ways I do not presume to comprehend, to direct and lead and persuade humankind toward harmony with nature as well as justice and peace in human community. Of course what God does is far more than I can suggest, and God's ultimate purpose lies beyond anything I can say. Nevertheless, as one involved in the biblical story that still continues, I believe eco-justice is God's project.

I live with hope because I find meaning and joy, excitement and adventure, companionship and community, and many small and large satisfactions by participating in God's project, the eco-justice journey. All this despite disappointment, dismay, and even outrage at the obstacles. God's time-frame is much longer than my own. The journey will continue beyond my participation. I do not say this to dispel a sense of urgency. As I once said to a student in the Eco-Justice Project, "You have to be patient. But do not lose your impatience!"

And I live with hope because hope is inseparable from grace. The first and last essential in Christian experience is the grace of God: the realization that the Source of all that is, the One who has brought us and all life into existence, is friend and not enemy.[23] This One is loving, just, and compassionate and wills love, justice, and compassion. Our lives therefore have meaning and purpose, in an affirming relationship with God, all human companions, all life, all that is. God is in nature and in history for their good, for reconciliation and fulfillment. God's love for humankind and otherkind is a given, uncontingent and prior to all efforts to gain God's favor. The Christ event makes this known. Those who hear and respond are freed to trust that nothing, not even death, can separate them from God's love in Christ Jesus (Romans 8:38f.). The future holds no final terror or defeat. God is the beginning and the end. "For [God] has made known to us . . . [God's] plan for the fulness of time, to unite all things in [Christ]. . . ." (Ephesians 1:9f.).

In the meantime, in the eco-justice crisis, God's judgment on the desecration of the earth, the oppression and violence within the human family, the anthropocentric attempt to be separate from and dominant over fellow creatures, the idolatrous worship of power and wealth, and the enthrallment with technological, material "progress," God's judgment on all this is an act of grace. It is instrumental to the new beginning that God wants. It needs to be heard within the priority of the first word, the good news of steadfast love, the assurance that the ultimate Source and Will is friend and not enemy.

Then the call and the gift are to live by love, the only absolute law of life, and to get involved, to get with God in the project, to undertake the journey, to accept the risks, to embrace the adventure. The call and the gift are grace, the summary word for what God does. In the realization and acceptance of grace—however grim the present situation, however rocky the road, however distant the destination—there is always hope to sustain the journey.

Notes

1. See *Hope for a Global Future: Toward Just and Sustainable Human Development* (Louisville, Ky.: Office of the General Assembly, Presbyterian Church [U.S.A.], 1996). Appendix B, 164–72, is an account of "Our Journey to Honduras."

2. Donella Meadows, "Living on Sun, Water, Wind, Grass, and Community," *Global Citizen*, March 12, 1998. Also see Alan Weisman, *Gaviotas: A Village to Reinvent the World* (White River Junction, Vt.: Chelsea Green, 1998). As guerilla and military violence in Colombia has increased (2001–03), I have not heard about the effects on Gaviotas.

3. See Peter W. Bakken, Joan Gibb Engel, and J. Ronald Engel, *Ecology, Justice, and Christian Faith: A Critical Guide to the Literature* (Westport, Conn.: Greenwood Press, 1995).

4. I do not find the statement of the stewardship theme in this document really satisfactory. It gives the impression that the rest of creation needed human beings to take care of it. Actually, the nonhuman creation got along very well for millions of years without humans. Their uniquely destructive impact on nature is what makes healing and renewal necessary.

5. The Policy Statement on Ecology is contained in the Bible study booklet *Our Only Home: Planet Earth* (Valley Forge, Pa.: Ecology and Racial Justice Program, National Ministries, American Baptist Churches, U.S.A., 1991), 32–39.

6. The Presbyterian statement is contained in *Restoring Creation for Ecology and Justice* (Louisville, Ky.: Office of the General Assembly, Presbyterian Church [U.S.A.], 1990).

7. This statement was printed as a booklet *Caring for Creation: Vision, Hope, and Justice* (Chicago: Evangelical Lutheran Church in America, 1993).

8. *Searching for the New Heavens and the New Earth: An Ecumenical Response to UNCED* (Geneva, Switzerland: World Council of Churches' UNCED Group, 1992), 9.

9. See, e.g., Michael Schut, ed., *Simpler Living, Compassionate Life: A Christian Perspective* (Denver, Colo.: Living the Good News, a division of The Morehouse Group, 1999).

10. Lester R. Brown, "The Future of Growth," in Lester R. Brown et al., *State of the World 1998* (New York: W. W. Norton, 1998).

11. Ibid., 3–11.

12. Ibid., 4.

13. Ibid., 19.

14. Ibid., 12. The World Bank projections came in the early stage of the Asian economic crisis that began in 1997. Precipitated by over-zealous investments and speculation in the global currency markets, this crisis severely interrupted anticipated economic growth. "Recovery" in the affected countries is understood, of course, as a resumption of the growth trajectory. Whatever the accuracy of the 1997 and later projections, they exemplify the firm assumptions of the leading actors in the economic sphere. Their criterion of economic health is growth, and they take little or no account of the sustainability factor.

15. Ibid., 14.

16. *Hope for a Global Future*, 124.

17. David C. Korten, *When Corporations Rule the World* (West Hartford, Conn.: Kumarian Press, 1995).

18. William E. Gibson, "The Sustainability Factor and the Work of God in Our Time," *Earth Letter*, November 1998, 5–8. See Herman E. Daly

and John B. Cobb, Jr., *For the Common Good: Redirecting the Economy toward Community, the Environment, and a Sustainable Future* (Boston: Beacon Press, 1989); James Robertson, *Future Wealth: A New Economics for the 21st Century* (New York: Bootstrap Press, 1990); Jerry Mander and Edward Goldsmith, eds., *The Case Against the Global Economy and For a Turn toward the Local* (San Francisco: Sierra Club Books, 1996); David C. Korten, *The Post-Corporate World: Life after Capitalism* (West Hartford, Conn.: Kumarian Press, 1999); and Dean Ritz, ed., *Defying Corporations, Defining Democracy: A Book of History and Strategy* (New York: Apex Press, 2001).

19. See Robert Costanza et al., "The Value of the World's Ecosystem Services and Natural Capital," *Nature* 387 (15), May 1997.

20. Larry L. Rasmussen, "Learning to Meet the Fourth Revolution," in *Theology for Earth Community: A Field Guide,* Dieter T. Hessel, ed. (Maryknoll, N.Y.: Orbis Books, 1996), 4.

21. Dieter T. Hessel, "How Will Theological Education and Religious Studies Respond?" in Hessel, ed., *op. cit.*, 11. Also see Hessel and Rosemary Radford Ruether, eds., *Christianity and Ecology: Seeking the Well-Being of Earth and Humans* (Cambridge, Mass.: Harvard University Press, 2000); and Dieter T. Hessel and Larry L. Rasmussen, eds., *Earth Habitat: Eco-Injustice and the Church's Response* (Minneapolis, Minn.: Fortress Press, 2001).

22. Reinhold Niebuhr, *Leaves from the Notebook of a Tamed Cynic* (1929; reprint, New York: Meridian, 1957), 224f.

23. See H. Richard Niebuhr, *The Responsible Self* (New York: Harper & Row, 1963), ch. 5.

Contributors

Peggy Antrobus was general coordinator of Fiji-based DAWN (Development Alternatives with Women for a New Era) from 1991 to 1996. She remains on DAWN's Steering Committee. She has worked in the field of women in development since her appointment in 1974 as advisor on Women's Affairs to the Government of Jamaica. In 1987 she set up the Women and Development Unit in the School of Continuing Studies at the University of the West Indies, and was its head until retirement in 1995. One of the most prominent feminist voices on global development, Dr. Antrobus has published widely and received regional and international awards. She is especially interested in transformative leadership—by "feminists with a passion for justice and a commitment to change things and change themselves."

John B. Cobb, Jr., is emeritus professor, Claremont School of Theology and Claremont Graduate School. He is currently a co-director of the Center for Process Studies in Claremont, California, as well as co-founder of Mobilization for the Human Family. He has written numerous articles and books on eco-justice and sustainability, including *Is It Too Late?; The Liberation of Life,* written with Charles Birch; *Sustainability: Economics, Ecology and Justice; The Earthist Challenge to Economism: A Theological Critique of the World Bank; The Green National Product,* written with Clifford W. Cobb; and *For the Common Good: Redirecting the Economy Toward Community, Environment, and a Sustainable Future,* written with economist Herman Daly, winner of the Grawemeyer Award for Ideas Improving World Order.

Carolyn A. (Chris) Cowap (1939-1988) graduated from Smith College and taught school for six years. Returning to her native England, she worked for the British Council of Churches on Christian Aid. Then, in the United States, she was consultant to Church Women United and staff member of the United Methodist Women's Division. From 1975 until her death she served the National Council of Churches as director of Economic and Social Justice, Division of Church and Society, developing policy and program on justice for women, eco-justice, and AIDS. She headed a major NCC study on "The Ethical Implications of Energy Production and Use"; and she led in forming the NCC's Eco-Justice Working Group in 1984-85.

Elizabeth Dodson Gray combines in her work several intellectual traditions. She is an environmentalist and futurist. And as a feminist theologian she is both heir and critic of the Judeo-Christian tradition. She has taught at MIT's Sloan School of Management, Williams College, Antioch New England Graduate School, and Boston College. Since 1978 she has been at Harvard Divinity School, where she is coordinator of the Theological Opportunities Program. She is the author of *Green Paradise Lost* (1979), *Patriarchy as a Conceptual Trap* (1982), and *Sunday School Manifesto* (1994), and editor of *Sacred Dimensions of Women's Experience* (1988). In 1989 the National Film Board of Canada produced a 19-minute film-for-television, "Adam's World," about her thought and work.

J. Ronald Engel is research professor in Environmental and Social Ethics at Meadville/Lombard Theological School, and co-director of Nature/Politics/Ethics: Chicago Regional Planning, a project of the Hastings Center and the Chicago Academy of Sciences. The theme of eco-justice has inspired his writing, teaching, and professional life for over thirty years. He has represented the Unitarian Universalist Association on the Eco-Justice Working Group of the National Council of Churches, co-founded the Theological Initiative for Eco-Justice Ministry in the Association of Chicago Theological Schools, co-directed the Program on Ecology, Justice and Faith, chaired the Ethics Working Group of the World Conservation Union, and served on the Earth Charter drafting committee. He is co-editor of *Ethics of Environment and Development: Global Challenge, International Response* (1990), and co-author of *Ecology, Justice, and Christian Faith: A Critical Guide to the Literature* (1995).

William E. Gibson is director emeritus of the Eco-Justice Project of the Center for Religion, Ethics and Social Policy at Cornell University, Ithaca, New York. An ordained Presbyterian minister, he has a Ph.D. in Christian Ethics from Union Theological Seminary in New York. After serving as a minister in higher education on several campuses, he came to Cornell in 1972 as one of the Protestant chaplains. There he led in the founding of the Eco-Justice Project in 1974. He was consultant and writer in the preparation of the policy statement of the Presbyterian Church (U.S.A.), *Restoring Creation for Ecology and Justice* (1990), and has undertaken other assignments, denominational and ecumenical, on the issues of ecology, justice, and Christian faith.

Richard Grossman, who lives in Milton Mills, New Hampshire, is co-founder and co-director of POCLAD, the Program on Corporations, Law and Democracy. Formerly, he was a Peace Corps volunteer in the Philippines, director of Environmentalists for Full Employment, organizer of the Labor Committee for Safe Energy and Full Employment, and co-founder of the Highlander Center's STP (Stop the Poisoning) Schools. He is the author of books and articles on labor, environment, job blackmail, energy, and economics.

Charles A. S. Hall is a systems ecologist with broad interests in energy and aquatic and tropical forested ecosystems. At the State University of New York, College of Environmental Science and Forestry (ESF), he teaches courses in the global environment, systems ecology, and resources and development. He has published six books and over 170 papers. On campus he and his wife have been especially interested in making ESF the environmental college for urban and downstate students in addition to its traditional rural and suburban students. Dr. Hall earned his Ph.D. from the University of North Carolina at Chapel Hill. In his spare time he enjoys reading history, gardening, and (especially) fly fishing.

Dieter T. Hessel, Ph.D., a Presbyterian minister specializing in social ethics, directs the foundation-supported ecumenical Program on Ecology, Justice and Faith, Princeton, New Jersey, and co-directs Theological Education to Meet the Environmental Challenge in partnership with the Center for Respect of Life and Environment, Washington, D.C. From 1965 to 1990 he coordinated adult social education and directed social policy studies for the Presbyterian Church (U.S.A.). He is editor or co-editor of these recent books: *Earth Habitat: Eco-Injustice and the Church's Response* (Fortress Press, 2001); *Christianity and Ecology: Seeking the Well-Being of Earth and Humans* (Harvard University Press, 2000); *Theology for Earth Community: A Field Guide* (Orbis Books, 1996); and *After Nature's Revolt: Eco-Justice and Theology* (Fortress Press, 1992).

Carol Holst is founder/director of Seeds of Simplicity, the first national nonprofit program for the general public centered on voluntary simplicity. Based in Los Angeles, her work (formerly the Ministry for Population Concerns) has been part of the Center for Religion, Ethics and Social Policy at Cornell University since 1992. She is also the administrator of the Simplicity Forum, a leadership alliance, and serves on the board of the Simple Living television series for PBS. Previously an early childhood educator, she founded

The Learning Place preschool in 1981. Her article, "Buying More Can Give Children Less," was published in *Young Children* by the National Association for the Education of Young Children in 1999. She is the single mother of two daughters in the fast lane, both born on her birthday five years apart.

Donald Quale Innis (1924-1988) was born in Toronto and began his study of geography at the University of Toronto. After working with Carl Sauer at Berkeley, he received his Ph.D. in 1959. He taught at the University of Chicago and Queen's University and then served as Professor (1963) and Chairman (1965) of the Geography Department at the State University of New York, Geneseo, until his death. His research concentrated on traditional farming practices in the tropics. He liked nothing better than studying small-scale agriculture around the villages of Jamaica, Mexico, India, Nepal, Thailand, and Togo, much of which is detailed in his book *Intercropping and the Scientific Basis of Traditional Agriculture*. In 1979 he received the Chancellor's Award for Excellence in Teaching.

Charles Lee is associate director for Policy and Interagency Liaison, in the Office of Environmental Justice of the Environmental Protection Agency. He has played a pioneering role in creating the field of environmental justice. When serving the United Church of Christ's Commission for Racial Justice, he was the architect of two landmark events—the 1987 *Toxic Waste and Race in the United States* report and the 1991 National People of Color Environmental Leadership Summit. He has spearheaded the emergence of federal policy on environmental justice and is the author of the National Environmental Justice Advisory Council report on "Public Dialogues on Urban Revitalization and Brownfields: Envisioning Healthy and Sustainable Communities." He carries major responsibility for developing the Integrated Interagency Environmental Justice Action Agenda.

Helen Locklear's heritage as a Native American lies with the Lumbee/Tuscarora peoples of southeastern North Carolina. An ordained Presbyterian minister, she is a graduate of Austin Presbyterian Theological Seminary. Her current position is as associate director, Racial Ethnic Ministries Program Area, of the Presbyterian Church (U.S.A.). Previously, she served as pastor, New Hope Chapel, and director, Pembroke (N.C.) Area Presbyterian Ministries (1990-1991); coordinator, Racial Justice Leadership Development in the Racial Ethnic Ministries Program Area (1991-1996); and executive director, Presbyterian Health, Education and Welfare Association (1997-1999). She has contributed, as editor or writer, to numerous publications, and has served on committees and boards of National Project Equality and the National Council of Churches.

Bernadine McRipley graduated from Michigan State University and Princeton Theological Seminary, and was ordained as a minister in the Presbyterian Church (U.S.A.). After holding positions as campus minister and pastor, she became an associate in the Presbyterian Washington Office, working on environmental and health issues, until her retirement. She is a former chair of the Eco-Justice Working Group of the National Council of Churches, and was co-editor of "For the Beauty of the Earth," a 1996 issue of *Church and Society* magazine. She contributed to the *Women of Color Bible* and was guest editor of the *Eco-Justice Quarterly* issue on "Linking Population and Development at Cairo," Winter 1994-95.

James A. Nash served as executive director of the Churches' Center for Theology and Public Policy in Washington, D.C. (1988-1998), editor of the Center's scholarly journal, and Lecturer in Social and Ecological Ethics at Wesley Theological Seminary. He now teaches at Boston University School of Theology. Previously, he served the Massachusetts Council of Churches for twenty-one years, first as associate director for Strategy and Action and then as executive director. He received his Ph.D. in social ethics from Boston University. Among his many writings is *Loving Nature: Ecological Integrity and Christian Responsibility* (Abingdon, 1991), a frequently used text. His research is now focused on the interaction of ecology, economics, and ethics; and he is writing on frugality as a subversive virtue, a pre-condition of social justice and ecological integrity.

Sabine O'Hara is vice president of Academic Affairs and dean of the College at Concordia College, Moorhead, Minnesota. Her work has been in ecological economics, environmental policy, social economics, economics and ethics, and sustainable development. Her research interests include sustainable development in urban and rural settings, and theoretical and applied work in the use of discourse ethics approaches and stakeholder models for integrated economic, social, and ecological valuation. In addition, she is active in developing innovative models for teaching economics in multidisciplinary settings. In previous positions she was provost of Green Mountain College, Pultney, Vermont, and a member of the Economics Department, Rensselaer Polytechnic Institute, Troy, New York. A native of West Germany, she has a Ph.D. in Environmental Economics from the University of Göttingen.

Ingrid Olsen-Tjensvold began working with the Eco-Justice Project in 1978, while finishing her doctorate in religious studies at Syracuse University. She was associate coordinator until 1981, when she became assistant director of Cornell United Religious Work. In 1984 she went to Cornell Law School. She started practicing privately in 1988, and in 1993 became an attorney for the Cortland County Department of Social Services with primary responsibility for cases involving child maltreatment. She is still an environmentalist. Her chosen cause, however, is animal welfare.

Larry L. Rasmussen has been the Reinhold Niebuhr Professor of Social Ethics at Union Theological Seminary, New York City since 1986. Prior to that, he was professor of Christian Ethics at Wesley Theological Seminary, Washington, D.C. His volume *Earth Community, Earth Ethics* (Orbis Books, 1996) won the prestigious Grawemeyer Award in Religion of 1997. With Dieter T. Hessel, he co-edited *Earth Habitat: Eco-Injustice and the Church's Response* (Fortress Press, 2001). He currently serves on the Science, Ethics, and Religion Advisory Committee of the American Association for the Advancement of Science, and on the Justice, Peace, Creation Advisory Committee of the World Council of Churches.

Karen Rindge is currently a full-time mother of two, doing part-time volunteer work on such issues as global climate change and energy consumption. She worked as an advocate for U.S. population aid and international reproductive rights as a legislative representative for Planned Parenthood Federation of America (1994-97), and as the Population Program Coordinator for the National Wildlife Federation (1991-94). She studied international development and African political economy at the University of Zimbabwe in 1989. Prior to that, she was a legislative assistant to Congressman James McClure Clarke (1987-88). She received her B.A. in political science from the University of North Carolina at Chapel Hill in 1986.

James Robertson read history and philosophy at Oxford; accompanied Harold MacMillan on his 1960 prime-ministerial "Wind of Change" tour of Africa; worked directly for the UK Cabinet Secretary and head of the Civil Service; set up an Inter-Bank Research Organization for the British banks; and in 1973 became an independent writer and speaker. In 1984-85 he co-founded the New Economics Foundation. His recent publications include: *The Transformation of Economic Life* (Green Books, 1998), also in Russian and Japanese; *The New Economics of Sustainable Development* (Kogan Page, 1999), for the European Commission, also in

French; and, with Joseph Huber, *Creating New Money: A Monetary Reform for the Information Age* (New Economics Foundation, 2000), also in Japanese.

Holmes Rolston III is University Distinguished Professor and professor of Philosophy at Colorado State University. He has written seven books, most recently *Genes, Genesis and God* (Cambridge University Press), *Philosophy Gone Wild* (Prometheus Books), *Environmental Ethics* (Temple University Press), *Science and Religion: A Critical Survey* (Random House, McGraw Hill, Harcourt Brace), and *Conserving Natural Value* (Columbia University Press). He gave the Gifford Lectures, University of Edinburgh, 1997-98, has lectured on seven continents, is featured in Joy A. Palmer, ed., *Fifty Key Thinkers on the Environment,* and is past and founding president of the International Society for Environmental Ethics.

Roger L. Shinn is the Reinhold Niebuhr Professor Emeritus of Social Ethics at Union Theological Seminary, New York. In recent years he has been visiting or adjunct professor at Columbia University, Jewish Theological Seminary of America, New York University Graduate School of Business Administration, Vanderbilt University, Drew University, Pacific School of Religion, and Princeton Theological Seminary. For several years, as a member of the working committee on Church and Society of the World Council of Churches, he investigated worldwide aspects of ecology and social justice. He is author of several books, including *Forced Options: Social Decisions for the 21ˢᵗ Century* (3ᵈ Edition with Reconsiderations, 1991) and *The New Genetics: Challenges for Science, Faith, and Politics* (1991).

J. Andy Smith III is president of Earth Ethics (www.earth ethics.com) and program director of the Earth Center in the Delaware Watershed. Consulting clients are from business, religious, and nonprofit groups. Former positions include director of Social and Ethical Responsibility in Investments for National Ministries, American Baptist Churches; Protestant Chaplain, Rensselaer Polytechnic Institute; and Baptist Chaplain, MIT. He is a founding board member of the Coalition for Environmentally Responsible Economies (CERES), a former chair of the board of the Interfaith Center for Corporate Responsibility, and a former member of the Public Advisory Panel for the Responsible Care Program of the American Chemistry Council. He has published one book and written extensively on social investing, corporate accountability, and environmental issues. He has a Ph.D. from Drew University.

George E. (Tink) Tinker is professor of American Indian Culture and Religions at Iliff School of Theology in Denver. He is a member of the Osage Nation and works and writes out of that heritage. He is an ordained Lutheran pastor and has a Ph.D. from Graduate Theological Union. His publications include *Missionary Conquest: The Gospel and Native American Genocide.* He is co-author, with Claire Sue Kidwell and Homer Noley, of *Native American Theology*, the first book to articulate a comprehensive and systematic Christian theology through Native American eyes. Dr. Tinker directs the Four Winds American Indian Survival Project in Denver, is past president of the Native American Theological Association, and a member of the Ecumenical Association of Third World Theologians.

Index

West Germany, 204
Wiesner, Jerome, 114
Wilberforce, William, 74
wilderness designation, 142–43
Wilken, Gene, 172–73
Willard, Dr. Bettie, 50
Wolfe, Alan, 37, 38
women: DAWN and structural adjustment, 190–92; development and, 228; naming and, 181, 189–90; Native American values, 194–95; need to affirm, 51; population issues and, 187–88, 192–93; value of and Cairo conference, 193–94; in workplace, 220–21
World Climate Conference, 123
World Commission on Environment and Development, 251
World Council of Churches, 262–63, 303
Worldwatch Institute, 307

Y
Yellowstone Park, wild animals in, 134–36, 140–41
York, Herbert, 114